WHY LOVE MATTERS

This book is part of the Peter Lang Education list.
Every volume is peer reviewed and meets
the highest quality standards for content and production.

PETER LANG
New York • Bern • Frankfurt • Berlin
Brussels • Vienna • Oxford • Warsaw

WHY LOVE MATTERS

Values in Governance

Edited by Scherto Gill & David Cadman

PETER LANG
New York • Bern • Frankfurt • Berlin
Brussels • Vienna • Oxford • Warsaw

Library of Congress Cataloging-in-Publication Data
Why love matters: values in governance /
edited by Scherto Gill, David Cadman.
pages cm
Includes bibliographical references and index.
1. Leadership—Social aspects. 2. Compassion. 3. Love. 4. Altruism. 5. Values.
I. Gill, Scherto, editor. II. Cadman, David, editor. III. Title.
HM1261.W49   303.3'4—dc23   2015023485
ISBN 978-1-4331-2929-2 (hardcover)
ISBN 978-1-4331-2928-5 (paperback)
ISBN 978-1-4539-1657-5 (e-book)

Bibliographic information published by **Die Deutsche Nationalbibliothek.**
Die Deutsche Nationalbibliothek lists this publication in the "Deutsche
Nationalbibliografie"; detailed bibliographic data are available
on the Internet at http://dnb.d-nb.de/.

The paper in this book meets the guidelines for permanence and durability
of the Committee on Production Guidelines for Book Longevity
of the Council of Library Resources.

© 2016 Peter Lang Publishing, Inc., New York
29 Broadway, 18th floor, New York, NY 10006
www.peterlang.com

All rights reserved.
Reprint or reproduction, even partially, in all forms such as microfilm,
xerography, microfiche, microcard, and offset strictly prohibited.

Printed in the United States of America

Contents

Foreword   vii
    By Archbishop Emeritus Desmond Tutu

List of Figures   ix

Acknowledgments   xi

General Introduction   1

    Part I: Love Matters: An Emerging Shift in Consciousness

    Introduction to Part One   9

1. The Leap in Consciousness   15
    Scilla Elworthy

2. Nourishing the Soul of a Leader   29
    Dadi Janki

3. The Need for Altruism   39
    Matthieu Ricard

4. A New Economic System Based on Core Human Values   51
    Stewart Wallis

5. Governance with a Human Face   63
    Kul Chandra Gautam

    Part II: Values in Governance: Towards a Compassionate System

    Introduction to Part Two   73

6. Compassionate Governance in Corporations   79
    Garrett Thomson

7. Love, Compassion and Respect in Earth System Governance: The Contribution of Convergence 93
Jenneth Parker

8. Globalisation of Compassion: The Example of Global Health 107
David G. Addiss

9. Communities and Freedom: Transforming Governance 121
Mohammed H. Mohammed and Kurian Thomas

10. Pillars of Peace 133
Steve Killelea

11. A New Form of Global Governance 149
Polly Higgins

Part III: Governance in Action

Introduction to Part Three 163

12. Governance and Politics 167
Thabo Makgoba

13. Reconciliation: From Hostility and Violence to Valuing the Other, Compassion and Altruism Born of Suffering 179
Ervin Staub

14. Caring Science 193
Jean Watson

15. Finding the Others: The Re-Imaging of Politics for a Brighter Future in Iceland and Canada 205
Heiða Kristín Helgadóttir and Derek Masselink

16. The Efforts of King Abdulaziz Center for National Dialogue to Promote a Culture of Dialogue and Tolerance in the Saudi Society 221
Amal y. al-Moallimi & Fatima M. Al-Bishri

Epilogue 235

References 237

Contributors 253

Index 259

Foreword

BY ARCHBISHOP EMERITUS DESMOND TUTU

About 15 years ago, at the Peace Centre that I gave my name to, we organised a Colloquium on Values-Based Leadership. Since then, I have been reflecting on values and governance and have come to understand a bit more about the most desirable qualities in leaders. From Nelson Mandela, for instance, I have learned that great leaders serve and lead for the sake of and on behalf of people; from his Holiness the Dalai Lama, I have learned that great leaders personify and exemplify by embodying and living the values they wish to instill in the community, in the nation; from Aung San Suu Kyi, I have learned that great leaders inspire and they invite others to share the spirit of magnanimity and purpose.

However, as South Africa continues celebrating its journey from apartheid into democracy, I am also learning that great qualities and great leaders are not enough. The future of South Africa lies in good governance. For most of us, good governance is about transparency, accountability, respect for human rights, rule of law and democracy. However, the more I observe South Africa's processes, the more I realise that good governance is more than that. Good governance is about a vision of what it means to be human, together.

In other words, good governance is to live out *Ubuntu* at a global scale. Ubuntu is a South African word suggesting that humans cannot exist in isolation because we are bound together in oneness. Ubuntu means that we can become who we truly are only through our relationship with others and through others being themselves. We are interconnected. Ubuntu is the ultimate philosophy of good governance. Without Ubuntu, without love and compassion, there will be no human dignity—dignity as the result of our caring for one another which underlies other moral pillars of our societies: respect, forgiveness, understanding and justice.

At the moment, our world is threatened by terror, fear, hatred and division and equally humanity is struggling to bring prosperity and well-being to all corners of our planet. The need for a new narrative that restores love and compassion as our core values and humanness as our way of being together has never been greater. Therefore, set in the context of such a global urgency, this deeply insightful book not only points out the need for a new narrative for our humanity, but in my view, it is itself part of the new narrative. In reading the collection of articles, we are once again reassured that we are each made for goodness and that ordinary acts of love and compassion speak to the extraordinary promise that every human life is of inestimable value. As one reflects on the ideas put forward in the book, is it not more clear that if such propositions are regarded as radical, it is a sorry commentary on all of us? And yet might it be that the acceptance of these truths and bringing them to the centre of our lives is now absolutely necessary for our very thriving—together?

Love Matters: Values in Governance, despite being provocative, speaks forcefully about the emergent shift in human consciousness. These articles offer compelling exemplars illustrating that Ubuntu is not just a philosophy but a possible reality if it is embedded in the fundamental considerations for a system of governance and leadership.

I commend the many thoughts, ideas and actions contained in this book. The wide range of different but connected aspects of our lives addressed in the book—sustainability, spirituality, community, health, well-being, economics, politics, peace and reconciliation—are helpful in enriching our understanding of values in governance.

I hope that the 'story' being told in this book is heard, understood and acted upon.

God bless you.

Archbishop Emeritus Desmond Tutu
Cape Town, South Africa

List of Figures

Chapter 7

Figure 1. How rocks, oil, fish, and grass lead to people (Koca, 2013).   98

Chapter 10

Figure 1. The Pillars of Peace.   139

Figure 2. Stronger Pillars Lead to More Peaceful Outcomes.   142

Figure 3. Effective Governance.   145

Figure 4. Causality.   146

Figure 5. Peace as a Guiding Principle.   147

Acknowledgments

The proposal for this book was originally put forward at the 2nd Spirit of Humanity (SoH) Forum held on April 10–12, 2014, in Reykjavik, Iceland. This volume is a collection of selected articles inspired by the Forum.

We first want to thank each of the contributors of this volume who were also participants, presenters, and speakers at the SoH Forum. We are grateful for their imagination and articulation of the emerging shift in governance as well as their invaluable insights into the global challenges and complexities confronting humanity today.

We are most indebted to the team at the SoH Forum without whose encouragement we wouldn't have been able to put together this collection. We are equally thankful for the Guerrand-Hermès Foundation for Peace for its trustees' understanding and appreciation of the meaningfulness of this volume and for their thoughtful contribution to this project.

We also thank the City of Reykjavik for its partnership in hosting the SoH Forum. The leaders of the City, in particular, the former Mayor Jón Gnarr, the Director of Culture and Tourism, Svanhildur Konradsdottir and MP Óttarr Proppé, have been exceptionally supportive of us in the process of editing this unique volume, which is also an expression of the City's dedication and commitment to values-based governance.

We owe a special note of thanks to Laura Hobson for her invaluable administrative support as well as to the team at Peter Lang for their assistance during the final production phase.

Scherto Gill and David Cadman

General Introduction

Our human compassion binds us the one to the other—not in pity or patronizingly, but as human beings who have learnt how to turn our common suffering into hope for the future.
—Nelson Mandela

Towards a New Story

We are storytellers.

From the beginning, we have told each other stories for comfort and for explanation. Indeed, it is by the telling of stories that we have held together as communities—families, tribes, nations, and civilizations; it is through stories that we belong—we share the story of who we are and who we aspire to be and become.

Stories are fundamentally about the values that we share and the ways in which our communities come together. In other words, stories articulate a value system through which we agree to live with one another. When we encounter the need for change, we must re-examine the old stories and their underlying value systems that have brought us to where we are and create new stories to live by. That is to say we must truly distance ourselves from the old narrative rather than looking from within its boundaries. This requires a shift in consciousness.

At present, humanity is between stories. We shall suggest that the old story is increasingly seen to be inadequate and even harmful and that a new story is yet to be imagined and to be told. If the old story is about competition, assertiveness, and unlimited consumption to support economic growth, the new story seems likely to be about collaboration, reciprocity, and an economy of enough, an emerging narrative that speaks of that *Ubuntu*, an African philosophy of solidarity and interdependence, to which Emeritus Archbishop Desmond Tutu refers in his Foreword.

The new story is not just an aspiration or dream; it also points to pragmatic action grounded in a necessary shift of human consciousness and already being pioneered by some individuals and organisations who have started to change. To make this shift, or rather this leap, in consciousness, is to see that to be truly human is to be part of a greater whole, whether this be the integration of the inner and outer being of the individual, the individual in the community, humanity as part of Nature, or indeed of our interconnected being within the universe.

At the core of this new story is a key message: core human values such as love, respect, compassion, justice, and dignity are not external to our life or our society; rather they are integral to our being. Indeed, they arise from our true being, which cannot be otherwise. This is so for all aspects of our lives, including family, personal relations, work, the way of our economic, corporate and institutional structures, our relationship with the natural environment, and all forms of political governance and decision-making.

It was within this context that the Spirit of Humanity (SoH) Forum began its work to explore core human values in decision-making. In September 2012, the first SoH Forum took place in Reykjavik and brought together over one hundred leaders from different parts of the world to examine the practical possibilities offered by this shift in human consciousness. Reykjavik was chosen as the birthplace of the Forum due to its uncompromising commitment to strive to become a world capital of peace. And here the idea of establishing a community of practice was born, aimed at connecting people from around the globe who share a passion for values-based work and who aspire to learn from each other through such connections.

In April 2014, over two hundred people from forty countries around the world again gathered in Reykjavik to take part in the second SoH Forum. Recognising the positive energy of love and compassion as one of the deepest and most enduring aspects of human nature and realising that these core human values are key guiding principles for good economy, peaceful society, and sustainable environment, Reykjavik 2014 made an explicit call for creatively re-imagining new forms of governance that respect people and Nature. It served to create a space for thinkers and activists to discuss and share value-based decision-making in many fields. Within this space, a community of practitioners came together with the possibility that they would continue their work feeling supported and invigorated by having shared with and learned from each other.

General Introduction

These two forums also prompted us to explore certain core values in depth and reflect on what might be meant by 'values in governance'. This book is, therefore, an attempt to undertake that exploration, in particular, to examine more closely the underlying principles that have sustained this active work around the globe, to make propositions with regard to ways to effect positive change at a systemic level, and to inquire into practical examples that illustrate how the work of values might have profound and beneficial impact on our societies and our planet.

The book thus serves as a platform for bringing together divergent voices from different fields of action to narrate this emergent story. The inspirational and pragmatic nature of the narrative suggests that it will have different kinds of 'plots'—plots that have to be brought together as a whole, brought into some kind of balance and harmony. This includes the balance of the global system in its entirety with the sum of its parts, spirituality and mysticism with political realism, philosophical reflection with social practices, critical analyses with compassionate concerns, and individual inner values with collective outer actions.

We believe that bringing these diverse voices together and letting them be heard will further strengthen the coherence of the new story that has started to be developed in the SoH Forums. Thus Stewart Wallis, the Executive Director of New Economics Foundation, and one of the speakers at Reykjavik 2014 and a contributor to this book, describes this story as our 'new world symphony' orchestrated in such a manner that the different instruments and voices play and sing to the same music score—a common narrative that compels us, the leaders and the led, to be, become and act from who we truly are and for the future of humanity.

Aims of the Book

In light of this, and with a sense of urgency, this book aims to explore the new story, the emerging narrative; to try and understand how such a shift in human consciousness could take place, and how it is, in effect, already taking place, and what insights we might gain in order to overcome the challenges.

Within the framework of 'Love Matters', we have chosen a much-debated theme, 'values and governance', to illustrate what is desirable and possible for systemic transformation.

We take 'Love' with a capital 'L' to be a fundamental shaping principle. It is the thread, the pulse, the ordering principle that gives shape to and is experienced by all that is. Love is present in every relationship and connection, however close or far away. It is only by dwelling in Love that we can be who we truly are. We cannot continue as one humanity without Love and we certainly cannot flourish together without Love. We take 'compassion' to be Love in action, the practice and virtue of kindness, respect, care, and justice for oneself and for others. This is a wholesome care from the deepest humanity, which is to say that it recognises the importance of relationship and interconnectedness, the importance of being a part of rather than apart from.

Governance has multiple meanings. In this book, it is concerned with how decisions are made, decisions related to achieving common goals that matter to all, whilst maintaining valued relationships and providing accountability to humankind and planet Earth. Governance is also about human beings in context, which is not just an organisation, an institution, a region, or a country. Instead, the context of governance is already, and will always be, global with all its complexity, and governance will always be concerned with decisions implemented at local and global levels.

We see that authentic leadership and collaborative decision-making are at the forefront in guiding our collective pathways towards this shift in governance. Leadership is essentially a process of social and political influence in order to achieve common good. Therefore, the exemplary acts of a true leader can call upon the good deeds of many; and the values they live by, and the ethical standards they set, can inspire real transformation. There is a simple truth here: Those who are governed from the perspectives of core human values of love, compassion, respect, and care are most likely to reflect back these qualities and values in their life and work.

In the SoH community, there are many activists and leaders, each of whom, in their particular field, is breaking new ground or at least trying to do so. Many have claimed that truly compassionate leadership has spiritual sustenance at its core. In other words, they say that it is the nourishment of our souls that ensures an attention to ourselves to each other and our planet as a whole. This spiritual sustenance helps to bring us closer to the practice of developing balanced lives and harmonious societies—where, for example, there can be enough for all to share and where, therefore, individuals and institutions are not tormented by neediness; where true meaning is found through being of service to each other and to the world at large.

This is why we have chosen a provocative title for the book: *Why Love Matters: Values in Governance* because each of these concepts has profound resonance with people and communities, and together these words put forward a new story—an innovative proposal that can serve as a luminous guiding force to lead our societies into becoming more humane, more caring, and more peaceful.

Essentially, therefore, this book seeks to awaken what is truly human in our perspective and our consciousness and to bring together both conceptual and pragmatic suggestions for incorporating core values in governance. In doing so, it urges the leaders and the led to look beyond a notion of happiness framed through the lenses of self-interest and economic growth, divorced from our relationships with each other and all that is. Instead, it encourages us to realise that dignity lies in the flourishing of all, including humankind and all other kinds on our planet.

Together, the contributors of the book explore those values in governance that nurture the wholeness of human life. As we shall see, it is clear that although each author's voice is distinct and of a unique colour, together they form a rich palette of colours that depicts a coherent story and narrates an understanding of a greater connectedness: an integration of personal responsibility with commitment to communal life, the unity of the scientific, the sociological, the creative, the technological, the poetic, and the spiritual.

The Outline of the Book

Across the globe there are similar concerns about transforming and transcending existing forms of governance towards an inspirational pathway into the future. However, despite this emerging new story, there remains a gap between human aspiration and policy pragmatism. The gap consists in the intellectual and practical steps needed to design and bring about compassionate governance.

In order to take these steps, we need to overcome three key challenges:

First, cultures and societies prioritise different values—some regard values as a set of rigid moral rules often unexamined, some of which are imposed by religion(s); others consider values as contextualised and emergent. So the challenge is: how can we, as one humanity, collectively agree on those common or core values that can constructively support an enduring humane culture?

Second, values in governance may be criticised as being too vague a concept as no leaders will claim that their system of decision-making is value-free. Therefore, the real challenge here lies in how we ought to define 'values' so that we can examine governance through such a lens in a manner that is rigorous and well grounded?

Third, governance is already a contested concept that is struggling to redefine itself and to be reborn from an increasingly ineffective and dysfunctional system. Hence there remains yet another challenge: How should we conceive the notion of 'governance' so that it is compassionate, fair, just and serves to support people, communities and planet? What are the practical examples of such governance?

In order to confront these challenges, we have divided the book into three parts.

Part One discusses what we see as an outline of the aforementioned new story, depicting an emergent shift in human consciousness and beginning to consider how this story might unfold in practice.

Part Two continues this exploration of governance in a more grounded way. These authors offer specific proposals highlighting the principles underpinning values-based decision-making in different fields, suggesting what is possible.

Part Three is a collection of 'stories' that aims to illustrate how such governance is being put into practice, how and where it succeeds, and what stands in its way.

Each part explores the theme through a number of interconnected lenses, such as politics, economy, environment, health, sustainability, community, and peace. These wide–ranging themes have been chosen because they reflect our proposition that an emerging consciousness is already being experienced. This, we argue, is not simply something required and felt in our private lives. Rather it is something much more important. It is something that is especially required, and now being felt, in our public lives. Even though this emergent 'story' may be resisted, it will not be pushed to the margin, but will insist upon being heard in the boardroom, in the marketplace, in corridors of power, in public policy, and every time we sit down together to resolve a disagreement or conflict.

Part I:
Love Matters: An Emerging Shift in Consciousness

Introduction to Part One

The gift of the gods is consciousness.

—Jim Harrison, 'In Search of Small Gods'

This part of the book sets out the contexts and key concerns of an emerging and pressing need for a radical investigation of values in governance. In particular, it explores the underlying story of a shift in human consciousness towards new and innovative forms of governance.

For the contributors of this book, the kind of governance required by the future of humanity must prioritise the 'flourishing of all'—not only the flourishing of human kind, but also all kinds of species and beings and, indeed, the planet Earth as a whole. The contributions argue that this aspiration can only be realised through a system of decision-making underpinned by core human values such as respect, love, compassion and care—a rigorous and deliberate move away from a declining way of being and towards something that is about interconnection and relationship.

In light of the much debated paradoxical role of religions and spirituality in determining values and systems of governance in the contemporary social and political contexts, as well as the potential of faith and spirituality to shape global governance, the chapters in this part make an explicit effort to explore the spiritual development of leaders and the need to nurture their innermost being.

Thus, each chapter of Part One is dedicated to the conceptual articulation of the relationship between values, governance and spirituality. Our contributors are mindful that key concepts such as love, compassion, spirituality, flourishing, and governance are highly contested. So the chapters in this part also ask if these disputes can be settled, and how they might be transformed in light of this radical shift in consciousness. Taking an inquiry-based approach, each chapter is able to avoid being limited by crisis discourse alone and draw attention to what is possible.

Questions considered by the contributors include this: 'How should our governance reflect core human values whilst taking into account our current cultural, economic and social situations?' In addressing this question, these chapters have been able to propose a shift in our awareness and understanding of humankind's relationship with each other and with our environment in a constructive way, grounded in current local and global challenges.

Another question investigated is: 'In what way can exemplary ways of integrating inner spiritual life with public services inform the overall social policy agenda?' This question is tackled in a manner that is aimed at exploring the inner nature of being human and how positive change in society might stem from our inner transformation. In considering this question, the contributors are able to suggest that pursuing a spiritual life is essentially the process of honouring greater life forces and of acting out the meanings and values inspired by them in an integrated way. When leaders are able to express all of their qualities, including those that are part of their higher and inner self, they are more able to enhance the systems of governance within their institutions or organisations, and the lives of the people associated with them. This understanding points to a need for a policy agenda to look at ways that foster compassion and wholeness in our ways of being in the world.

Each of the five chapters in Part One discusses these questions from somewhat different but connected perspectives, and has done so creatively and convincingly.

The first chapter is by Scilla Elworthy, the Founder of the Oxford Peace Research Group, who describes a necessary 'Leap in Consciousness.' Speaking from her personal experience and her work for peace, Scilla proposes four essential elements that are constituted in this shift. These are *perspective, interconnectedness, blazing intelligence,* and *balance between the masculine and the feminine*, all pointing to the interdependent nature of being, and being human.

In articulating the meanings and significance of these elements, Scilla offers the reader an opportunity to truly understand what Einstein once said, that 'No problem can be solved from the consciousness that created it.' In light of the current challenges that confront us, Scilla encourages us to wake up to and act from a new consciousness, because only such a new consciousness can give us the guidance, wisdom, and strength needed to transform our future.

Following from this strong opening narrative, Dadi Janki, the Spiritual Head of Brahma Kumaris World Spiritual University, maintains that the shift

Introduction to Part One

of our consciousness is a change in our inner reality, which comes from each person cultivating an 'inner strength', the feeling of peacefulness. In particular, she asks that we consider what it is that gives the inner strength to leaders that helps support wise and values-based decision-making. Dadi Janki also draws our attention to the quality of our thoughts through self-awareness, the power of love and the deep intention to serve. She describes Love and the power of Love as the most transformative energy in the world, and attributes such power to a Greater Being, which is recognised by people of religions and of non-religions as the Source of Love. Her central message is that when leaders lead themselves by practising such profoundly spiritual ways of being, they will be followed by many who are inspired to follow their own inner capacity for greatness towards the good.

It is this idea of goodness that concerns Matthieu Ricard, a Tibetan Buddhist Monk and philosopher, who, in the third chapter of this book, discusses the nature of altruism and how to develop a system of governance that helps move towards a more altruistic society. Altruism, Matthieu proposes, is a benevolent state of mind, consisting of feeling concerned for the fate of all those around us, and wishing them well, strengthened by our determination to act for their benefit. Valuing others is the most fundamental state of mind that leads to altruism. When it is our 'default mode', it expresses itself as benevolence towards anyone who might come into the field of our attention and translates itself as goodwill, readiness and willingness to care. As shown by psychologist Daniel Batson, when there is a need that is perceived in others, we readily develop empathic concern, bringing about the urge to fulfil that need. When the need is related to a yearning for happiness, valuing others and benevolence will foster the realisation of that aspiration. When the need is related to suffering, valuing others and being compassionate will induce us to remedy the suffering and its causes.

Matthieu suggests that altruism and compassion are skills that can be cultivated with training, for instance through contemplative practices such as meditation. To introduce a shift towards a more altruistic, compassionate culture in the world, Matthieu proposes, we must dare to cultivate altruism in each one of us; dare to ensure that governance and economy listen to the voices of caring, dare to commence a radical re-orientation that takes into account the interests of others as well as our own. He thus concludes that real happiness and good governance are entwined with altruism, because they are part of an essential kindness that is accompanied by a profound desire that everyone can flourish in life.

Continuing to address a similar concern, Stewart Wallis, the Executive Director of New Economics Foundation, proposes in Chapter Four that as our current economic system is unsustainable, unfair, unstable and deeply unfulfilling for many, a transformation is needed urgently to an economic system that remains within planetary limits and has as its goal the equitable satisfaction of human needs (as opposed to wants) and the maximisation of human well-being. The barriers to this transformation, he says, are not technical, but human, they are set within our values, which reinforce the concerns of policy and practice change. For Stewart, core human values are the ones widely recognised and accepted by most cultures, faiths, religions and enlightened civilisations. They rest on a shared understanding of human dignity which comes from both how we treat others and are treated by others—human reciprocity. Such reciprocity, according to Stewart, can be extended to our systems and institutions so that all of our institutions, markets and political systems can be designed explicitly to promote the common good—goodness for all. He concludes that the new narrative thus 'plotted' is so compelling that it can inspire solidarity amongst groups towards a united political will for true socio-economic transformation.

Following this call for a compelling plot, in the last chapter of Part One, Chapter Five, Kul Gautam, the former deputy executive director of UNICEF and assistant secretary-general of the United Nations, explores compassionate governance in the work of international agencies, such as UNICEF. He maintains that core values, such as compassion and solidarity, are part of the greater human spirit that has guided our collective journeys throughout human history. Although suspicion, indifference, animosity, and hatred have also typified the relationships between some tribes, religions, and groups, they should never be taken as the underlying design for systems of governance or our public and private institutions. Echoing Scilla and Matthieu, Kul points out that our only response to the threats from climate change, terrorism, and other humanitarian crisis must be to dare to be and to work from what is truly noble in the spirit of humanity—Love. He then offers a few stories from his experiences at UNICEF to illustrate that 'governance with a human face' can have genuine positive impact on public policy, governance and human well-being across countries, sectors, and from local to global.

In their diverse voices, these five authors thus provide an excellent context for the emerging narrative. We see that there are two important aspects to moving towards compassionate governance—the first is the prerequisite to transform our consciousness or perspective; the second is the imperative to act on and from this new consciousness. As the chapters make clear, how we see the world and the values that we adopt in shaping our governance, lie at the root of how things can become. Values matter, which is why Love matters. If our perception is rooted in Love and our being, including ourselves

Introduction to Part One

and the world, is touched and irrevocably affected by Love, everything else flows from that.

At the same time, the contributors in Part One also suggest that this new paradigm of thought should not just be restricted to the mere materialistic and the social realm. Instead, this new consciousness is seen as being originated in our innermost self, born from the same source that gives rise to all that is sacred. Although cultures offer multitudes of images, symbols and myths to describe what this source is, the chapters in this book express the meaning arising from the sacred in ways that transcend these differences.

What truly gives hope is that this book not only makes a radical proposition for a new paradigm towards values-based and compassionate governance, but also provides principles and guidance to show how acting with such values is possible. This is the focus of Part Two of the book.

1. The Leap in Consciousness

SCILLA ELWORTHY

Edgar Mitchell, the pragmatic young US Navy captain who was the lunar module pilot on Apollo 14, was the sixth person to walk on the moon. On the return trip, as he watched the earth float freely in the vastness of space, he realized that the story of the world and humanity as told by science was incomplete and likely flawed. 'I recognized that the Newtonian idea of separate, independent, discreet things in the universe wasn't a fully accurate description. What was needed was a new story of who we are and what we are capable of becoming'(Mitchell). What 'new story' is Mitchell talking about? What are human beings capable of becoming?

As far as I can see what is required to discover the new story is not a shift in consciousness, not something incremental. What is required is a great leap into a fundamentally different way of perceiving ourselves and the world we inhabit. It will alter everything, and I believe its time has come.

This has nothing to do with religion. This leap in consciousness is spiritual as well as practical, emanating from a deep desire in human beings for meaning in life and for a profound connection with a greater intelligence, the divine source of All That Is.

And so, in this chapter, in two parts, I will describe, from my own experience, what this leap in consciousness is and why it is urgently needed before, at the end raising a question about whether or not it will come about—in time.

What Is This New Consciousness?

My experience tells me that there are many aspects to this leap in consciousness and that there are four essential elements: perspective, interconnectedness, blazing intelligence, and balance between the masculine and the feminine.

Perspective

What Edgar Mitchell saw from space was our exquisite planet in its entirety. That sight of our home floating in space allows us humans to perceive the wholeness of our home—the weather systems swirling around it, the vast oceans held to its surface by gravity, and its agonizing beauty. Here we are, sitting on this planet, and we are also able to see it. We are conscious that we are an active part of something vast—living, interconnected cells in one huge body. We can no longer claim to be millions of tiny entities whirling about randomly, victims of circumstances beyond our control. No longer does a person need to be a scientist to begin to grasp the enormity of the planetary systems that our home is part of and the interconnectedness of all things.

For the first time, we have a bird's-eye view of the human race. We can see where we live and whom we live among, and we can begin to see what effect our actions have on our home (Arthus-Bertrand & Besson, 2009). We are the first species on this earth to be aware that we can destroy not only ourselves but also our habitat by the decisions we make. This alone is a huge wake-up call to consciousness, to the miraculous universe we are part of, and to the responsibility that brings. It is vastly accelerated by the internet, which now means that the majority of the earth's human population can find out, in seconds, what's happening anywhere—and what's happening to our planet as a whole.

Many people experience this kind of perspective when they climb high mountains. For me this was in the Himalaya, when, after a strange series of events, I found myself alone with a depressed guide and two Ladakhi pony men on a twenty-four-day trek, climbing up and over seven passes between 15,000 and 17,000 feet high. It was the beginning of a spiritual journey, and like all worthwhile spiritual journeys, it got tough at times. At the halfway mark—a dilapidated village called Padum—I was asked if I wanted to carry on walking or catch a bus. I sat on a hillock to contemplate this matter. When I opened my eyes, a bird was hovering, fluttering its wings, right in front of my face. And I wasn't sitting on its nest. I closed my eyes again for some time, and when I opened them again, the same thing happened. I took this to mean 'get up and fly,' and so I got up and went on. Little did I know what was about to happen.

The next pass was the toughest we'd faced yet—and the highest; after a steep, fifteen-mile trek, I crawled the last distance to the summit on hands and knees. When I got to the top, all I could see was more of the same—arid, barren, spiky mountains—for miles. No relief of green. No single resemblance to the photos I had seen of wide, fertile Zanskari valleys.

'Where do we go now?' I asked

'Down,' came the reply. 'And then up.'

What I saw at my feet was an almost vertical drop to a gorge far below and a vertical mountainside opposite, up which was a zigzag path going considerably higher than we already were

I said, 'I don't want to go there.'

What I actually wanted was to go home. I cried all the way down the vertical mountainside, put up my tent, and sobbed myself to sleep.

The next day we began the dreaded ascent. About halfway up, we came upon willow trees, which meant water. And, indeed, there was water, a gurgling stream. I sat down, put my feet in the icy water, and began to laugh. I washed my clothes and stretched them on stones to dry. I washed my hair for the first time in two weeks, climbed on a rock, and lay in the sun. Later that night I cooked dinner for the four of us with dried mushrooms that I had brought and felt a sense of well-being.

The next morning brought the real wonder. We climbed a high gorge and after three hours the gorge opened into a stony ascent with perfectly symmetrical sides. As I walked, I began to feel that I did not seem to have a head. It was a strange, inexplicable feeling, full of lightness (Harding, 2002). Energy seemed to be resonating everywhere and entering my body through the top of my shoulders. Soon I could see the pass itself—always a sacred place—with a stupa decked with prayer flags carrying messages of love on the mountain winds. When I got to the stupa, I fell on my knees, eyes closed. When I opened my eyes, what I saw took my breath away. Below me, stretched out for hundreds of miles, was the entire exquisite panorama of the snow-clad Himalaya.

What this experience gave me was perspective. It gave me a new perspective on life. I saw everything through an entirely different lens, one belonging not to my brain, but to my awakened heart. I wished for everyone on earth to have that experience of spaciousness and peace. I drank in a whole new understanding of the boundless beauty of this planet, seen from the highest place on it that I had ever visited. Everything I saw, I fell in love with.

Interconnectedness

Unless we have gone numb and want only to turn a blind eye to what's happening to the earth, we cannot avoid the reality that we are affecting our own evolution with everything we do. We have learned, for example, that the gases produced by refrigerators destroy the ozone layer; the thinning of the ozone layer, in turn, permits harmful ultraviolet rays to reach our bodies.

This kind of awareness may be jarring and demanding, but it is real. And it is exciting. It is the most unusual opportunity to move toward what some people call 'unity consciousness'—a direct, intuitive awareness of the oneness of reality. With this realization comes—inescapably—the knowledge that whatever we think, however we react, and whatever we do has an immediate and positive or negative effect on others. This affects not only those close to us but also those far away whom we have never met.

People across the planet are discovering processes that increase awareness—meditation, reflection, creativity, attention to intuition, and bodywork such as yoga or martial arts. Moreover, they are discovering that these practices are enabling them to connect with others in intriguing ways. Thousands of people around the globe now meditate together, at coordinated times, and observe the results.

This sense of interconnectedness is driving change, even in the poorest places on earth—the 'informal settlements' in major cities all over Africa and Asia, where thousands arrive every day, desperate to find work. In Mumbai, for example, Shaheen Mistri is the founder and CEO of Teach for India, a movement of young people that has, over the past four years, placed more than seven hundred teachers in under-resourced classrooms. These teachers are willing to forego more lucrative posts because they feel a sense of connectedness to children in need of education.

Explaining this, Shaheen stopped fifty Western visitors in their tracks when she said that when we face a challenge we can use either a mirror or a magnifying glass. The magnifying glass reveals the detail of the problem, which can be useful if we want to externalize it, but the mirror shows us who *we* are. Seeing who we are and how we interact with the problem is the fastest and most efficient route to transforming it. She says, 'When I walk out in the street, do I see the kids as my kids? Do I clean out my house and dump the garbage in the street?'

Imagine a world in which activists on the front line are supported by activist meditators dedicated to the marriage of radical action with inner meditation. This could ultimately stop war. In fact, it has already. An experiment, described by quantum physicist Dr. John Hagelin, was conducted in the Middle East during the war in Lebanon in the 1980s (Hagelin, 2009). The hypothesis was that if enough people were collectively stimulating peace within, that would be reflected in the wider society. The results showed that the numbers of people meditating correlated exactly with lessening violence and progress toward peace.

Eventually, after endless review processes, this was published in the Yale University *Journal of Conflict Resolution*, with an accompanying letter requesting that other studies be carried out, since the results were so unexpected. In about six different studies at different times and in several different countries, the fluctuations in the size of the meditating groups were compared to officially collected data on daily rates of crime, violence, war deaths, and other problems. The correlation between the size of the meditating group and reductions in violence and crime was dramatic and statistically significant. The statistical likelihood that the results were due to chance was one in ten million—which is a far higher level of significance than most pharmaceuticals or other social interventions have been required to show to prove that their products work as claimed.

Something astonishing is becoming clear in this evolving marriage of science and mysticism, and it is this. The whole universe is being recognized as a 'Unified Field' of brilliantly intelligent, interconnected energy. Like many others, I have had my own personal experiences of this field. What happened in 2012, however, showed me the enormity of the resources this field makes available for exactly the kind of social and political transformation we now need.

In the summer of 2012, at the Celebrate Life Festival in northern Germany, a teacher named Thomas Hübl explained the Unified Field to an audience of about eight hundred people. Hübl said the Unified Field was a social process for higher understanding. At the festival, my colleagues and I were facilitating a five-day working group of about sixty people, and we were curious to investigate whether this Unified Field had any effect on the transformation of conflict.

During the next few days, our experience was as follows: as conflicts erupted in the group, we found that a key decision on the part of individuals was whether to move 'toward' the conflict or to shy away from it. Those willing to move toward the conflict—to unearth it, face it, and listen to others involved in it—found that they could move through the conflict to a place where it was transformed. A key factor seemed to be that they were supported in doing this by a number of people consistently meditating.

As a result of this experience, which was documented, Thomas Hübl asked me if I knew of a community in a zone of hot conflict who might like to work on a further experiment. He wanted to be connected with a community who were thoughtful and reflective, so I put him in touch with the Tree of Life in Zimbabwe.[1] The Tree of Life is a network of five different community groups comprising several hundred people, who have been meeting across the country for years of dedicated work to heal the victims of electoral brutality, torture, rape, and murder that have proliferated under the vicious political regime of Zimbabwean president Robert Mugabe. At the time, they were also gearing up to support activists and community organizers to prevent violence in the run-up to the elections announced for July 2013.

Thomas suggested that those in Zimbabwe meet in meditation at specific times on the first and third Tuesday of every month, connecting with his group sitting in meditation in Germany. As he said, 'Many people sitting at the same time generates a very strong energy field. I think this will be very supportive for you… I would suggest that everyone invite consciously that a new level of awakening or light or consciousness will take place. This invitation will draw the energy in.' The coordinated meditation groups started in March 2013. In mid-July I received an email from Zimbabwe telling me that this work had been successful in helping to foster conditions of greater peace and calm between the different political parties and their supporters (Reeler, 2013).

Zimbabweans lined up to vote on July 31, and the absence of violence was noted by all observers; this election was quite different to previous ones. Then came the official result of an overwhelming victory to Mugabe. Most non-African observers expressed concern over electoral fraud, including alleged bribery, bussing of voters to opposition strongholds and manipulation of the electoral roll. Nevertheless, the peaceful atmosphere continued.

What is emerging has several names: it's known by biochemist Rupert Sheldrake as the Morphogenetic Field, and it's also called the Amplified Field and the Unified Field. This field develops when people choose to come together to communicate with the intention to tell their deepest heart truth. Frontier scientists from across the planet have produced remarkable evidence that an energy field connects everything in the universe and that humanity is part of this vast exchange of energy. Lynne McTaggart, in her remarkable explanation of how this field was discovered and how it works, says that some scientists suggest that all of our higher cognitive processes result from an interaction with this field, and that this 'might account for intuition or creativity—and how ideas come to us in bursts of insight, sometimes as fragments but often as a miraculous whole' (McTaggart, 2001).

McTaggart records how the Transcendental Meditation organization had systematically tested—through dozens and dozens of studies conducted over a twenty-year span—whether group meditation could reduce violence and discord in the world. The organization had elected to call this 'Super Radiance'—after the super-radiance in the brain or in a laser that creates coherence and unity—because they believed meditation would have the same effect on society.

Many of the studies were published in peer-reviewed journals. One study of twenty-four US cities 'showed that whenever a city reached a point where

1 percent of the population was carrying out regular [Transcendental Meditation], the crime rate dropped [by] 24 percent. In a follow up study of 48 cities, half of which had a 1 percent population which meditated, the 1 percent cities achieved a 22 percent decrease in crime, compared with an increase of 2 percent in the control cities' (Ibid).

Our understanding of this field is in its infancy, but it is clear to me and to many others that an extraordinary power of transformation awaits us if we can establish a humble and transparent relationship with it, if we can foster interconnection.

Blazing Intelligence

One day not so long ago, I suddenly saw the amazing feat that is a tree. In this case, it was a towering oak tree near where I live; it was in April. It dawned on me that this massive edifice, which has been standing there for at least two hundred winters, was conveying liquids and nourishment vertically upward through solid wood. In a few weeks, this rich moisture was going to produce tiny leaves from the buds I could already see swelling. In autumn there would be acorns falling to the ground, each one carrying a four-hundred year blueprint plan of its own.

I stood there stunned.

As I look around me now, there are literally thousands of such organisms and plants and animals and insects, all going through the most intricate cycles, without any instruction from anyone. I see the exquisite perfection of a butterfly's wing and realize that however hard we humans try, we can't produce that level of live beauty.

When my daughter became the mother of twins, I stared in awe at these beautiful beings who—at the moment of taking their first breath—possessed functioning internal organs that would last them for perhaps a hundred years, who had genes reaching back over millions of years, who had nervous systems and endocrine glands and hormones perfectly designed to function smoothly with no instruction from a human or a computer

Daniel Siegel, clinical professor of psychiatry at the UCLA School of Medicine, makes the following observations: 'Given the number of synaptic connections, the brain's possible on-off firing patterns—its potential for various states of activation—has been calculated to be ten to the millionth power—or ten times ten one million times. This number is thought to be larger than the number of atoms in the known universe. It also far exceeds our ability to experience in one lifetime even a small percentage of these firing possibilities' (Siegel, 2010).

Observing these things, I have awoken to the sheer extent of the blazing intelligence that must have produced everything that we see around us. We and everything else are made from the stardust of the Big Bang. I remain astounded by the beauty of this system, in the midst of which we humans live. Any day, any one of us can go into a public park—or even a patch of waste ground—and see the extravagant elegance of what nature has produced over billions of years. A two-year-old child looking at a snail or a wildflower is rightly mesmerized and astonished. If an adult—gazing out of the window of a jet passing over the remaining great tropical forests of the earth is not astonished and mesmerized, something is…well…not in working order.

Balance between the Masculine and the Feminine

For three thousand years—at least—power and decision making worldwide has been in the hands of men. While this has brought us obvious advances in science and great discoveries in many fields, it has also led to an imbalance, a distorted way of doing things that excludes or marginalizes essential aspects of human intelligence.

When I was researching a book on power and sex in 1995, I found that nearly all recorded thinking on power and the use of power has been androcentric—that is, done by men and based on male values. The male norm and the human norm, even today, tend to be thought of as identical. Nations operate according to distorted male notions of power, and that is the way they assume others will respond. There is a whole set of preconceptions underlying this way of thinking, including the conviction that humans are inherently aggressive, inveterately competitive, and socially separate and independent, and that they have no need to be responsible in a collective manner (Elworthy, 1996).

This has led to a dangerous imbalance between the masculine and feminine in most of us today—regardless of gender—and it is prevalent almost everywhere in the world. For example, we see women in the City of London and on Wall Street dressing exactly like men (except for the high heels) and competing to outperform men in focus, logic, ruthlessness, and achievement.

What has become devalued in this way of living are essential elements of being human, elements such as: the skill of listening; the ability to nurture and to include; the choice to exercise 'power with' rather than 'power over'; the attention to intuition and the creative imagination that makes for great art and invention; the ability to stand in the shoes of another person; the practice of dialogue with our inner world; the compassion and stamina to look after those who are weak or in need; and reverence for the sacredness of creation and of our bodies.

This loss of the feminine principle of the soul has also resulted in the devaluation of the deep masculine, also known as the sacred masculine and exemplified in the great saints and sages of our global traditions. In our contemporary world's lethal addiction to the grasping and dominating aspects of the male, we have lost sight of the more profound and life nurturing gifts of the masculine. These include the passion to protect life and the vulnerable, the sense of honour in duty to the community; the profound depth of brotherhood in goals that transcend personal agendas; the courtesy and modesty of the code of chivalry; the rigorous patience devoted to discovery and verification in scholarship and science; the love of order, clarity, and law (not as goals in themselves, but as a way of structuring life); the capacity for one-pointed focus and the stamina to complete the task; and the courage to be in the service of the rights of the weak, to stand up and be counted, and to blow the whistle on corruption.

This devaluation of the qualities of the deep feminine and the deep masculine—in women as in men—has led to untold suffering all over the world. It is a fundamental cause of the dissociation from ourselves, our bodies, and the natural world—and the avalanche of disasters caused by that dissociation.

What is essential for human survival now is the rebalancing of the masculine and feminine qualities possessed by both men and women. We recognize and admire the extraordinary power of individuals who have managed it, who can call equally on their courage and their compassion, on their logic and their love, on their intention and their intuition. Think of how Nelson Mandela had the empathy to understand the needs of the white supremacists in South Africa, combined with a steely courage such as the world has rarely seen. Think of how the compassionate heart of Mother Teresa worked in tandem with a mind as sharp as a razor.

This principle of balance between the feminine and masculine parts of ourselves has long been recognized. For thousands of years, Eastern spiritual traditions have worked with the balance of *yin* and *yang* and Eastern health practices and medical expertise—such as acupuncture—are based on achieving this balance in the body's energy. The balance is superbly evoked in the Kabbalah, the eloquent archive of Jewish mysticism, and it is found in the Hindu tradition of Shiva and Shakti, as well as in ancient Egypt, and in the stories and folklore of indigenous peoples the world over.

This rebalancing of the masculine and feminine over time creates a being that, like a great dancer, combines peace and passion, rigor and spontaneity, discipline and surrender, being and doing, heart and head, and clear interaction between the right and left hemispheres of the brain.

The 'wise mind' is in the space created where these two circles of the masculine and the feminine overlap. It is this mind that can be the vehicle of the leap in consciousness that I am calling for, because by its nature it is connected to all modes of being and becoming in the Unified Field, and because it is able to draw on whatever is needed for the situation in hand. Imagine for a moment what resources we would discover for the regeneration of the planet if our educational systems were devoted to drawing out this wise mind.

With all its challenges, the age we face now demands that human beings access their wholeness—their ability to use body, soul, and spirit, as well as mind. Women and men of wisdom have a key part to play in showing how this rebalanced power works, awakening in humanity the love of and devotion to life on earth that will enable not just survival, but transformation and a future full of possibility. This can be an evolutionary awakening of global proportions.

Why Do We Need a Leap in Consciousness and Shall We Get There?

The kind of leap in consciousness that we are interested in could be compared to the transformation of a caterpillar into a butterfly. A caterpillar eats hundreds of times its weight in a day—day after day—until it is too bloated to continue and hangs itself up, its skin then hardening into a chrysalis. Inside this chrysalis, deep in the caterpillar's body, tiny things that biologists call 'imaginal discs' begin to form. These discs contain the blueprint of a whole new being. At first they are attacked and resisted by the caterpillar, but they keep coming faster and faster, becoming the 'imaginal cells' that build the butterfly by feeding on the soupy meltdown of the caterpillar's body.

It took a long time for biologists to understand the reason for the immune system attack on the incipient butterfly cells, but eventually they discovered that the butterfly has its own unique genome, carried by the caterpillar, inherited from long ago in evolution, yet not part of it as such, but coming to be (Margulis and Sagan, 2002).

Before we examine the extent to which the leap in consciousness is occurring, we need to understand the paradoxical nature of our current crisis. It is at once a great birth and a great death. On the one hand, we are living in a time of stupendous scientific discoveries and spiritual renaissance that are transforming our concept of the universe and shattering old ideas about the nature of reality. On the other, our mindless plundering of the earth's resources and our destruction of nature's balance are threatening the delicate organism of life on our planet and the survival of our species as never before.

Since 1900, the percentage of the world's overexploited or fully exploited oceans has risen from less than 10 percent to 87 percent. 'Fully exploited' means there are no fish left in the sea. Ivan MacFadyen has twice raced a yacht from Melbourne in Australia to Osaka in Japan. The first time, in 2003, his isolation was relieved by regular sightings of turtles, dolphins, and flurries of feeding birds. But ten years later, in 2013, he says that 'for 3,000 nautical miles there was nothing alive to be seen.' What modern mariners do notice is plenty of floating plastic debris. The long overfishing of course explains the scarcity of maritime creatures. But the debris is lethal. Albatrosses, for example, mistake plastic debris for food and give it to their young. 'Chicks starve with full bellies, and when their bodies rot away, they leave tragic piles of bottle tops, pens, cigarette lighters and plastic fragments to bleach in the sun' (Ray, 2013).

The International Union for the Conservation of Nature—the world's leading authority on biodiversity—estimates that, as of 2013, species at imminent risk of extinction include 196 mammals, 197 birds, 151 reptiles, 519 amphibians, 413 fishes, 120 insects, 548 molluscs, and 1920 plants (IUCN, 2013). It does not take much imagination to realize the effect such disappearances have on food chains—and thus on human survival.

There is an accelerating change in our entire earth system, of which climate is but one component. Without realizing it, molecule by molecule, we have upset the earth's climatic balance. Arctic coastlines, for example, are retreating by fourteen meters per year. Greenland's surface ice melt season reached peak levels in late July 2013.[2] This will contribute to rising sea levels (Rignot et al., 2011).

The World Meteorological Organization (WMO) reports that the first decade of the twenty-first century was the warmest ever recorded for both northern and southern hemispheres. According to the WMO, the rate of temperature rise in the past two decades has been unprecedented

The combination of the melting of the Antarctic and Greenland ice sheets and the thermal expansion of the oceans as they warm means not only are sea levels rising but also that the rate of this rise is speeding up. From 2000 to 2010, the rise averaged 3 millimetres per year, nearly double the yearly average of 1.6 millimetres in the twentieth century. The global sea level average in 2010 was 20 centimetres (nearly 8 inches) above the level in 1880. Rising sea levels mean that vast populations will have to move. On an already grotesquely overcrowded planet, where will they go?

Melting sea ice is now, in turn, causing the release of vast quantities of methane from the Arctic Ocean. For the first time, hundreds of plumes of methane—many of them over a mile wide—have been observed rising from previously frozen methane stores in the Lapdev Sea, off the East Siberian Arctic shelf. This may just be the beginning of what increased global warming can release, and because methane is many times more potent a greenhouse gas than carbon dioxide, this could pose the ultimate death knell to our environment.

Here are figures quoted by the 2009 award-winning film *Home*, made by Yann Arthus-Bertrand that give some idea of what is happening: (Arthus-Bertrand et al., 2009).

1. In fifty years—a single lifetime—the earth has been more radically changed than by all previous generations of humanity combined.
2. Before the end of this century, excessive mining will have exhausted nearly all the planet's reserves of minerals.
3. The Arctic icecap has lost 40 percent of its thickness in forty years.
4. Across the planet, one major river in ten no longer flows into the sea for several months of the year.
5. In India 30 percent of wells have had to be abandoned because the underground aquifers have dried out.
6. It takes nearly 3,500 gallons of water to produce a little over two pounds of beef.
7. One billion people worldwide have no access to clean water.
8. Fish is the staple diet of one in five humans, yet three-quarters of fishing grounds worldwide are depleted or in dangerous decline.
9. Half the world's poor live in resource-rich countries.
10. Half the world's wealth is in the hands of the richest two percent of the world's population.
11. Every week over a million people swell the population of the world's cities.
12. In one hour the sun gives the earth the same amount of energy as that consumed by all of humanity in one year. Yet in some countries bathed by the sun, you see almost no solar panels.

Every one of these examples shocks and frightens me. These are examples of human violence—unconscious violence, perhaps, but on a massive scale. Added to that lack of awareness is the desperate race to make money and the hubris of thinking that advanced technology has no consequences.

How can humans wake up to the mortal danger of our interference with the fragile web of relationships upon which life on this planet depends? Is there a way that we can see that we are an integral part of this great web of life, formed over countless millions of years? That we certainly cannot control it? That we will not survive unless we respect it?

It is now clear to many observers that this mortal danger is challenging us to take a great leap in our evolution—one that we might not have confronted were we not pushed right up against chaos and collapse. We have never had to think as a planet before. Why? Because our capacity for destruction—whether military, societal, or environmental—is now so much greater than it was fifty years ago. Because the advances we have made in the technology of destruction—combined with our belief in our right to ravage the planet for our own purposes means that this destruction will be greater tomorrow. We have, at most, only a few decades in which to heal ourselves and help regenerate the planet.

Historian Karen Armstrong writes, 'We risk environmental catastrophe because we no longer see the earth as holy, but regard it simply as a resource.' She goes on: 'Unless there is some kind of spiritual revolution that can keep abreast of our technological genius, it is unlikely we will save our planet' (Armstrong, 2006). More and more outstanding writers and broadcasters are now saying the same thing.[3]

Is this kind of revolution happening? Might it happen? I don't know the answer to this question, and I want to know. I am astonished that there are no serious studies of the growth in global awareness, since it is the key to human survival.

In 2010, I asked the head of Google's School of Personal Growth if Google could set up a simple poll, asking five questions to determine awakening, but so far this the idea has not been taken up, and the next obvious question is, aren't governments and world organizations dealing with global warming and climate change? The organizations that we would hope could do this—like the United Nations, the International Monetary Fund, and the World Bank—are taking stabs at it, but these have been disastrously ineffective. The UN Framework Convention on Climate Change, whose job for the past twenty years has been to ensure the stabilization of greenhouse gases, has failed in its goals. Likewise, the Convention on Biological Diversity, whose job has been to reduce the rate of biodiversity loss, has failed. And the UN Convention to Combat Desertification has also failed. Governments either cannot make the necessary agreements to halt the devastation of the planet, or they cannot stick to them.

A recent article in the *Economist* concludes, in effect, that no one wants to be responsible unilaterally, since all want to profit from the world's resources.

We are in the grip of a classic—and this time global—case of the 'tragedy of the commons', which is the depletion of a shared resource by individuals acting independently and 'rationally', each according to his or her own self-interest. Given the extent and complexity of the crisis and the lack of leadership in response, it is hardly surprising that most people feel helpless and allow their instinctive common sense to be dulled by the media.

Andrew Harvey, a teacher of mystic traditions, says that 95 percent of us are in denial and 4 percent are beginning to wake up, but then getting lost in magical thinking (by 'magical thinking,' he means New Age dreaming). In his view, only one percent of us are actually waking up to the extent of what must be done and girding ourselves with the powerful energy of the new consciousness (Harvey, 2012).

What is clear is that time is running out. Now, more than ever before, we have to wake up and act from a new consciousness. Only such a consciousness can give us the guidance, wisdom, and strength we need to transform our future. As Eckhart Tolle says, 'The history of Communism, originally inspired by noble ideals, clearly illustrates what happens when people attempt to change external reality—create a new earth—without any prior change in their inner reality, their state of consciousness' (Tolle, 2005).

So, what would happen if we were able to access the consciousness of the Unified Field—and how can we gain this access? How can we discover and use a higher level of human consciousness? How can we make this leap in consciousness?

It seems to me that these are questions we must address if we are to make those necessary changes in our governance, personal, corporate and political, to discover and give expression to that 'new story of who we are and what we are capable of becoming,' that Edgar Mitchell called for when, from Apollo 14, he saw our world as a whole.

Notes

1. The Tree of Life is a healing and empowerment process of storytelling and time in nature with circles of around eight participants and two facilitators using the tree as a metaphor for life (roots, trunk, branches, wounding, fruit), which takes place over three days.
2. National Snow and Ice Data Center (NSIDC), http://nsidc.org.
3. Cultural historian and theologian Thomas Berry in *The Great Work* (1999) and *The Dream of the Earth*, biologist and business consultant Dr. Elisabet Sahtouris in *Biology Revisited*, physicist Fritjof Capra in *The Web of Life* (1997), biology professor Christopher Uhl in *Developing Ecological Consciousness: Paths to a Sustainable World* (2003), and many others—all give the same urgent message.

2. Nourishing the Soul of a Leader

Dadi Janki

> *If I wish others to respect me, I need to respect myself; if I wish others to love me, I need to love myself. A leader always has to be active and alert. The foremost quality of a leader is humility*
> —Dadi Prakasmani, Spiritual Head of the Brahma Kumaris, 1969–2007

Effective leadership requires inner strength, because clarity of purpose can so easily be lost when other people press their own ideas and opinions. But where does that strength come from, and how can it be sustained?

Growing My Inner Strength

When I have inner strength, I feel at peace with myself and decision-making, even in difficult circumstances, happens with a depth of clarity and a feeling of knowing what is the right thing to do. There is a flow of positive, uplifting ideas that others also come to accept. The more I draw on my inner strength, the momentum of positive energy increases. This is reciprocated by the positive attitudes of others towards me. Consequently, my thoughts, feelings, attitudes, words and actions begin to make a real difference in the world.

To develop this kind of leadership, the quality of my thoughts is extremely important. Thoughts that are optimistic, clear and filled with goodness increase our energy, whereas thoughts of worry, fear and confusion drain our energy. If I think of my mind as a garden, a good gardener needs to weed the garden and also water and feed it with good, productive thinking. Weeding out the thoughts of worry, fear or doubt clears away the veil that is obscuring my true potential as a human being.

The mind therefore acts as a gateway between the outer and inner worlds. Whatever is within is reflected without. I can either live my life allowing what is outside of me to penetrate my thinking and feeling, or I can access my inner strength and allow the qualities I have within to be a positive influence in my life and in the world. There are three aspects at the root of such powerful, productive thinking: self-awareness, the power of love and the deep intention to serve.

Self-awareness tells us that before I can begin to lead others I have to be able to lead myself; that is to become the master not only of my thoughts, but also of my feelings, words and actions. Self-awareness sifts through the layers of memories, good and bad, habitual thinking and past influences. Self-awareness steps beyond the many changing roles that I may play in life and brings me to my original self, the self that is unchanging and stable. Self-awareness brings me to the innermost soul of I, the human being. To experience myself in this true way is not difficult; I just need to decide to take the time to sit quietly, silently, with myself.

Silence does not have to be a physical silence; I can be silent within in the midst of noise. Silence is to consciously move away from thoughts of the external world—maybe of people, situations or of the tasks not yet accomplished—allowing space for me to go on my journey within. In silence I am no longer connecting with all the many influences around me, or even the influences of my own past; in silence I go beneath the surface of my thoughts and begin to experience something that is only accessible through silence—a state of inner peace that carries with it calm and ease. I begin to experience my true original self—a gentle self that is extremely strong. It can never be influenced into being anything other than it is; a being of peace, love and wisdom. The human soul *is* this and it is the soul that inhabits the costume of the body, rather like an actor donning a costume to play a part in a play. The soul and the body together make up a human being. However, the master is the soul itself. This is why it is important to use the phrase 'I am a soul' rather than 'I have a soul'. This change of phrase creates the difference between being a master of the self and a servant of external influences. The consciousness of 'I *am* a soul' is experienced as the 'I am the master'. The consciousness of 'I *have* a soul' is experienced as being overpowered by external influences. It is important to ask oneself the question each day: who am I? And to then experience the greater truth of who I am. Thus, self-awareness is not something to theorise about, it is something to be practised and experienced.

The experience of self-awareness can answer an age-old question: is the original nature of human beings good or evil? Together with witnessing human greatness, far too often we see violent traits dominating human behaviour. How is this possible? When I am aware of my true self I experience the original goodness that is the core of the soul itself. However when I allow external influences to rule me, I suppress that goodness deeply inside so that it no longer has the power to influence my thoughts, attitudes and actions. To suppress my inherent goodness in this way is the very first violence that I perform—towards my own self. This leaves an emptiness and insecurity inside, so that I lose touch with my true identity and instead rely on many other aspects to give me a sense of self. These 'external identities' include gender, culture, ethnicity, power, position, wealth and so on. When these identities are challenged I move into a state of fear, whether subtle or overt. Fear is the root cause of anger. I therefore move from the state of non-violence to violence.

This is why it is so important to keep nourishing the self with self-awareness and thoughts of our inner state of goodness; to keep reminding myself of the peace, love and wisdom that I hold inside. It is something that I cherish about myself.

The Power of Love

Over the years—I am now 99 years young—I have seen the power of love work in my own life and in the lives of others. I am now convinced that love is the most transformative energy in the world. This is because love is inherent to the soul itself and exists in and of itself. It is a love that is strong. It can transform negativity because it is not influenced by it; it continues to give, independently of whether or not this is reciprocated by others. It has no need for revenge; instead true love seeks to forgive. It is not selfish in any way. It is also a great healing force. When two people or communities have animosity for one another, feelings of love from the heart can reach the heart of the other, more powerfully than words. Love can reach across the divides of gender, culture and religion. This is because love is more powerful than fear.

How can love transform to this extent? It is important to understand the difference between 'being' loving and 'loving' something or someone. In the latter, there is the possibility that love can become too narrow and possessive. Whether it is an idea, an opinion or a relationship, if I become possessive, I cannot let go and be open to change, and I sacrifice my inner strength. 'Being' loving is to experience love that is inherent to who I am. This state of being creates an atmosphere of love around me and opens up the possibility of letting go of whatever is putting a limit on who I can be or what I can do in the world.

This takes a generosity of spirit, which is possible when I have accumulated a stock of love inside. From where do I take love? If I seek it from human relationships, it is uncertain. Today someone will give me love and tomorrow it may be taken away or the relationship may take on a different form. However, if I seek love from a higher Source of love, I have the possibility of accumulating love and as I give love, it accumulates even more. As it is said, 'To give is to receive.'

As with all things that nourish the soul, the connection with the Source of love happens in inner silence. For this, my mind needs to be totally still, away from thinking about others and from the thoughts of the past or the future. As I focus on my self-awareness, the being of spiritual energy that I am, I kindle the flame of love and begin to open my heart to the Source of love. Then the energy of love begins to flow. Pure love enters my heart. It is like receiving a current of love. It is a cool, healing energy, clearing away the negativity that may have been with me for a long time. As I allow the current of love to flow, I am accumulating love and I experience my original, loving state of being.

You may feel that you cannot survive in a harsh world in this way, especially as many eyes are on a leader's every movement. At present we are witnessing a lot of violence in society. In particular if someone feels disrespected, they can react in very unpredictable ways. This can happen in personal relationships and between communities. Often the solution applied to overcoming violence is yet more violence. This creates a cycle of violence from which it is very difficult, if not impossible to escape. This is because we have not understood the root of violence; it is a lack of love.

Wherever people have the humility and patience to listen, to learn and to begin to give respect, the atmosphere of love begins to transform the most intransigent of situations. It takes courage to start to deal with situations with love. Love in my attitude creates a loving and enabling atmosphere. My presence will speak louder than my words and the atmosphere I create will generate good feelings in others. This is the basis of trust. It does not mean that I cannot take tough decisions; in fact with the energy of love accumulated within I have greater courage and strength to do the unexpected, to follow my inner voice of truth.

I then need to keep the energy of love alive within me so that the transformation is lasting. There is so much anger in the world because people cannot have what they want or because they feel devalued or dehumanised by others. Embedded in the energy of love is the awareness that each human being is of inherent value and has a unique gift to offer to the world, however large or small. As I nourish myself, I begin to see the connection between my own state of being and the way I relate to others. If I value myself, I will naturally value those around me; it does not take effort. In turn, they begin to value themselves. This brings with it the experience of inner peace and happiness and most of all hope. Thus, I can inspire others by my way of being. This is why it is so necessary to keep nourishing the self within and to keep accumulating from the Source of love every day and to make that Higher power my quiet, reassuring companion. This is what keeps me strong and free from burdens.

Wise Decision-Making

Every day a leader faces challenges either personal or collective. Some may be waiting for me to fail so that they have a chance to prove that they can do the task better. Others may try to deceive me so that I come to accept their opinions. I may be offered many 'gifts' of this kind. I have noticed that the more I think about a difficult situation, the more fearsome it becomes. A small problem assumes gigantic proportions and my imagination can run wild. Along with this, if we are habituated in seeing what is wrong with the world and in particular what is wrong with people, we make assumptions about how a person may respond: 'He/she is always like that!' This kind of thinking makes me and the other person a prisoner of the past and sets up a chain reaction of confusion and fear. When my vision becomes myopic in this way, usually tolerance and understanding are also in short supply. Solutions seem very far away. Any decision I take will be based on fear and decisions based on fear divide. As my thoughts are the seeds of my words and actions, let me ask myself, what quality of seeds am I sowing and what is the fruit that I will reap?

When I feel nourished inside, the awareness of my gentle yet strong self will help me to broaden my vision and open up new possibilities. This gives me courage and will power, and naturally lessens the fear inside. I literally begin to see things differently. The more positive I am inside, the more clarity I have and my power to discern is heightened. I begin to sow seeds that will bring the fruit of solutions that will nourish all concerned. I am able to get to the root of the problem, which is often different to what presents itself on the surface. For this there are key questions that I like to ask myself: 'What can I say or do to help that person feel more positive about herself or himself? What other influences are contributing to a particular behaviour? How can I create an atmosphere in which others can feel more relaxed so that we can truly listen to and respect each other?'

It takes a lot of inner, strong determination to set the past aside and to allow something new to emerge. The world needs new solutions and, as a leader, I cannot presume that anything today will be the same as yesterday. There are an unlimited number of influences that can bring change at any given moment. At such times, it is important not to be tempted to take sides—we need to work for the good of all; for reconciliation; for peace. This is wisdom. Peace within will bring peace in our attitude, vision and behaviour.

There is a deep connection between the awareness of my true self, a being of peace, love and wisdom, and my values. My values provide an interface between the self and the world; they are clearly visible not only in my attitude, but also through my decision-making and action. I become aware of the difference between values that result from the influence of external factors such as culture or the prevailing trends in society, and values that somehow rise above these factors, values that are constant and nourished by self-awareness and the accumulation of love within. Even in the most challenging of situations, I will not compromise my values. This has the effect of encouraging togetherness and co-operation.

For example, if I show respect to someone because it is expected of me, that respect will not touch the heart of another. Its superficiality will be felt. If I show someone respect, not because of my own need, but because I truly have love for and respect people for who they are, the impact of that will be profound. The words may be the same, but the interaction will be totally different. As I live by values that are nourished by love, my burdens are lessened. It is as if I am 'handing them over' to the Source of love, allowing love to do its work. Love becomes the underlying intention of all that I say and do. I no longer carry the burden of worrying about the results of my decisions; if my intentions are truly to serve, I have the confidence that only good will result, often in unexpected ways. Love truly sets me free.

This is not an abdication of responsibility, but an even greater responsibility to be true to my inner self at every moment. This is why it is important to take times of silence, to reconnect and to remain strong. This is because the highest quality of decision-making involves the arts of listening and reflecting, without my own needs, ideas or opinions interfering. Two things result from this; firstly others feel validated and heard, and secondly I will be calm enough to draw on my own experience and so bring understanding and wisdom to the outcome. Too many thoughts can cloud the decision-making process. With a clear and calm mind, decisions are taken in an instant; it is the careful preparation within that takes time. Having prepared the ground of my own being and having sowed the seed of benevolent thoughts, I reap the fruit of knowing in an instant what needs to be done, and the actions that follow will be filled with benevolence. I will not hesitate; I will have the strength to act.

What is described above is an expression of true compassion; decisions and actions based on the underlying intention of love, understanding the heart of another, looking beyond immediate outcomes and working for the welfare of all. Another way of expressing this is: the restoration of humanity and dignity. Compassion acts to alleviate suffering by empowering others to experience self-love. It is about true independence and freedom; freedom for each individual to give of the best and the highest of themselves as citizens of the Earth. It is essential for these principles to inform our major development agendas such as the greater sharing of resources, care for the planet and education and healthcare for all. Putting love and compassion at the heart of the decision-making process will create a better future for the whole of humanity.

Serving Society

Therefore the vision of a leader is both broad and deep, beyond the usual limits that society may place on me. In my whole life I have sought never to allow anyone to suppress my own inner feelings of truth, nor have I allowed anyone to deceive me. In deceiving others we are only deceiving ourselves. In allowing others to suppress me, I am in fact suppressing myself. My spirit needs to be free to look over distant horizons to a new landscape. For such inspiration, I need to connect with something greater than myself. As a human being I am prone to many influences and doubts, but in the consciousness of being an instrument for a greater task, I will be stretched beyond my own limits; in fact I realise that limits are an illusion. I connect with a greater Being that is not only the Source of love but also of inspiration. However, as well as clearing my mind, ready for inner silence, there is one more important aspect to pay attention to; I need to imbibe the quality of humility, of being a server. If there is ego, I can never gain the highest inspiration and I will limit myself and the task in front of me. Humility allows the power of truth to work. I never need to prove the truth; truth always reveals itself at the right time and in the right place. Therefore humility is the simplest, most powerful expression of truth.

The Source of truth is a Source of spiritual energy that is ever pure, untainted by the changes that take place in the physical dimension, and is beyond space and time. As I take my own consciousness beyond these limitations-fears, worries and doubts are left behind-I connect with that Source of energy, an unlimited Source of all that is true and benevolent. Such benevolence makes me feel safe and secure and engenders my trust. It is an act of surrender to something much greater than myself. In this awareness, inspiration is altruistic, compassionate and just, and I gain the strength to move forward. As an instrument, I am constantly learning and growing. To stop learning is to stop living. By accepting the task in front of me, I will receive the strength and wisdom that I need. This courage comes from seeing with a broader vision, beyond human-made boundaries and borders. Without this I cannot see the possibilities for transformation and if I cannot see them, I cannot work towards them. I will experience the constant struggle of remaining stuck in the problems at hand. A true instrument can always see a solution. Implementing such a vision often challenges the status quo, which is why I need to return time and again to nourishing my inner self.

Taking Time to Nourish the Self

There is a deep connection between my thoughts, breath, energy and time. If I have many thoughts, my breathing will be shallow and I will have less energy. It will take me twice as long to complete the simplest task. If I have few, yet productive thoughts, I will conserve my energy and I will use my time well. Even a complex task will be accomplished easily. It is important to use my thoughts, time and energy in a worthwhile way and not to waste these valuable resources. For this it is important to take time to nourish the self in silence. The soul needs silence to replenish its stock of power; the mind needs silence to maintain inner peace and stability and my body needs silence to rest and remain healthy. As a leader, there may be many demands on me, so I need to nourish myself otherwise I will run out of steam.

The early morning is the best time for silence. At that time the atmosphere around is calm and there is nothing else that I need to do. By consciously mastering my thoughts and connecting with the Source of love as the first act of my day, I create a foundation for the whole day to be productive. I also begin with inner strength so that I will be able to face challenges calmly, with patience and wisdom. The deep feelings of connecting nourish the soul. It is like feeding the self nourishing and fresh food. This is the most important task of the day. Otherwise I shall be chasing my mind all day long and will be drained of my energy. Taking time in this way will save time. And the interesting thing is that I begin to see the strong connection between thoughts and time. Productive thoughts enable me to use time well. By worrying, my time is wasted. At the end of the day, let me take time for silence, to contemplate on the lessons learned, new discoveries, aspects that could have been improved upon. It is necessary to have closure to each day in my mind and heart otherwise things of the day will continue to pull my mind and will not allow me to rest or to move on to new things. During the day, whenever I can, let me take a moment or two of silence. There are times when the mind is not thinking about anything in particular; when I am walking somewhere or doing an automatic task. I can take those opportunities to nourish my mind with thoughts of my true self. We do not value silence enough in our society and yet, without silence, sound itself loses its meaning. My words will be empty. Inner silence is like a cooling balm or a fresh breeze to a heated mind.

When a leader leads himself or herself in this way, many will follow. They will not follow the leader, but rather follow their own inner capacity for greatness. The world needs silence, peace, love, truth and wisdom and yet they are already within us just waiting to be released into our lives.

3. The Need for Altruism

MATTHIEU RICARD

In the modern western world, individualism is often appreciated as strength and as a virtue, sometimes to the point of selfishness and narcissism. This is a bit puzzling, since it does not seem to foster an optimal way to live in society. Should we be discouraged, then, by the assertions of the likes of Plautus, for whom 'man is a wolf to man,' Thomas Hobbes, who speaks of the 'war of every man against every man,' or Freud who asserts he has 'found little that is 'good' among human beings on the whole'? Perhaps not since, despite the violence that afflicts our world, in the reality of the every day our existence is usually woven from deeds of cooperation, friendship, affection, and care. What is more, contrary to conventional wisdom and to the impression the media give us, all in-depth studies gathered together by Harvard professor Steven Pinker in *The Better Angels of Our Nature*, show that violence, in all its forms, has continued to diminish over the course of the last few centuries (Pinker, 2012).

Indeed, over the years in which I have been working with scientist colleagues, I have been reassured to note that during the last thirty years the deformed vision of human nature has been challenged by an increasing number of researchers who demonstrate that the hypothesis of universal selfishness is disproven by scientific investigation. This, in particular, includes the work of Daniel Batson who was the first psychologist to investigate, through rigorous scientific protocols, whether real altruism existed and was not limited to a disguised form of selfishness (Batson, 2011).

The experience of thousands of years of contemplative practices attests that individual transformation is possible. And this age-old experience has now been corroborated by research in the neurosciences that has shown that any form of training—learning how to read or learning a musical instrument, for example—induces a restructuring in the brain, at both the functional and structural levels. This is also what happens when one trains in developing altruistic love and compassion (Ricard, Lutz, & Davidson, 2014).

Twenty years ago, it was almost universally accepted by neuroscientists that the brain could not be reorganized after its initial phase of development during childhood. But we now know that major functional and structural changes can occur throughout a person's life. We speak of 'neuroplasticity', a term which takes into account the fact that the brain evolves continuously in relation to our experiences, and that a particular training, such as learning a musical instrument or a sport, can bring about a profound change. During the last twelve years, major neuroscientists have conducted research with expert and novice meditators indicating that, like any other skill, altruism and compassion can be greatly enhanced through proper training. Increasingly powerful MRI techniques and electroencephalograms (EEG), combined with the participation of experienced contemplatives, have led us towards the golden age of a new domain of research called 'contemplative neuroscience' (Davidson & Begley, 2012).

A strictly genetic evolution such as this, under pressure by global, environmental constraints, would require several tens of thousands of years (50,000 according to some estimates). On the other hand, an evolution of our cultures can lead to significant changes of our behaviour within a much shorter period of time. Recent work by theorists of evolution, particularly Richerson and Boyd (2004), has emphasized the crucial importance of cultural evolution in major transformations that have taken place in human society since the appearance of our species. This evolution is cumulative and is transmitted over the course of generations by education and imitation. The influence of a particular culture can also transform individuals through neuroplasticity and epigenetics. In this way, society and individuals transform each other like the two blades of a knife sharpening each other.

Numerous studies have shown that, from a very early age, children demonstrate empathic responses to other children in distress. From the age of six months, before they have developed the most rudimentary sense of self, infants prefer individuals who help rather than hinder others. Other studies have shown that by eighteen months of age, children are able to perform altruistic acts themselves and often express a pure sense of altruism—offering help with no expectation of getting something in return (Warneken & Tomasello, 2006).

Put more simply, the Dalai Lama, for whom I have had the honour to work as an interpreter since 1989, often states, 'My religion is kindness.' The essence of his teaching is as follows:

The Need for Altruism

> Every sentient being, even my enemy, fears suffering as I do and wants to be happy. This thought leads us to feel profoundly concerned for the happiness of others, be they friends or enemies. That is the basis for true compassion. Seeking happiness while remaining indifferent to others is a tragic mistake.

I accept that we are presently confronted with many challenges and that one of our main problems consists of reconciling the demands of the economy, with the search for happiness and respect for the environment. These imperatives correspond to three time scales—short, middle, and long term—onto which three types of interests are superimposed: ours, the interests of those close to us, and those of all sentient beings.

The economy, with its world of finance, appears to be evolving at an ever-faster pace, and those who thereby live in ease are often reluctant to alter their lifestyle for the good of those who are less fortunate and for the benefit of generations to come. At the same time, those who live in need aspire understandably not only to more wealth, but also to be able to enter a consumer society.

And yet, although satisfaction with life is often measured in terms of a life plan, a career, a family, and a generation, it can also be measured according to the quality of each passing instant, the joys and sufferings that colour our existence, and our relationships to others; satisfaction can be given or denied both by the nature of external conditions and by the way in which our mind translates these conditions into happiness or misery.

As for the environment, except for the occurrence of a few global catastrophes such as when the collision of a giant asteroid caused the fifth massive extinction of species on earth, its evolution has been measured over dozens of millennia or millions of years as a continuous process in terms of geological, biological, and climatic eras. However, in our time this slow evolution has been disturbed because of ecological upheavals provoked by human activities. In particular, the swift changes that have occurred since 1950 have defined a new era for our planet, the *Anthropocene* (literally the 'era of humans') that, for the first time in the history of the world, is bringing about a time when human activities are profoundly modifying (and, at present, degrading) the entire system that maintains life on earth. This is a completely new challenge and it has has taken us by surprise (Rockström & Klum, 2012).

Set within this context, we can see that individualism, which in its good aspects can foster a spirit of initiative, creativity, can also very quickly degenerate into irresponsible selfishness and rampant narcissism, to the detriment of the well-being of all. Selfishness, then, is at the heart of most of the problems we face today: the growing gap between rich and poor, the attitude of 'everybody for himself,' which is only increasing; and indifference about the well-being of generations to come.

We need, therefore, a unifying concept that will allow us to find constructive solutions in this maze of problems. And altruism is the thread that will allow us to do this, allow us naturally to connect the three scales of time-short, middle and long term—by reconciling their demands (Ricard, 2015).

The Nature of Altruism

What, then is altruism, and what are the benefits of altruism with respect to the major problems we have described?

Altruism is a *motivation*, a momentary state of mind that aims at accomplishing the good of others. It can also be a *disposition* to care for others in a benevolent way, pointing to a more lasting character trait. The American philosopher Thomas Nagel explains that altruism is 'a willingness to act in consideration of the interests of the other person, without the need of ulterior motive' (Nagel, 1970). Philosopher Stephen Post (2003) defines altruistic love as:

> unselfish delight in the well-being of others, and engagement in acts of care and service on their behalf. Unlimited love extends this love to all others without exception, in an enduring and constant way.

This is the *agapē* of Christianity, an unconditional love for other human beings, while altruistic love and compassion in Buddhism, *maitri* and *karuna*, is to be extended to all sentient beings, humans and non-humans.

In writing about this, some authors emphasize putting intentions into practice, while others think it is the quality of motivation that defines altruism. For example, the psychologist Daniel Batson, to whom I have already referred, and who has devoted his career to the study of altruism, points out that 'altruism is a motivational state with the ultimate goal of increasing another's welfare' (Batson, 2008). He clearly distinguishes altruism as ultimate goal (my explicit aim is to accomplish others' welfare) from altruism as means (I accomplish others' welfare with a view to fulfilling my own well-being). In his eyes, for a motivation to be altruistic, the well-being of others must constitute a goal in itself.

However this may be, it seems to me that if each of us cultivated altruism more, that is if we had more consideration for the well-being of others, much would change for the better. Financiers, for example, would not engage in wild speculation with the savings of small investors who have entrusted themselves to them, just to gather larger bonuses at year's end. And if, in making decisions, all decision makers had more consideration for the quality of life of those around them, they would be concerned with the improvement of their working conditions, their family and social life, and many other aspects of their lives. They would be led to acknowledge the divide that is growing ever wider between the poorest and the richest, and to act with the view of remedying injustice, discrimination, and poverty. They would be led to reconsider the way we treat animals, not reducing them to nothing but instruments of our blind domination and thereby transforming them into mere products of consumption. Finally, if we were all to care for the fate of future generations, we would not blindly sacrifice their well-being to our ephemeral interests, leaving only a polluted, impoverished planet to those who come after us.

Developing altruism would become a determining factor of the quality of our existence, and as such it should not be relegated to the realm of utopian thinking maintained by a few big-hearted but perhaps naïve people. We must all have the perspicacity to acknowledge this and the audacity to say it. Our motivations, whether they are benevolent, malevolent or neutral, colour our actions. One cannot always distinguish altruistic behaviour from selfish behaviour by the sole appearance of actions, and we cannot always qualify an act as altruistic or selfish only on the basis of the simple observation of its immediate consequences. On the other hand, in every circumstance, it is possible for us to examine our motivations attentively and honestly, and to do our best to determine if they are selfish or altruistic, which is why it is crucial for us to look again and again into the mirror of our mind to check our motivations.

Altruism does not require that we sacrifice our own happiness in order to help others. On the contrary, altruism and compassion constitute some of the core virtues that contribute to a truly fulfilled life. Cultivating altruistic love and compassion, both in intention and in action, often turns out to be the best means for simultaneously benefitting others and ourselves. The pursuit of a 'selfish happiness' leads to a lose-lose situation in which we become miserable and makes the lives of others miserable as well. Conversely, altruism and compassion, which are based on a correct understanding of our interdependent reality, lead to a win-win situation. Our benevolent frame of mind contributes to our own flourishing in addition to being beneficial to others.

The fact of experiencing joy in working for the good of others, or of coming away with unexpected benefits for oneself, does not, in itself, make an action selfish. Authentic altruism does not require that you suffer from helping others, and it does not lose its authenticity if it is accompanied by a feeling of profound satisfaction.

Altruistic Love, Compassion and Empathy

Whilst, for most of us, it is natural to feel benevolently inclined towards someone dear to us, or to anyone who is well intentioned towards us, it seems more difficult to extend that benevolence to many individuals, especially to those who treat us badly. But we have the ability, through reasoning and through mental training, to include them in the sphere of altruism by realizing that kindness and compassion are not simply 'rewards' given for good behaviour, but that their essential aim is to promote the happiness of beings and to remedy their suffering. These qualities are part of what the Dalai Lama calls the promotion of human values or secular ethics, an ethics that is not opposed, in principle, to religions, yet depends on none of them (1999).

Buddhism defines altruistic love as 'the wish that all beings find happiness and the causes of happiness.' By 'happiness,' Buddhism means not just a temporary state of well-being or a pleasant sensation, but rather a way of being based on an array of qualities that include altruism, inner freedom, inner strength, as well as an accurate view of reality. By 'causes of happiness,' Buddhism is referring not merely to the immediate triggers of happiness, but to its profound roots, namely the pursuit of wisdom and a more accurate understanding of reality. This altruistic wish is accompanied by a steady readiness and availability towards others, allied with a determination to do everything in our power to help each individual being to attain authentic happiness.

It is not a question here of making a simple dogmatic assertion that 'suffering is evil'. Rather it is about taking into consideration the desire of every sentient being to escape suffering. A purely normative attitude, the aim of which would be to bring an end to suffering as an abstract entity, might involve a risk that one might be less attentive to the beings themselves and to their specific sufferings. That is why the Dalai Lama gives this advice:

> We must use a real individual as the focus of our meditation, and then enhance our compassion and loving-kindness toward that person so that we can really experience compassion and loving-kindness toward others. We work on one person at a time. Otherwise, we might end up meditating on compassion for all in a very general sense, with no specific focus or power to our meditation. (Dalai Lama, 2001)

Altruistic love is characterized by unconditional kindness toward all beings and is apt to be expressed at any time in favour of every particular being in particular. It permeates the mind and is expressed appropriately, according to the circumstances, to answer the needs of all.

Compassion is the form that altruistic love takes when it is confronted with others' sufferings. Buddhism defines it as 'the wish that all beings be freed from suffering and the causes of suffering' or, as the Buddhist teacher Bhante Henepola Gunaratana poetically writes: 'Compassion is a melting of the heart at the thought of another's suffering' (Gunaratana, 2001). This aspiration should be followed by putting every method possible into action to remedy their torments.

Here again, the 'causes of suffering' include not only the immediate and visible causes of suffering, but also the deep-seated causes, chief of which is ignorance. Ignorance here is understood as a mistaken understanding of reality leading us to have disturbing mental states like hatred and compulsive desire, and to act under their influence. This kind of ignorance leads us to perpetuate the cycle of suffering and to our turning our backs upon lasting well-being.

Loving-kindness and compassion are the two faces of altruism. It is their object that distinguishes them: loving-kindness wants all beings to experience happiness, while compassion focuses on eradicating their suffering. Both should last as long as there are beings and as long as they are suffering. And so empathy is defined as the ability to enter into affective resonance with the other's feelings and to become cognitively aware of their situation. Empathy alerts us in particular to the nature and intensity of the sufferings experienced by the other. One could say that it catalyzes the transformation of altruistic love into compassion (Klimecki, Leiberg, Ricard & Singer, 2013).

Altruism should also be enlightened by lucidity and wisdom. It is not a question of inconsiderately gaining access to all the desires and whims of others. True love consists in combining unlimited benevolence with flawless discernment. Love thus defined should involve taking into account the full picture of each situation and asking oneself: 'What will be the short- and long-term benefits and drawbacks of what I am about to do? Will my action affect a smaller or larger number of individuals?' Transcending all partiality, altruistic love should lucidly consider the best way to carry out the good of others.

The Dalai Lama distinguishes two types of altruistic love: the first manifests spontaneously because of the biological dispositions that we have inherited from evolution. It reflects our instinct to take care of our children, those close to us, and more generally whoever treats us with kindness. This 'natural altruism' is innate and requires no training. Its most powerful form is parental love. Still, it remains limited and partial, for it usually depends on our links of parentage or the way we perceive others, favourably or unfavourably, as well as the way they treat us. Solicitude toward a child, an elderly person or a sick person is often born from our perception of their vulnerability and their need for protection. We indeed have the ability to be moved by the fate of children other than our own and of people other than those close to us, but natural altruism is not easily extended to strangers, and even less so to our enemies. It is also fickle since it can disappear when a friend or a parent, who until then had been well-disposed toward us, changes their attitude and suddenly treats us with indifference, or even hostility.

However, the second form of altruistic love, 'extended altruism', is impartial. In most people, it is not spontaneous and must be cultivated. 'The social instinct, together with sympathy, is, like any other instinct, greatly strengthened by habit,' wrote Darwin (Darwin, 1839). Whatever our point of departure, we all have the possibility of cultivating altruism and transcending the limits that restrict it to the circle of those close to us. But natural altruism, especially the mother's for her child, can serve as a basis for this more extended altruism, even if that was not its initial function. This extension has two main stages: on one hand, one perceives the needs of a larger number of beings, especially those we had regarded till then as strangers or enemies. On the other hand, one learns to value a vaster totality of sentient beings, beyond the circle of those close to us, our social, ethnic, religious, national group, and even beyond the human species.

This more extended form of altruism begins with the following realization: If I look deep inside myself, I want not to suffer. I do not wake up in the morning thinking: 'May I suffer all day and, if possible, all my life' (Ricard, 2006). When I have recognized this aspiration not to suffer within myself, what happens if I mentally project myself into the awareness of another being? Like me, he or she is perhaps under the sway of all kinds of torments and great mental confusion, but, like me, would prefer, if possible, not to suffer. He or she shares my desire to escape suffering, and this wish is worthy of respect.

It should also be noted that the practice of altruistic love and compassion does not have the aim of rewarding good conduct, and its absence is not a penalty for punishing bad behaviour. Altruism and compassion are not based on moral judgments, even if they do not exclude them. As French philosopher André Comte-Sponville writes, 'We only need morality if we lack love' (Comte-Sponville, 1996). Compassion in particular has the aim of eliminating all individual sufferings, whatever they may be, wherever they are, and whatever the causes might be. Considered in this way, altruism and compassion can be impartial and limitless.

Altruism and an End to Suffering

'One grows out of pity when it's useless,' wrote Albert Camus (Sagi, 2002). Powerless and distant pity becomes compassion, that is, an intense desire to free others from suffering when we become aware of the possibility of eliminating it and when we recognize the ways to accomplish it. These various stages correspond to the *Four Noble Truths* stated by the Buddha during his first teaching, at the Deer Park in Sarnath, near Varanasi. The first Noble Truth is the *truth of suffering*, which must be recognized for what it is, in all its forms, visible and subtle. The second is the truth of the *causes of suffering*, which is ignorance that leads to anger, greed and many other mental obscurations. Since these mental poisons have causes that can be eliminated, the *cessation of suffering*—the third Noble Truth—is thus possible. The fourth Noble Truth is that of the *path* that transforms this possibility into a reality. This path is the process that puts into play all the methods allowing us to eliminate the fundamental causes of suffering. It is known as the Noble Eightfold Path—right view, right intention, right speech, right action, right livelihood, right effort, right mindfulness and right concentration.

Since ignorance is finally nothing more than an error, a distortion of reality, it is always possible to dissipate it. Mistaking a piece of rope for a snake in the twilight can give rise to fear, but as soon as you shed light on the rope and recognize its true nature, this fear has no reason to exist. Ignorance, then, is an adventitious phenomenon that does not affect the ultimate nature of things: it simply hides it from our comprehension. That is why knowledge is liberating. As we can read in the *Ornament of Sutras*: 'Liberation is the exhaustion of delusion.'

If suffering were a fate linked to the human condition, worrying endlessly about it would only add uselessly to our torment. As the Dalai Lama said playfully: 'If there is no remedy for suffering, think about it as little as possible, go to the beach and have a nice beer' (Ricard, 2015). On the other hand, if the causes of our sufferings can be eliminated, it would be regrettable to ignore that possibility. Realization of the possibility of freeing oneself from suffering gives compassion an entirely different dimension that differentiates it from impotent pity.

Obstacles to Overcome

In order to bring about a more altruistic and compassionate society, it is essential to identify and overcome the major obstacles that stand in the path of altruism, chiefly the lack of concern for the suffering and welfare of others. The devaluation of others may lead to unapologetic selfishness, domestic violence, dehumanization of fellow human beings and degenerate into genocide. Similarly, the devaluation of the lives of animals has led to their merciless exploitation and continued mass slaughter.

Economist Dennis Snower has been able to show convincingly that reason alone, without the help of some pro-social motivation, is not enough to persuade individuals to widen their sphere of responsibility to include all those who are affected by their actions (Snower, 2014). What's more, if the balance of power tips in your favour, nothing will stop you from serving yourself shamelessly at the expense of others. Devoid of care and spurred on by selfishness, reason can lead to deplorable behaviour, to manipulation, exploitation, and merciless opportunism.

This is why we need the voice of care. It is founded on a different interpretation of human nature and can naturally accommodate empathy in economics, as we do in life, not to mention the capacity to put ourselves in others' places, compassion for those who are suffering, and the altruism that encompasses all these qualities. Combined with the voice of reason, the voice of care can fundamentally change our will to contribute to collective goods. Such ideas echo the Buddhist teachings on uniting wisdom and compassion: without wisdom, compassion can be blind; without compassion, wisdom becomes sterile.

For anyone who holds that it is more rational to be selfish than altruistic, on the basis that it is the most realistic and effective way of guaranteeing their prosperity and survival, and that altruists are utopian and irrational idealists ripe for exploitation, Robert Frank of Cornell University has this to say: 'Altruists are neither more nor less rational than non-altruists. They are simply pursuing different goals' (Frank, 1988).

In the governance of our lives, therefore, we cannot exempt ourselves from asking about the consequences of our actions and our way of life. It is perfectly normal for us not to ransack the house that we intend to bequeath to our grandchildren. Why not grant the same attention to the future inhabitants of the planet? This is the view of Edith Brown Weiss of Georgetown University, who talks of the 'principle of intergenerational equity', which states that each generation leaves its successor a planet that is in at least as good a condition as that generation had inherited it (Weiss, 1989).

What good is an extremely rich and all-powerful nation full of unhappy people? An enlightened human society, as we have seen, must provide an appropriate way of life for the present generation by alleviating poverty, and at the same time serve future generations by staving off the planet's destruction. According to this philosophy, growth is secondary to establishing a balance between everyone's aspirations and a 'sustainable harmony' that factors in the fortunes of generations to come, and which is only conceivable in a context where altruism and cooperation prevail. Nowadays, we are better advised to pursue qualitative growth based on better living conditions than a quantitative growth based on ever-increasing consumption.

The middle way between growth and decline can be found in 'sustainable harmony', in other words a situation that guarantees everyone a decent way of life and reduces inequality at the same time as ceasing to exploit the planet at such a drastic speed. To bring about and maintain this harmony, we must on the one hand lift a billion people out of poverty as soon as possible, and on the other, reduce the rampant consumption taking place in rich countries. We must also gain awareness of the fact that unbridled material growth is not remotely necessary for our well-being.

Conclusion

For things truly to change we must dare to promote altruism; dare to say that real altruism exists, that it can be cultivated by every one of us, and that the evolution of cultures can favour its expansion. We must dare to teach it in schools as a precious tool allowing children to realize their natural potential for kindness and cooperation. We must dare to assert that the economy cannot content itself with the voice of rationality and strict personal interest alone, but that it must also listen to the voice of caring and ensure that it is heard. We must dare to take the fate of future generations seriously, and dare to change the way we are exploiting the planet today, which will be their home tomorrow. And, finally, we must dare to proclaim that altruism is not a luxury, but a necessity.

As we approach a dangerous point of no-return in terms of the environment, we still have the power to overcome these difficulties by fully engaging our extraordinary ability to cooperate with each other: 'Cooperation,' the evolutionist Martin Nowak reminds us, 'was the principal architect of four billion years of evolution. It is the greatest hope for the future of humanity, and it will allow us to meet the serious challenges that lie ahead' (Nowak & Highfield, 2011).

The Dalai Lama, with his 'religion of kindness,' asserts that love and compassion are the very foundations of society, and explains his thinking in his book *Ancient Wisdom, Modern World: Ethics for a New Millennium* (2000):

> The spiritual revolution I advocate is not a religious revolution. Nor does it have to do with a style of life that, in a way, would be from another world. It has even less to do with anything magical or mysterious. Rather it is a matter of radical re-orientation, far from our usual selfish preoccupations, for the benefit of the community that is ours. It is a kind of conduct that takes into account the interests of others as well as our own.

Real happiness and good governance are entwined with altruism, since they are part of an essential kindness that is accompanied by a profound desire that everyone can flourish in life. It is a love that is always available, and that stems from the unchanging simplicity, serenity, and strength of a good heart.

4. A New Economic System Based on Core Human Values

STEWART WALLIS

Introduction

A transformation is needed urgently to move us towards an economic system that remains within the planet's limits and has as its goal the equitable satisfaction of human needs (as opposed to wants) and the maximisation of both human well-being and that of all living things.

In this chapter, I show that the barriers to this transformation are not technical, but human, and that a focus on policy and practice change alone is insufficient. We have to start by being clear about the values we want to live by and from these derive the design principles of a new economic system. Transformational change then requires the creation of a simple and powerful new story or narrative about how we want to live as well as the creation of a movement for change that will shift values and generate the necessary political will. I set out how such a new story and movement can be created and draw lessons from the systemic changes achieved in western economies in the twentieth century by the Keynesians and the Neo-liberals.

Current Economic System: Unsustainable, Unfair, Unstable and Unfulfilling

Our current dominant economic system, based as it is upon western market capitalism, has undoubtedly brought great benefits to huge numbers of people across the world. However, we have now entered a period of major crisis where our current system is no longer fit for purpose. The economic crash of 2008/2009 is still seen by some people as a temporary blip—a very painful one, of course, but for all that, a short-term blip. Nothing could be further from the truth. The economic system that we currently have is unsustainable, unfair, unstable and deeply unfulfilling for many. Let me explain.

Firstly, unsustainable: For the two hundred thousand years that humans have inhabited this planet, we have lived within the planet's ability to regenerate itself…until forty years ago. Around 1970, humankind began to live beyond this capacity. We now use the equivalent of 1.5 planets to provide the resources we use and to absorb our waste. In these forty short years, we have exceeded the planet's capacity by 50%. On our current path, by 2050 we will require three planets worth of resources to sustain humankind—a 300% overshoot on our planet's ability to sustain us (Footprint Network, 2015).

The stresses on our planet's system are already becoming apparent. Climate change is a reality and extreme weather events are becoming more frequent. Even on very optimistic de-carbonisation scenarios, most scientists believe that we only have a fifty-fifty chance of limiting global warming to 2° above pre-industrial levels by 2050, and our current path means we are on track for a 4° rise above such levels (IPCC, 2014; Climate Change, 2014). Two degrees is potentially perilous—four degrees would most likely trigger a whole range of catastrophic events around the planet which would particularly affect the poorest people and do untold harm to other species. Already, the number of non-human vertebrates has halved over the last forty years (WWF Global–Living Planet Index n.d.). The UN Millennium Ecosystems Report of 2005 indicated that fifteen out of twenty-five crucial ecosystems that provide our planet's life support systems are either in decline or are in serious decline. These include our atmosphere's carrying capacity as well as fresh water, pollination systems, coral reefs and topsoil.

We are entering a new geological era—the Anthropocene—so called because now, humans are radically affecting how the planet operates. This future is deeply unsustainable and technological change, while necessary, is clearly not going to be sufficient.

This unsustainable situation is compounded by the unfairness of the current system. Inequality is growing rapidly within many countries around the world and there are insufficient good jobs for the young people entering the workforce. At the time of this writing, for example, the youth unemployment in Spain is over 50%. Some 50 million new jobs are needed in the Middle East/North Africa alone, in the next ten years which will require a year-on-year GDP growth rate of 10% in the current economic structure; but these countries currently have either negative GDP growth rates or 1% growth per annum, at the most. The most startling statistic of all is from Oxfam's report in January 2014, *Even It Up: Time to End Extreme Inequality* (Oxfam

International, 2014), which indicated that the richest eighty-five people in the world (this number would fit on a London bus) have as much wealth as the poorest 3.5 billion on the planet—the poorest half of humanity. In the UK, the ratio of the 100 largest companies' CEO pay compared to the average employee's pay has risen from sixty-nine times, in 1999, to 145 times in 2009. Such levels of inequality are unsustainable on a societal level as well as being the cause for many other human ills. A book called *The Spirit Level*, by Richard Wilkinson and Kate Pickett, demonstrated the correlation between inequality and a range of social ills, including alcoholism, teenage pregnancy and drug use (Wilkinson & Pickett, 2010). A recent book by French academic Thomas Piketty called *Capital in the 21st Century* indicates why large levels of inequality are not only socially harmful but affect the functioning of the whole economy (Piketty & Goldhammer, 2014).

In the current economic model, using a car analogy, if we put our foot on the economic accelerator we can create more jobs, but we drive even faster through critical ecological boundaries and cause irreparable harm to our planet and ourselves. If we put our foot on the brake and lower our consumption and slow economic growth, we fail to create enough jobs for everyone. In the current system, neither the accelerator nor the brake is working. The only solution is a different economic system.

The unfairness and unsustainability of the current system are further compounded by the growing levels of instability. We have seen the growing frequency of financial crises around the world. These include currency issues, chronic fiscal imbalances, as characterised by the Eurozone, and major banking crises. A sub-prime mortgage crisis in the USA in 2008 rippled through the entire financial system and nearly stopped cash machines throughout Europe. We have built a system that is highly interlinked and built for efficiency rather than resilience. Natural systems are a mixture of both efficiency and resilience and our economic systems need to have the same balance. As a result of building for efficiency only, we have developed systems that are not resilient and, as a consequence, are not efficient. Recently, the IMF has warned that there are still major risks to the banking system despite the measures that have recently been taken to improve capital requirements (Monaghan, 2014).

Finally one would hope that, at the very least, the harm we have caused the planet would have had a trade-off in human happiness. This is certainly not the case. In many of the richer countries around the world, the correlation between more growth and better lives seems to have completely broken down. In the UK, for example, during the period between 1973 and 2003 GDP doubled, but human life satisfaction flat-lined. Over the same period in the USA, life satisfaction actually declined. 'More' and 'Better' have departed company. This is clearly not the case if one is poor, where more income would mean (all other things considered) better well-being. However, where people get past a relatively modest level of income, this relationship becomes far more tenuous. What is clear is that in the richest countries the current economic system is not generating better well-being (where well-being is defined as people functioning well and having positive feelings, both, day-to-day and longer term) (New Economics Foundation, 2004).

In summary, we are running faster and faster and doing untold harm to our planet; creating worsening inequality; failing to create enough good jobs; facing considerable instability; and we are not even making ourselves any happier. Clearly, we need a different system.

There Is an Alternative

Is it possible, then, to transform our economic system into a different model? The answer is an unequivocal YES.

We could keep the benefits of a market system in terms of creativity and enterprise, but harness it to a different set of values, institutions, measurement systems, and incentives. A radically different system would have to have, as its main goal, the maximisation of well-being of all living species. It would have to focus on meeting human needs for all rather than the infinite wants of a few. It would also have to operate within planetary limits, which would require a radical change in incentives—for instance to focus taxes on things that are harmful rather than things like labour and value-added. All of this is feasible. The economy is a human system and can be changed by humans. So, the obvious question is: Why isn't this happening?

Barriers to Change

There are four main barriers to change. Firstly, there is the concentration of economic power and the reluctance of those with power to relinquish it. Secondly, economics is treated as an exact science rather than an inexact social science. Thirdly are the myths and half-truths that surround economics. And fourthly there are the prominent values promulgated in society and the effects that they have on people's wants and choices

When people gain economic or political power, they are reluctant to give up that power. There are democratic political systems that are designed to ensure successful transformation of political power from one group to another when there is a popular will for that to happen. But, in economic terms, as people become more wealthy and have more economic power, the markets do not act to equalise or share it. The truth about markets is that unless action is taken to mitigate that power, if one player goes into a market with far more power than the others, even more economic power is gained. In *The Wealth of Nations* and *The Theory of Moral Sentiments*, Adam Smith showed that the common good was only served when two key conditions were in play: firstly, that no buyers or sellers had enough power to affect the market outcomes, and secondly, that all players were acting as moral actors. In most markets, neither of these conditions exists. Furthermore, as can be seen in the American economic system, concentrations of economic power can have a significant effect on political outcomes. It is now impossible to become president of the United States, or even a senator, unless one has a personal fortune.

These problems are exacerbated by the fact that economics is now treated as a science where outcomes are predicted mathematically. Just some of the reasons why this is not the case are: the fact that most economists don't recognise that the economy is a subset of the eco-system; economic theory is not based on explicit values, it mixes means and ends (GDP is a means and not an end); it is not focused on meeting human needs (physical and psychological); the theory is insufficiently focused on economic inequality, and there is a lack of an explicit power analysis. In addition, neoclassical economics is based on a number of dangerously simplistic assumptions that distort reality. These include: that humans are rational utility maximising actors; that markets tend toward equilibrium and market failures are exceptional; and that sufficient money is always provided when there is demand. I could go on, but I believe that neo-classical and neo-liberal economics, in many ways, are practically, intellectually and morally bankrupt.

These factors are further compounded by the fact that economics is littered with myths and half-truths. This is not a particular failure of economics as a discipline. It is, rather, a failure of how politicians and many other economic actors interpret economics and use 'half-baked' theories of economics in their political decision-making. As Maynard Keynes, one of the most famous economists, stated, 'Practical men who believe themselves exempt from any intellectual influences are usually the slaves of some defunct economist' (Keynes, 1936). Amongst the myths and half-truths are: we can have infinite growth in a finite world; markets are fair; prices tell the truth; salaries reflect value; and more income equals more happiness. These contribute significantly to the malfunctioning of the current economic system.

Since World War II, we have seen a massive increase in advertising. This has been accompanied by the growth of all types of media and, more recently, by the ever-increasing digital world. Much of this tends to model the values of celebrity, success, notoriety and riches. The work by psychologists such as Tim Kasser, which has more recently been incorporated into the work of Tom Crompton and others in Common Cause (Tom Crompton et al. 2010) shows that humans hold a variety of values. Some are called extrinsic values, such as fame, power, success and wealth; some are called intrinsic values, such as community, spirituality, friendship, love and health. We all have all of these values. What is interesting, though, is how certain sets of values and principles are triggered by external stimuli or by group behaviour. Hence, the extrinsic values are heavily triggered by what people see, hear and read in the media and via social media. Studies further show that people who regularly have those extrinsic values triggered tend to be less environmentally conscious, less pro-social, and even live shorter lives than those whose intrinsic values are triggered more regularly. So, the messages that trigger our values and principles are vitally important. They determine how the mass of any population are likely to behave and what they are likely to ask for through their political voice.

Focusing on Core Values

I am part of the World Economic Forum's Global Agenda Council on Values. Over the past few years, we have spent time answering the question, 'Are there some common core human values or are all values relative to culture and determined by different political and economic systems?' We have come to the conclusion that there are some common human values and these are values that are widely recognised by most faiths and many of the most enlightened civilisations over human history. They are very simple. At the level of the individual, the core value is human dignity. This is not just about a full set of rights and having our needs met, where those needs are both physical and psychological. This is also about our responsibilities. Dignity comes from both how we are treated and how we treat others. At the level of our systems and institutions, the key value is promoting the common good. All of our institutions, markets and political systems need to be designed explicitly to promote the common good. At the planetary and inter-generational level, there is the core value of stewardship—stewardship of the planet and stewardship of resources for all creatures and future generations.

These values can sound very simple; like 'motherhood and apple pie'! However, if we used them to build an economic system, that system would look radically different than the economic system we have today.

How to Change the System

Before I go into what a new economic system might look like, it is critical that we understand how previous economic transformations have taken place in western economies and how the type of economic transformation now needed, can happen. In advanced western economies of the twentieth century, there have been two major economic transformations. In the 1940s, 1950s and 1960s there was a transformation to Keynesianism, with its emphasis on the management of markets and the provision of social safety nets and social security. In the late 1970s, early 1980s, 1990s and early 2000s, there was a shift to neo-liberalism with its focus on individualism and markets. According to this, the answer to the common good was the freeing of markets and getting governments off the backs of their peoples.

What is fascinating in each of these cases is how they came about: the discrediting of the existing story or narrative; the creation of a compelling new story or narrative; the weakening of existing power bases; and the construction of new power bases. In the Keynesian case, its introduction was hastened by the Great Depression and the Second World War. In the case of the neo-liberals, there was a very clear strategy to bring about change by these four means. In 1947, a group of intellectuals and academics, led by Friedrich Hayek (Austrian, later British, economist and philosopher best known for his defence of classical liberalism), met in the small Swiss town of Mont Pèlerin (to form the Mont Pèlerin Society) to set out how they were going to change the economic system. Amongst this group were Milton Friedman (who later created the University of Chicago's School of Economics) and Antony Fischer. Antony Fischer told Hayek that he was going to return to the UK to become a prominent conservative Member of Parliament and, hopefully, in a few years after that, be in a position of government. The story goes that Hayek told Fischer not to be so stupid; he should go and create a think tank. Fischer did, in fact, return to the UK and established the Institute of Economic Affairs—one of the most powerful, right-wing think tanks in the world.

The neo-liberals set out not to change policies and practice, but to create new institutions and to alter the story. They set up think tanks such as Heritage, Cato and the Institute of Economic Affairs. They 'captured' some of most important economic departments of the world and became prominent on editorial boards of key economic publications. They created conditions for a new power base which much later translated into Margaret Thatcher and Ronald Reagan coming into power in the late 1970s and putting into force the neo-liberal economic theory. It took thirty years to do this.

However, if the population was not convinced that change was needed, the creation of new power structures and institutions, alone, would not be enough. In this, the neo-liberals were brilliant (and still are). They created and disseminated a simple message that rested on four principles: small government, free markets, freedom of the individual, and strong defence.

Many of the think tanks and supporters of the right political spectrum in many different counties would still, today, come up with those same four principles. In other words, the neo-liberals constructed a compelling, positive new story based on the view that government was too big; that markets would serve everyone if allowed to be more free; and that freedom of the individual was vital and a right. Therefore the power of trade unions and similar groups were stopping economic progress as well as obstructing the potential for individuals to become wealthy. This was an incredibly powerful credo and did have elements of truth (there was, at that time, excessive power by some of the trade unions). What is fascinating, however, is how it has become all-encompassing. The idea is continually repeated: economic growth, the freeing of markets, the encouragement in all walks of life of competition—this has been set into our thinking, our minds, our subconscious and it is important that the new story that needs to be told finds a positive way of countering this mind-set.

The New Story and the Movement for a New Economy

So, what would a compelling New Story look like? A story that gives hope to people-that allows the values and principles discussed earlier to really come to the fore. This is something that is still being worked on by my organisation in the UK, the New Economics Foundation (NEF) and others. It is not that we don't know what changes are needed; but it is important to know what form of narrative is going to resonate most with people: how can we tell a positive and compelling story about how we might live? We do know that the story needs to be positive; that it needs to be based on those core values (human dignity, common good and stewardship); that it needs to appeal to a sense that an economic system can be created which has values of love and compassion and of cooperation, as well as necessary elements of competition. A discussion around the values we want to live by is an important priority.

In 2009, the World Economic Forum conducted a survey of 140,000 people working in businesses across the world. Three-quarters of those surveyed indicated that they felt the economic crisis was not just a crisis of economics but also a crisis of values. A different sample indicated that they wished they could exercise the same values in the economy as they exercised in their home. This gives us a clue—we need a new economic system based around the same values that we use with family and children, values that First Nation(s) peoples have always used in relation to the natural environment, where they focus on how the environment in which they live can be preserved, sustained and strengthened for the benefit of not just the next generation but for the seventh generation. It is clear that we need a new set of principles for the new economy.

At the preliminary stage of discussions with other groups, NEF has posited six core principles, which we believe must underlie any New Story, any new economic system. These must be universal, must apply everywhere, and must be fundamental determinants of the type of change we want to move towards:

The first principle is strong, democratic economic governance. There needs to be democratic control by governments and other key stakeholders of economic power and of the functioning of markets.

The second is diversified ownership. This requires a move from shareholder ownership to a variety of diversified ownership models and a diversity of scale and form of economic enterprises; it also requires major redistribution of income, wealth and time.

The third is strong, non-market economy. It recognises that the market economy rests on both the non-marketised economy (the public sector) and the core economy (non-financial transactions such as caring, child rearing, and other such activities that take place outside of the formal economic system); these must be strengthened and supported.

The fourth is harnessing the creativity of all people. Such aspiration involves a focus on cooperation as well as competition; it must be clear where competition is relevant and where cooperation is relevant.

The fifth is the regeneration of natural systems. This is because it is no longer sufficient to simply sustain our natural systems; we urgently need to regenerate them.

The last principle is long-term decision-making and investment. There must be a focus on prevention rather than simply dealing with symptoms, long-term thinking for the seventh generation, and new investment models.

These six principles could form the basis of the new economic system. The goal of that system would be the meeting of human needs and the maximisation of well-being of all living species. These would be measured as the key determinants of progress, alongside measurement of regeneration of natural systems. The economy then becomes a means for achieving these ends rather than being an end in itself. GDP is a useful 'speedometer' to indicate whether the economy is going faster or slower, but there is no use going faster if one is going in the wrong direction! These measures assist in indicating if we are going in the right or the wrong direction.

If we are going to proceed in the right direction, we need to see a radical transformation in the models of business based on these principles. Built into the DNA of business would, therefore, be the creation of good jobs and the strengthening of the environment, and taxes would shift from labour and value-added to wastes and non-renewables. Once organisations grew past a certain size, power would be shared amongst the critical equity holders who would include not just investors but also those employed within the organisations. All organisations past a certain size would have a specific charter setting out their societal purpose and would be measured on whether or not they were achieving that purpose. Their charter would not be renewed if they failed to do so. This would be a radical reform of the engine of the economic system.

There would need to be major shifts in our financial systems, with much greater emphasis on the creation of money for socially useful purposes and much greater diversity of form and size of financial institutions, as well as ownership of such institutions.

Democratic governance and markets would mean that no one actor would be permitted to become too powerful in any market, whether local, national or international; and no one actor would be allowed to become too powerful in the running of any large organisation. There would also be clarity on which areas were more effectively run in a market system, with competition built into this system; and which areas would be more effectively run, cooperatively, outside of a market system.

Distribution of income, wealth, time and land would be critical and would bring more people into the economic system. In addition, many activities that could be, and would be, carried out in a more local and de-centralised way. For example, energy production and food production are areas that could and would more often be carried out at a local level. Other industries would be required to remain at a national or international level. A strong industrial policy would help achieve such changes.

A focus on well-being would mean the design of not just jobs, but of good jobs that gave people meaning, and all policies would be focused around how they maximise well-being. Policies would need to increase people's contact with each other, facilitate lifelong learning and encourage people to give of their time, resources and love. This would also include policies at a wider level that would reduce inequality, reduce debt levels and reduce environmental harm. Most critical would be the obligation to meet the needs and guarantee the rights for all. Our economies would run mostly on renewable resources and, therefore, the idea of a circular economy would become important. Such an economy would be focused on reusing, repairing and restoring—not on consuming and discarding. Finally, we would need to live within our planet's limits. This would not need to be a 'hair shirt' operation; it could mean that we have far better lives than we do at the moment.

All of the above are feasible, but they require an economy based on the values and principles set out in this chapter. This is what a New Story can bring about.

The New Economic Movement

Even with the construction of a compelling new story, change will not happen unless enough people who are leaders in society and different walks of life demand it. This is why the construction of a new economy movement will be critical. Politicians, by nature of the electoral cycle, tend to be followers and are concerned by whether or not they can persuade enough voters at their next election. Therefore, unless I am being too pessimistic, an emphasis on trying, in the short term, to get politicians to lead on systemic change is unlikely to be successful. What is needed now is for those people (from all walks of life) who see the need for a new economic system to come together to form a new power base, a new group pressing for change, and this diverse group could assist in creating and disseminating a New Story.

At the moment, those people who see the need for a new economic system are still playing their own instruments, to different scores and in different orchestras. As a result, politicians only hear a discordant noise. We want people to play their own instruments, but to a number of common scores in one orchestra. This will not be easy; it requires hard work to change governance build leadership, develop institutions, bring people together, and to construct a common story. But in the spirit of love and compassion and given the urgency of what we face—it is entirely possible. This is our task; this is the most critical thing for all of us to do.

5. Governance With a Human Face

Kul Chandra Gautam

Introduction

Traditional concepts of governance emphasizing economy, efficiency, accountability, checks and balances, audit and inspection, transparency, measurable results and sustainable impact, have served humanity well. However, in a world wracked with the evils of greed and intolerance, hatred and mistrust, violence and vitriol, there is a need to invoke the power of love, compassion and solidarity as part of humane governance. Citing practical examples of how such positive primordial human values have been harnessed for the betterment of humanity, this chapter makes a case for a new paradigm of 'governance with a human face'.

Governance is a process of managing the affairs of a state or an institution through rules, regulations, laws and norms that are negotiated and agreed upon by all key stakeholders. In a modern democracy, the rules of governance are normally formulated by people's elected representatives, with the help of specialist civil servants, academics and other experts. Such approach to governance seeks to maximize the well-being of citizens, in a cost-effective, user-friendly and efficient manner.

Similar principles apply in the governance of public institutions, private companies, and community organizations that seek to maximize the benefits for their members, and often to society at large. Whenever it involves management of public resources, good governance practices emphasize economy, transparency, accountability, checks and balances, audit and inspection, measurable results and sustainable impact.

The World Bank defines governance as the manner in which power is exercised in the management of a country's economic and social resources for development. Popular participation, non-discrimination, non-violent resolution of conflicts, rule of law, control of corruption or other abuse of power, are some measures of good governance.

Missing from these modern definitions of governance are certain primordial human values such as love, compassion, charity and solidarity that have driven human civilization from time immemorial. These values are deeply felt personal emotions and sentiments of individuals, family and community groups that do not seem to have a legitimate place in the modern concepts of governance.

However, love, compassion and solidarity are parts of the positive spirit of humanity that have guided the best of individual human behavior and values throughout human history. On the other hand, suspicion, indifference, animosity and hatred have also characterized human relations—particularly in dealing with people of different tribes, religions and cultures. Because of the subjective nature of these sentiments, these are rarely factored in designing systems of governance of our public or private institutions.

The Ups and Downs of the Spirit of Humanity in History

It is worth recalling that throughout human history, there have been great epochs when the lofty spirit of humanity soared to new heights. During what the Hindus call *satya yuga* or the Era of the Truth, humanity was apparently governed by the ideals of divinity, when the intrinsic goodness of humanity ruled supreme.

Over two millennia ago, Siddartha Gautam Buddha, born as a Hindu Prince in Lumbini, in today's southern Nepal, spread the message of peace and compassion in South Asia. The Great Indian Emperor Ashoka, after executing a cruel and brutal war, came to the conclusion that his imperial victory was in fact a defeat for humanity, and became the foremost proponent of Buddha's teachings of peace and compassion all over Asia, the Orient and beyond.

The Renaissance in Europe uplifted the spirit of humanity and profoundly impacted the literature, philosophy, art, music, politics, science, religion, and other aspects of intellectual inquiry with deeply humanistic values.

There are many similar epochs of the uplifting of the spirit of humanity in different cultures and civilizations around the world. But there have also been dark chapters in human history when the spirit of humanity was seriously dampened with evils, such as greed, hatred, aggression and megalomania, temporarily overpowering the innate goodness of humanity.

The last such period of evil that engulfed the whole world seriously for half a century was the global Cold War that spread an unhealthy ideological rivalry that divided nations and weakened our efforts to create a strong United Nations.

From the Cold War to Millennium Development Goals

Thankfully, the positive spirit of humanity resumed again when the historic Summit between the American President Ronald Reagan and Soviet President Mikhail Gorbachev, in Reykjavik, Iceland in October 1986 planted the seeds of the end of the Cold War.

The Reykjavik Summit brought great hope to humanity. The whole world breathed a sigh of relief as the Cold War ended. We started seeing significant decline in global military expenditures, and there was high hope that some of the savings from military budgets would be invested as peace-dividend for development.

The end of the Cold War brought about a whole new dynamics in international relations. The United Nations that had been paralyzed by the bitter divisions between the world's two major super-powers and their followers began to act in greater unison. The collapse of the Soviet Union, the fall of the Berlin Wall, the spread of democracy in Eastern Europe and many other parts of the world greatly uplifted the spirit of humanity.

A series of world summits were held in the 1990s on important topics— starting with the very first World Summit on Children in 1990 at the United Nations (at which, as a senior UNICEF official, I had the great privilege to contribute to drafting its declaration and plan of action containing ambitious goals for children, which eventually evolved into the Millennium Development Goals); the path-breaking 1992 Earth Summit; the 1993 Vienna World Conference on Human Rights; the 1994 Cairo International Conference on Population and Development; the 1995 Copenhagen Summit on Social Development: the 1996 Beijing Conference on Women, etc. We also saw the end of *apartheid* in South Africa; and even some signs of the possible end of the long-festering Arab-Israeli conflict in the Middle East.

But the pace of human progress is not straightforward. It often goes two steps forward and one step backward. And so it is that although wars between countries declined after the end of the Cold War, wars within countries, especially of an ethnic and sectarian nature, proliferated. At the turn of the millennium, the spectre of terrorism haunted the whole world. The existence of nuclear arms and other weapons of mass destruction, and dangers of climate change and global warming still hang over our heads as the sword of Damocles.

In some parts of the world, like in my home country of Nepal, we even saw a temporary rise of Marxist-Leninist-Stalinist-Maoist ideology which many thought had been thrown into the dustbin of history, except in some of its last strongholds such as in the Democratic Peoples Republic of Korea, which, contrary to its name, is neither democratic nor representative of its people's wishes, certainly not a republic, but an authoritarian outpost in the North of the Korean peninsula.

The phenomena of religious extremism as represented by groups like the Taliban, Al Qaida, Boko Haram and the Islamic Caliphate, have led to the unintended consequence of Islamophobia, which is a sad blot in the march of human civilization.

Amidst these developments, at one point at the beginning of this decade, we saw the promise of the Arab Spring, rekindling our hopes for humanity again. But it did not last very long, as we can see in the headline news coming from the Middle East. The most recent upheavals in Ukraine, Syria and elsewhere make one wonder if the Cold War might raise its ugly head again.

Yet, the positive spirit of humanity chugs along. The half-fulfilled promises of the Millennium Development Goals are now being succeeded by even more ambitious post-2015 Sustainable Development Goals. We can expect more scientific and technological breakthroughs and more material progress for humanity in the coming decades, even as the spectre of global warming, new forms of terrorism and cruelty to humanity cannot be ruled out. Humanity is destined to flourish—perhaps two steps forward and one step backward—but making net progress and keeping our faith alive.

The UNICEF Child Survival Campaign

In 1980 more than 15 million children died annually—or 41,000 every day—from causes that were readily preventable at very low cost. The head of UNICEF at that time, James P. Grant, was surprised how people were not shocked or outraged by such statistics, and how politicians felt no shame or sense of accountability for allowing such genocide. He was determined to change this indifference through a global campaign for child survival.

Grant adopted a strategy that appealed to people's hearts, to their feelings of love and compassion, to take bold and decisive action to save children's lives and to promote their well-being. He reached out to heads of state and government, and civic leaders, inquiring if they had experienced deaths of children in their own families; how they felt about it; and what they would be prepared to do to prevent such tragedies. Many leaders in the Third World had direct personal experience of such tragedies, but felt helpless to do anything about it on a mass scale.

When told that there were many low-tech, low-cost remedies like immunization, oral rehydration therapy and breastfeeding that even poor countries could afford, and we could mobilize massive international support, many Third World leaders sprang into action.

Similarly, leaders of rich countries were motivated to act when the case was presented in a manner that touched their hearts. For example, asked how they would react if a jumbo jet full of children crashed in their shores every few hours, and how a tiny fraction of their aid budget could help avert such daily tragedies in developing countries, many donors showed great empathy and support.

Besides the compelling scientific evidence, economic rationale, or public health argument, it was the appeal to their human feelings of love and compassion that motivated world leaders to support a global movement for child survival and development. This resulted in dramatic expansion of childhood immunization, improved nutrition and control of infectious diseases that saved the lives of millions of children in Asia, Africa and Latin America.

The governance of the public health system itself changed dramatically in many countries with increased focus on low-cost and low-tech primary health care interventions rather than expensive, high-tech prestige projects of sophisticated hospitals that were beyond the reach of ordinary people. Millions of children's lives were saved and the health and well-being of hundreds of millions of children improved. As the *New York Times* columnist Nicolas Kristoff remarked, the child survival campaign that UNICEF's Jim Grant led in the 1980s and '90s, saved more children's lives than were killed by Hitler, Stalin and Mao Zedong combined.

Pele and Breastfeeding in Brazil

In Brazil, the life-saving practice of breastfeeding had declined dramatically in the 1980s, because of advertising of bottle feeding of infant formula, and changes in life-styles of 'modern' women. In a counter-advertising campaign, UNICEF enlisted the support of the great Brazilian football star Pele. In widely publicized posters and billboards showing Pele and his mother, the latter proclaimed proudly that her son was: 'the Best football player in the world because I breast-fed him,' and she commended all mothers to do so. Within a few years, exclusive breastfeeding rates in early childhood in Brazil increased from 8 percent to 40 percent, saving the lives of tens of thousands of children every year.

Inspired by Pele's example, the government of Brazil adopted a strong breast-feeding campaign as part of its public health strategy. This was an example of how the power of love and compassion influenced the governance of health sector in Brazil, and many other countries.

Days of Tranquility in El Salvador

In yet another example, during the civil war in El Salvador in the 1980s, many children were killed in the war, but even more children died because they were deprived of childhood immunization. UNICEF approached President Jose Napoleon Duarte and asked him to declare a cease-fire to allow children to be immunized throughout the country. He readily agreed, but asked how the rebel forces could be convinced to reciprocate his gesture.

We learned that the Catholic Church could be a trusted intermediary with the rebel guerillas. We approached the senior-most leadership of the Church in San Salvador and at the Vatican itself. The Church was initially reluctant to get involved in a politically polarized conflict. But when UNICEF made the case that saving children lives and protecting their well-being would be a gesture of great compassion fully consistent with the Church's religious and humanitarian mission, it agreed and persuaded the rebels to honor several 'Days of Tranquility for Children'.

The guns fell silent during a series of 'Days of Tranquility' when children were immunized and given other health care on both sides of the conflict, saving many lives and ultimately creating an atmosphere for the end of the war. This was a dramatic example of how the power of love and compassion influenced a nation's governance, and even led to conflict resolution.

Since this pioneering experience in El Salvador, humanitarian cease-fires have been organized in many other countries in conflict, e.g. for immunization against polio and for provision of emergency relief supplies.

Nepal's Female Community Health Volunteers

My home country of Nepal is one of the poorest in the world with very high rates of illiteracy, illnesses, and underdevelopment. But over the past two decades, we have seen dramatic progress in improving maternal and child health and women's empowerment. More than the government's efforts or international aid, one of the decisive factors in this progress has been the extraordinary role of ordinary community-based women health workers whose love and compassion led to massive service outreach and dramatic reduction in maternal and child mortality.

Given its difficult mountainous terrain, underdeveloped infrastructure and shortage of trained medical personnel who were willing to serve in remote areas, Nepal had extraordinary challenges to expand basic health service in rural communities. So the government, with support from UNICEF and USAID, devised a strategy of empowering ordinary village women with a little bit of training to act as local health promoters, known as Female Community Health Volunteers (FCHV).

There are now some 52,000 FCHVs throughout the country. They are given periodic training on simple health messages such as the importance of hygiene and sanitation, proper diet during pregnancy, encouragement for antenatal care, safe motherhood, breastfeeding and good infant feeding practices, childhood immunization, oral rehydration therapy, diagnosis and simple treatment of respiratory infections, etc.

The FCHVs personally administer to young children Vitamin A and deworming medications. As a result of their loving, caring and dedicated effort, Vitamin A coverage in Nepal is over 95 percent, one of the highest in the world. Even during Nepal's decade-long civil war, the FCHVs continued to operate in all 75 districts and thousands of villages across the country when most other basic services were interrupted. If any children were missed during the Vitamin A campaign, the FCHVs would personally visit them at their homes and ensure they are protected.

This is the kind of loving and compassionate care that government officials do not provide, but these highly motivated volunteer women do cheerfully.

As a result of their effort, in the past decade maternal mortality declined by 75 percent and child mortality by 60 percent—making Nepal one of the few least developed countries on track to achieve these important Millennium Development Goals. The FCHVs, along with the local Mothers' Clubs (Aamaa Samuha), and paralegal women's clubs, have done more to promote maternal and child health and to combat domestic violence and empower women than any other government program.

The work of these women's groups has also helped weaken traditional caste barriers in Nepali society as their services are inclusive and non-discriminatory. This is an outstanding example of governance with a human face, harnessing the power of love and compassion to help change a society's age-old negative cultural traditions and to promote new egalitarian values.

Embedding Positive Human Values in Governance and Leadership

The above are just a few examples of how love and compassion have influenced public policy, governance and human well-being across many countries, in many sectors and at different scale-from local to global. After all, love and compassion are the underlying sentiments that lead to solidarity, mutual self-help and cooperation. In modern societies we cannot survive and thrive without such compassionate solidarity.

As the whole world becomes increasingly a global village, where interdependence rather than independence in a narrow, parochial sense becomes the basis for our collective security and prosperity, there is no alternative to harnessing the positive potential of love and compassion in the governance of all human institutions.

The examples explored here illustrated that governance with a human face could have profoundly influenced public policy, governance and human well-being. Our global institutions like the United Nations, national governments and local neighbourhood groups need to use the 'appreciative inquiry' approach to identify how the power of love and compassion can be further harnessed to address the serious governance deficits in our societies in dealing with issues ranging from genocide to ecocide. Promoting value-based education is key to foster such value-based governance.

The world needs to support and nurture humane and compassionate governance as our evolving gold standard for global and local governance in the 21st century.

Part II:
Values in Governance: Towards a Compassionate System

Introduction to Part Two

Part Two of this book aims to ground the new narrative of consciousness and governance within key fields of action. The contributors have thus explored some general principles through the lens of an innovative conception of corporation, ecology, global health, communal life, peace and then through the laws that govern our relationship with our planet's eco-system.

The first clarification that these chapters make, which is also at the heart of our contemporary debates, is about our conception of value. The authors in Part Two pose this question: 'What is fundamentally valuable?', and set out to address a connected question: 'What value does a system of governance aim to serve?' It is here where an important distinction is drawn between instrumental value and non-instrumental or intrinsic value. According to our contributors, what is instrumentally valuable only has value in terms of what it leads to, prevents or facilitates. In other words, what makes something instrumentally valuable is that it serves as a means to some other end(s). By contrast, what is non-instrumentally value does not have value outside of itself. That is why it is intrinsically valuable. Some things can have both kinds of value, such as human health, and the planetary eco-system. This distinction may appear to be simple at first glance. However, as our authors illustrate, our society and governance tend to be situated within a false assumption of the relationships between instrumental and intrinsic values and the means and ends and results in a system that prioritises materialistic gains at human and environmental costs.

The second clarification that these authors make is around the nature of well-being. To further the previous point on values, they argue that humans and human life have intrinsic value and therefore human well-being is constituted in the processes, activities, experiences and relationships for those who are living them. Perceiving well-being as a lived reality helps shift our awareness and understanding of what counts as human dignity. As much as it is conceived to be rights-based and responsibility-inspired, according to the chapters in this second part of the book, human dignity is fundamentally about each individual pursuing and living a good life with others. The authors maintain that there is no dignity nor true well-being if our personal 'happiness' is achieved at the cost of or the exploitation of others, including other human beings, other creatures on the planet and the Earth's eco-system itself. Therefore, through the lens of dignity, the chapters put forward the notion of the 'flourishing of all' as the ultimate expression of Love and Peace—a central aim of governance.

The third point that Part Two sets out to elucidate is that to re-imagine or re-envision governance, it is necessary to understand what it means for humans to live together. The authors suggest that it is in community or in communion (in a non-religious sense) with others that we become who we really are. The higher forces that reside in us, referred to by authors in Part One, are what prompt us to seek genuine friendship with our fellow human beings. However, Part Two also proposes that the real mission of governance lies in our intention and action to design, develop and sustain community and live out a compassionate relationship with each other in communities.

It is within these three key propositions that each chapter puts forward the underlying principles for structuring new governance.

In the first of these chapters, in Chapter Six, Garrett Thomson, Compton Professor of Philosophy at Wooster College, Ohio and CEO of the Guerrand-Hermès Foundation for Peace, introduces the notion of value(s). He makes a distinction between instrumental and non-instrumental value, and there is a suggestion that our common conception of rationality does not allow us logically to articulate what is valuable because it implies that nothing has intrinsic value. This leads us to rethink the relationship between our activities and our goals.

Applying this analysis to corporations, Garrett introduces a discussion on the nature of profits and profitability—what are they and what are they for? From here, he develops a wholesale redefinition of what a corporation is and argues that the central value of a corporation is the intrinsic valuable nature of work as a set of lived processes for the people concerned. In this sense, good governance must be compassionate and must recognise that people matter primarily within an organisation or institution. The basis of compassion is an understanding of the feelings, experiences and life processes of others from the perspectives of those who are living them. Understanding this is the first

Introduction to Part Two

step in constructing a human-centred vision of political economy, and developing humanising corporations and organisations.

To extend the human-centred vision to our planet, in Chapter Seven, Jenneth Parker, Director of Schumacher Institute, argues that in the light of unfolding climate change, which reveals the inter-dependence of humanity and the Planet Earth, we must extend compassion and care to other human beings and to the eco-system itself. This is because the well-being of humans and other inhabitants of Earth and our planetary bio-capacity are profoundly interconnected. By highlighting humanity's and the planet's finitude and interdependence, Jenneth challenges the currently dominant narrative of human growth which is based on unending extraction and consumption of Earth's resources, and making human impacts decisive for the future of our planet. She proposes to engage peoples and communities in all their diversity in envisioning global governance for the protection and restoration of our shared inheritance of the Earth's bio-capacity. One suggestion she brings to the book is for humanity to adopt a Convergence vision that calls for a conscious transformation of social and economic organisation and of human relations—across the scales from local to global.

Following on the thread of compassionate care, in Chapter Eight, David Addiss, the Founder of the Centre of Compassion and Global Health, takes the discussion to a completely different realm, the field of health and in fact, the field of global health. Why global health? David maintains that global health is a compassionate, coordinated response to human suffering on a global scale. Its core values mirror those of the great religious and spiritual traditions, including interconnection, justice, and interdependence. Within complex political and social contexts, this vision highlights the imperative to extend compassion beyond our usual circles, borders and bonds, and to commit to improving the well-being and flourishing of all, towards the possibility of globalisation of compassion. David reinforces the message of the book that values are at the essence of global health and if these values were to be integrated into a system of governance, they could provide a renewed sense of meaning for leaders and individuals who work in this field, and empower them to connect more deeply with those they seek to serve.

Recognising that we can only connect with each other through being truly ourselves, and that our true selves can only be nurtured and liberated through an environment that encourages authentic exploration, Mohammed H. Mohammed and Kurian Thomas, Programme Officers at the Fetzer Institute, argue, in Chapter Nine, that governance must empower humans to connect with each other deeply and act upon our interdependence as opposed to systems of fragmentation, exclusion and alienation. They return to the theme of leaders' qualities that was touched upon by Dadi Janki in Part One. Mohammed and Kurian argue that to live together in community requires an individual commitment and sustained collaborative practices. The key to an enduring community lies in the fundamental principles underpinning the leadership which ought to be based on 'power with' rather than 'power over'. Cooperation and collaboration are persistent and effective ways that leaders can live out the community's core values, which in turn can sustain a compassionate web of connections. Similarly, leaders coming to embody ethical ways of being together through a process of listening, reflecting and dialogue can also be nourishing for both the leaders themselves and the members. Only in following such key principles and values can human communities serve as containers of deep affinity, which is an expression of a sacred bond. The reason why such a bond is considered sacred is because, through such profound connections between people, we may have a glimpse of the transcendent reality that is common to all sentient beings.

In Chapter Ten, Steve Killelea, the Founder and Executive Chairman of the Institute for Economics and Peace, extends the interest in the sacred human bond by exploring an ideal structure for peace and peaceful environment and its implication for leadership and governance. Steve argues that focusing on systems and structures can support and enable the presence of serenity and harmony in our being and our well-being, an experience of peacefulness. When an environment is created which is optimal for achieving sustainable peace as well as providing the conditions for humans and the planet to thrive together, the sacred human bonds described by Mohammed and Kurian will emerge and prevail. As Steve further explains, peace requires a global set of values to underpin the attitudes, institutions and social policies, which are pillars that can support and cultivate our compassionate nature, empathy, altruistic orientation and authentic connection.

Steve explains that as a society focuses on strengthening its pillars of peace, individuals will be less distressed, have more access to resources, experience less fear and therefore become more capable and more proactive in pursuing peaceful acts. This creates a virtuous cycle in which we have the freedom to become better human beings so that society becomes more compassionate and humane. However, as Steve points out, the key to structural peace lies in finding leaders who are not only dedicated to pursuing a personal and professional life of values, but also to developing their own capacity and capability for public service.

Lastly, for this part of the book, Chapter Eleven challenges present forms of governance from the point of view of the legal duty of care. Polly Higgins, the celebrated author, barrister and environmental lawyer, proposes a new

Introduction to Part Two

form of global governance that works for the interests of people, planet and community from an integrated perspective. Endorsing other contributors' earlier pleas for voices of caring, and reiterating Part Two's insistence on perceiving humans, human life and our eco-system as intrinsically value, Polly argues that when laws place human interests above the integrity of our eco-system, the outcome is Ecocide. By establishing a Law of Ecocide, a law that would make bringing harm to the natural environment an international crime, we can truly carry out our duty of care as responsible trustees and guardians of the Earth's eco-system. Polly's most powerful message to humanity is that there is a great powerfulness that can be harnessed through each individual's courage to pursue greatness. This is the power to effect greatness within our personal and public lives, which in turn contributes to a greater world. Like Matthieu Ricard, Polly invites us all to dare to be great, and urges us to take up the greater virtues inherent in our nature.

In accepting this call for new forms of governance, and in appreciating the importance of leaders and leadership in modelling an authentic way of being, Part Two of this book takes the imaginative leap outlined in Part One further and deeper into ourselves and into the everyday realm of practice. It makes clear the responsibility we have not only to analyse and propose, but also to embody and to act.

6. Compassionate Governance in Corporations

Garrett Thomson

Introduction

Any account of good governance needs to include what the governance in question is for, what it is supposed to serve. This means that it must be guided by intrinsic values and pertain to the well-being of people. This paper argues that this requirement of good governance implies that we ought to change our conception of what a corporation is. The institution itself needs reform. In part this is because standard answers to the question 'What is a company?' do not make sense. Such views are based on a mistaken understanding of values.

Any account of good governance has to touch what is fundamentally valuable. A central contention of this chapter is that what is of fundamental value is the living of life. Our lives are comprised of various experiences, activities, engagements and processes. The fundamental bearer of value is the person who is living these parts of his or her life. Because the person has value, these parts of her life do.

To explain the significance of this point, the first section will show how a common conception of value is erroneous. The rest of the paper will apply these ideas to the nature of corporations and their good governance.

Conceptions of Value

The standard answers to the question 'What is a corporation?' don't make sense because they operate within a misconception of the nature of value. I will bring this out in two steps.

1) The first is the distinction between instrumental and non-instrumental value. Something is instrumentally valuable insofar as it has value simply because of what it leads to, prevents or facilitates. For example, money has purely instrumental value; it is good only because of it can buy. On the other hand, happiness has non-instrumental value. Some things such as health can have both kinds of value.[1]

This distinction shows that instrumental value is entirely derivative. Things that have only instrumental value have absolutely *no* value apart from their contribution to what is intrinsically valuable.

We often fail to draw this distinction properly in practice. This kind of inappropriate instrumentalization constitutes a systematic value-error that abounds in society and our institutions. To instrumentalize is to treat something that is intrinsically valuable as if it had only instrumental value, and vice versa.

Let us apply this point to the aims of a company. Money has only instrumental value, and never intrinsic value. This does not mean that money is not important. On the contrary, it indicates the kind of value that money has, which is precisely what constitutes the fact that money is important. However, the value of money is essentially derivative. This means that 'making money or profit' is always an incomplete answer to the question 'What is the purpose of a company?' The money gained must serve some other purpose, and to understand the ultimate values of a corporation, we require a characterization of these intrinsic values beyond the financial. In short, a complete characterization of the value of the aims of a company cannot be couched entirely in instrumental and financial terms.

This does not mean that profit should not be a goal of a company's activities. Acquiring more things of instrumental value is clearly a legitimate end. Likewise, it is in our individual self-interest to earn more money. All other things being equal, it is to our benefit to acquire means of purely instrumental value, and harmful to lose and waste them. Nevertheless, the obtaining such benefits does not take us beyond instrumental value, which is entirely derivative.[2] Thus, purely financial specifications of the aims of a corporation are necessarily incomplete.

This simple point turns some standard understanding on its head. Common conceptions of the rational aims of a company are incomplete because purely financial goals do not specify any relevant non-instrumental values. A company that defines its mission and goals solely in these terms has failed to connect to the intrinsic values implicit in its own operation.

2) The second step is that our common conception of rationality does not allow us logically to articulate what is valuable. This is because it implies that

nothing has intrinsic value. This problem can be avoided, but the solution transforms our understanding of what is valuable in life, and the relationship between our activities and our goals (Thomson, 2002; Gill & Thomson, 2012).

i) The standard assumption identifies means with instrumental value and ends with intrinsic value. I shall argue that this assumption is false. Given this assumption, we can define instrumental rationality as follows. If a person wants X, and if to obtain X she has to perform certain actions that are means to X then, according to instrumental rationality, the following theses will be true:

- As means, these actions have only instrumental value;
- The goal or end, X itself, has intrinsic value as such;
- Thus, the person ought rationally to choose always the most efficient means to this given end.

This view of rationality is concerned *exclusively* with the most efficient means to a given set of goals. It underlies many economic theories, such as those that characterise production and consumption as merely means to maximise utility.

The principle that things that are only instrumentally valuable should be used efficiently is true. This principle also *seems* to apply to our goal-directed actions, which, after all, are means to some end. However, as we shall see, this application is severely problematic.

ii) To understand why, we must separate two pairs of distinctions. We can distinguish: first, instrumental and non-instrumental value, and second, means and ends. Instrumental rationality fails to separate the two pairs of distinctions.

iii) We need to separate these two distinctions for two reasons. First, without doing so, one would be committed to the claim that all of our goal-directed actions have only instrumental value. Actions are means to goals and if all means *as such* have only instrumental value then actions cannot be intrinsically valuable. Second, instrumental rationality implies that the only thing of intrinsic value is the attaining of some goal or end as such.

iv) The instrumental view of rationality cannot be correct. It contradicts the possibility that the activities themselves as processes can have intrinsic value. In other words, if intrinsic values and goals are identified, then all goal-seeking activity necessarily has only instrumental value. However, such a claim cannot be correct because such activities constitute part of one's life and one's life constitutes oneself. Thus, to treat all one's actions as merely instrumental is akin to treating oneself as merely instrumentally valuable. It is like saying 'My life has no significance; what is valuable is only the results that I attain.' Such a claim would defeat the very idea of anything having value. If everyone were to accept the principle that they themselves have no intrinsic value, then nothing could have value.

In order to matter, goals must be relevant to some aspect of the intrinsic value of living a life. Without such a condition, the whole process of achieving a goal in order to attain another goal in order to achieve yet another goal, and so on would be without value. This is because ends or goals *as such* don't have intrinsic value. Whether they do depends on what the end is and how it is relevant to the intrinsic value of living a life. In summary, instrumentalizing our actions dehumanizes our lives, and makes value impossible.

Thus, we need to separate the two distinctions: means and ends, and instrumental and intrinsic value. Furthermore, we need to deny the assumption of instrumental rationality that all means *as such* have only instrumental value, and that the only things that have intrinsic value are ends.

v) This point is vitally important because it transforms the way that we think about our goals and their relationship to our activities, including work. We are accustomed to the idea that the value of what we are doing is fundamentally the results that we attain. As we have seen, this idea cannot be correct.

The point here isn't simply that work is intrinsically valuable. It is rather that this simple truth cannot be recognized within a common conception of rationality that underlies the normal view of corporate governance. Typically we have core value relationships the wrong way around. The value isn't in the end; ultimately, it is in the means, when those means are human activities.

Consequently, we need to rethink the relationship between our activities and their goals. Work is intrinsically valuable as a process that we live through. It is part of a life. Having ends to attain can improve such lived experiences. Having a set of goals to attain can make intrinsically valuable processes more valuable. Metaphorically, we run to win because trying to win improves the running. Also, winning allows us to run again. We run to win but the intrinsic value isn't in the winning, it is in the running. In that sense, we win to run.

Likewise, although work is defined by its goals, this doesn't mean that the goals have intrinsic value and that the work is merely instrumentally valuable. On the contrary: having separated means/ends and instrumental/intrinsic value, we can affirm that although work is a means to an end, the activity of working has intrinsic value. Furthermore, the goals of work have instrumental value in three ways. First, the goal improves the activity of working. Second, the salary earned enables the person to work more. Third, the achieved goal provides products such as cars that are instrumentally valuable for other people in their working lives. In conclusion, among other things, the results of working enable more and better working. In each case, the intrinsic value is in the lived activities, which include working.

The idea that the activities of working have intrinsic value has two important implications. First, it contradicts the standard micro-economic conception of work according to which work is a personal cost, i.e. working involves giving up leisure time in order to receive a financial payment as recompense. This economic model implies a purely instrumental view of the value of work, and makes the contrast between work and leisure time activities absolute. It can't see work as sometimes like play.

Second, the idea that the activities of work have intrinsic value implies that different kinds of work and work conditions will accord in different degrees with that value. One's actual working may accord more or less with this intrinsic value. We shall return to this theme later.

What Is a Corporation?

What is a corporation? The question defines whether instrumental rationality applies to corporations, and whether corporations can have their own interests. Ultimately, our objective is to understand the ways in which the activities of companies can have value. According to contemporary theories of management, the minimal rational aims of a company are:

1. To make profits
2. To survive
3. To grow

We can contrast two ways of thinking about a corporation on the basis of these aims. First, according to the conception of a company as the instrument of shareholders, the survival and growth of the company are only instrumentally valuable as a means to distributable profit. This traditional answer to the question 'What is the purpose of a company?' is 'To survive and grow in order to maximize profits.' Second, the contemporary conception of a company as a person in its own right implies that profits are really only an instrumentally valuable means to the survival and growth of the company (Norman, 2010).[3] I shall argue that neither of these replies can be correct.

a) The Corporation as an Instrument
The first private companies were formed in 19th century Britain, when the law established limited liability as a way to encourage people to employ their

capital in new ventures. Investors could lose no more than their original capital injection into a venture instead of having a potentially unlimited liability for any possible debts incurred by the enterprise. Limited liability protected investors by transferring the legal responsibility to repay loans to the company itself.

These first companies were established as the legal instruments of investors for their personal financial gain. The stockholders controlled the company and were clearly its owners. They appointed agents, who were beholden to them, to manage the company on their behalf. As a result, these first companies can be regarded as instruments of the owners. In this sense, we might view such companies as machines for making profit for their owners.

However, many contemporary public corporations do not fit this original model because equity holders cannot be regarded straightforwardly as owners of the company.

1) First, because shares are negotiable instruments traded on the market, public corporations cannot be regarded as the property of specific investors. There is no longer a relatively fixed group of shareholders who can treat the corporation as their personal property.

2) In these circumstances, the voting right of any individual shareholder is less effective, all other things being equal. In fact, the voting rights of equity holders are limited. The company directors propose how much profit shall be distributed. The shareholders vote for or against a proposed set of directors, the annual accounts, and for or against mergers and voluntary dissolution (Norman, 2010).

3) Shareholders increasingly include other corporations, such as investment funds and their interests in the corporation are strictly financial. They don't have or typically see themselves as having the obligations that come with ownership.[4] In short, they own specific right-claims against a corporation rather than owning the corporation itself. Such corporate equity holders regard themselves as outside the organization rather than being its proprietor.

Let us bring these points together into an argument. With the original joint-stock company, the distinction between shareholder and creditor was a difference of kind. The shareholder could regard the company as his or her private property. On the other hand, people who had merely lent the company money only had the right to receive the capital and interest on their loan.

In contrast, for many public corporations today, the equity/loan distinction has become a difference of degree rather than one of kind. Equity can be regarded as a non-repayable loan stock with a variable rate of return, voting rights and specific rights on the dissolution of the company. In other words, the shareholder is an owner of specifiable financial and non-financial rights against the company, but should not be thought of as its outright owner.

Because loans have themselves become a negotiable instrument like equity, there are many possible types of negotiable instruments that would be intermediate between equity and loans, as traditionally conceived. For example, bonds can have variable rates of interest linked to company performance, and some preferential bonds carry voting rights under special circumstances. Such bonds are virtually indistinguishable from equity. In short, shareholders are capital creditors with a right to a variable rate of return, to vote at company annual general meetings, and a restricted right to the assets of the company when it is sold. We can conclude that, the distinction between shareholders and loan holders is one of degree and therefore, that, in many cases, shareholders should be regarded as suppliers of capital.

This point means that, for these public corporations, maximizing distributed profit should not rationally be regarded as an aim. Instead, dividends paid to equity rationally ought to be regarded as a cost to the company: as the cost of capital. Consequently, the aim of these corporations rationally should not be to maximize distributed profits. Such an idea confuses the point of view of the corporation and that of the shareholder.[5] Rationally, the company ought to work out what dividends would suffice to keep shareholders and the equity markets happy so that the company can raise more capital later when it needs to.[6]

In reviewing the idea that the purpose of a corporation is to maximize shareholder return, we must remember the earlier critique of instrumental rationality. This critique shows us that a purely financial characterization of the aims of a company is incomplete because it is entirely derivative on some intrinsic values that are left unspecified.

b) Corporations as Persons

An alternative and more contemporary view of corporations regards them as persons. This view has some advantages.

First, a corporation can have aims. In contrast, conceived as an instrument or machine, it cannot. Furthermore, as a person, the corporation can have beliefs, and it can learn. It can have a self-image and a culture. In brief, under the contemporary conception, we can employ psychological verbs to describe what the corporation does. This permits a powerful diagnosis of company performance and modes of operation compared to the machine or instrumental model.

Second, with regard to persons, it does not make sense to ask: 'What is the purpose of that?' The question applies only to artifacts and other instruments. Consequently, if a corporation really is a person, we should not ask: 'What purpose does it serve?' because, as a person, a corporation has its own purposes.

Third, insofar as a corporation is a person, it cannot be owned. This shows that it would be a contradiction to regard shareholders as proprietors and, at the same time, the corporation as a person with its own interests. Hence, our earlier point is strengthened: dividends are the cost for the service of supplying capital. Shareholders are suppliers of capital.

Fourth, if a corporation is a person with aims, then it becomes plausible to defend the view that a company has as a rational aim its own survival and growth, and that retained profits are instrumentally valuable for this purpose.

However, even if large public corporations increasingly are regarded as persons, we can still ask whether this is an adequate model. Indeed, corporations are not persons at all, even if they are regarded as such in law. Legally, a person is defined in terms of its powers and responsibilities, such as the ability to own and to enter into a contract. In the law, a corporation is in a twilight zone, considered as a person in some respects, and not in others. For example, it can buy and sell, borrow and lend, but it cannot murder, get married, kidnap or be put in jail. The law treats companies as legal persons, but within limits and only for certain purposes.

The fact that corporate law assigns financial rights and obligations to companies does not make a corporation a living person. The fact that the term 'person' is used in such legal contexts ought not confuse us into thinking that a corporation really is a person. Given these clarifications, it is obvious that corporations are not persons. A corporation cannot consciously think and want. It does not undergo life's processes. In this sense, my cat is more akin to a person than General Electric.

Given this, a corporation cannot be harmed. Affirming that an institution is harmed is a shorthand way of claiming that certain stakeholders will be harmed. We are tempted to think that a corporation can be harmed only because it can own things, and because we mistakenly think of harm in purely financial terms. However, harm cannot be so defined because money has only instrumental value. Although damage to purely instrumental interests often *causes* people harm, such interests do not *constitute* harm. Harm should not be *defined* in terms of ownership 'interests', but rather in terms of the processes of experiencing and living valuably.

Another reason why corporations aren't persons is their relation to their stakeholders, such as its employees. If a corporation were a person, then its employees couldn't be persons; they would be organs or parts of a person defined by their function. But such a view contradicts the principle that people are and should be treated as persons. In short, viewing a corporation as a person excludes regarding individuals in the workplace as persons. Personalizing institutions usually dehumanizes people.

If we dismantle the idea of a company as a person, then we remove the power behind the claim that what benefits a corporation is good *per se*. Of course, this does not imply that the continued survival and growth of companies is not a good thing; it just means that this good has to be explained in other terms. It has instrumental and not intrinsic worth.

Summary

In the first part, we argued that public companies cannot be regarded rationally as the instrument of shareholders and that, to this extent, maximizing distributed profits cannot be the rational end of a corporation. In the second part, we argued that public companies cannot be regarded as persons or organisms and that, to this extent, it is a mistake to treat them as having aims and interests that can be harmed.

Understanding the Value of Corporation

In Conceptions of Value, we outlined important points about what is valuable. Now we can apply these to the conception of a corporation. To transcend the limitations of purely financial characterizations of the corporation, we require a suitably non-economic understanding of its value. This is as follows: the activities of working for the end of servicing customer wants or needs (Thomson, 1987).[7] In short, a company should be viewed as an association formed for the sake of working together, which is a process that is valuable in itself. According to this view, a company provides the opportunity for working with other people. It is an organization that enables a certain kind of valuable work (social, productive and economically self-sustaining).

1) Working as intrinsically valuable
Working constitutes a vital part of a person's life and, as such, it has non-instrumental value. If anything has intrinsic value then persons do, and then, so do their lives and the activities that comprise their lives. Thus, work has intrinsic value. Consequently, good work cannot be conceived adequately in terms of instrumental reasoning, which identifies means with instrumental values and intrinsic values with ends. Work may be a means, but this doesn't

imply that it has only instrumental value. Working is a lived through process that has intrinsic value.

These points indicate that the drive to make profits for reinvestment within the company should be understood partly in terms of facilitating or enabling more opportunities for more and better quality work for the people involved with the corporation.

2) Customer Wants

In work, goals are very important. However, this point needs reframing. Instrumental reasoning wrongly identifies intrinsic value with goals, and this implies the disastrous idea that all activities are means that have only instrumental value. This way of thinking is destructive of value.

Consequently, we must reconceptualize the goals of work. Work for work's sake needn't exclude goals but the goals do need to connect to intrinsic values. Goals must contribute to the intrinsic values of some processes. Otherwise, we would return to the instrumentalism and a pointless infinite regress rejected earlier. Claiming that a company is trying to make money is akin to asserting 'John is larger'. 'Larger than what?' The assertion is essentially incomplete. Likewise, purely instrumental characterizations of value are incomplete.

Consequently, work must be a way to connect to the intrinsic value of people's lives. In other words, what has intrinsic value is work that serves and enhances the life processes of other people. This aspect of the work of the corporation (its goal) needs to be specified well. By conceiving of itself in this way, a company can connect to the intrinsic value of its activities.

This point should transform the way we conceive the value of what a company makes and sells. These goods and services are more than a way to make money; they are a way to respond and connect to the intrinsic value of people's lives. In this manner, a company can connect to the intrinsic value of its activities. Given this, it matters, or ought to matter, to the company *why* its clients purchase its products or services. In other words, for a company to connect to the intrinsic values of its activities, it must aim to sell products that people buy because they recognize the value, rather than because of false expectations and desires created by marketing and advertising. In this way, we arrive at the strange idea that businesses ought to have an interest in consumer education.

These are not moral injunctions. Our aim is to transcend instrumental values and the normal purely financial measurements of corporate performance in order to characterize the intrinsic value of the activities of a corporation. Our objective is to provide an alternative vision of a corporation that goes to the heart of the matter and that does not remain at the level of instrumental values and reasoning.

In conclusion, the second ingredient in the non-economic answer to the question 'What is a corporation?' or 'How should it be redefined?' is that, by associating and working together, the people concerned may respond to non-instrumental values beyond themselves, as expressed by market demand and the needs of society beyond, in ways that no individual could alone.

3) The Importance of Revenue and Profit
A by-product of the work process must be sufficient revenue to meet all costs, including the capital costs of investment, and retained profits or reinvestment necessary in order to be able to continue and improve working processes in the future. Viewed in this way, profits do not constitute an intrinsic value of the work process, but they are instrumentally valuable insofar as they enable more working activities in the future. Profits are only derivatively valuable. Consequently, although making profits is a rational aim, it cannot be a complete aim and, in this sense, the standard view of company rationality is defective. It doesn't get at what is valuable.

Normally, the decision to retain profits is explained in one of two ways, neither of which makes ultimate sense. First, the decision is understood in terms of the good of the company. However, this reply is not reasonable because it appeals to the idea of promoting the aims and interests of a fictitious person (i.e. the company). Second, the reinvestment decision is explained in terms of the longer-term interests of shareholders (i.e. reinvestment for the sake of yielding increased distributed profits in the longer term future). Since distributed profits function financially as costs, this explanation is also unsatisfactory. Because these two standard views fail, we may suggest that retained profits are important in part because they provide an opportunity for future activity and work. In this sense, the ultimate instrumental benefit of work is more work (and hopefully better quality work).

Often companies do not connect to the intrinsic values of their activities, but rather only to instrumental values and their numerical measurement. When one defines one's goals and success purely in financial and numerical terms, rather than in ways that also connect to the intrinsic values of one's activities, then *ipso facto* work is conceived as only instrumentally valuable as a means to certain results. And if the results are identified with their financial measurement, then work can become no more than an instrument to good performance ratios. The instrumental conception of the corporation denies intrinsic value by confusing a goal with its measurement, and the goals with the intrinsic values of the work processes. The possibility of a company connecting to the real values of its work is extinguished by aims defined only in numerical terms that measure performance.

In short, the current instrumental conception of a company is an institutional reflection writ large of the common understanding at the personal level of the value relationship between our activities and their goals. At the personal level, many people think that the goals and results of our activities define the value of the activities. They implicitly assume that because the activities are means, then, as such, they must be merely of instrumental value. They ignore the intrinsic value of the activities. The purely instrumental view of companies reflects on a larger scale this same personal misunderstanding. It characterizes the value relationships the wrong way around.

In conclusion, since economic and financial aims are essentially incomplete, they are a hidden postponement of answering the questions, 'what is the point?' and 'what is the value of what we are doing?' Achieving goals defined in terms of the financial measurement of success is no guarantee of connecting to values. On the contrary, necessarily, defining one's goals solely in such terms entails conceiving the activities as intrinsically valueless.

4) Objections and Conclusions
It might be argued that the central claims of this chapter cannot be applied to corporations working in current very competitive market conditions. In short, they are forced to employ instrumental rationality to stay alive. Of course, within very competitive market conditions, companies may not be able to afford the additional costs that the kind of shift argued for here would require. The thesis is not, however, that they should. It is rather argument for a wholesale redefinition of what a corporation is. It points a general direction in which we should be heading. It doesn't say anything about how to get there.

The view argued for here doesn't imply that we should abandon free-market economy for certain goods. It claims that the kinds of institutions that compete in a free economy should be different from what they are today.

How different? The view suggests a radical rewrite of what corporate culture consists in. A corporation should be an institution that facilitates good work for people within economic, ecological and other constraints. These conclusions mean that it is urgent that we acquire a better understanding of the intrinsically valuable nature of work and what constitutes higher quality working activities. How do different kinds of work fit best into a flourishing life? What kinds of work are best suited to what kinds of people? How can we know what people are talented at? Under what conditions do people find their work more enjoyable and meaningful? How do people best understand the meanings and challenges of their work? How does work contribute to the overall processes of individual human development? These aren't straightforward empirical questions because they require a clarification of the relevant criteria. For instance, part of what makes work good is that it challenges us to use our talents and energies in innovative and entrepreneurial ways.

Conclusion

We have arrived at the conclusion that a corporation should be viewed as an organization or association that enables intrinsically valuable social working activities that are productive in financially self-sustaining ways. In other words, the central value of a corporation is the intrinsic valuable nature of work as a set of lived processes for the people concerned. This means that it is essential to what a corporation is that it should recognize the intrinsically valuable quality of the working activities and processes of the people who form part of it.

Good governance must recognize what the relevant institution is for, and respond to the pertinent intrinsic values. Given that what is of fundamental value is the living of life, good governance must track and be sensitive to the well-being of persons. In this sense, good governance must be compassionate. It must recognize that people matter first or primordially. The basis of compassion is an understanding of the feelings, experiences and life processes of others as if from their point of view. Compassion is acting in accordance with such understanding.

When we apply these principles to corporations, we see that good corporate governance isn't simply a question of marshalling resources to produce goods that meet market demand in a profitable way within a competitive market. Fundamentally this is because the people who work in the company aren't simply resources to attain a financially defined set of aims. Their working processes should be the core *raison d'etre* of the corporation. This doesn't mean that companies so defined wouldn't be competitive and profitable. It means that we wouldn't be creating institutions that require us to put the cart before the horse. In this sense, the very idea of good corporate governance requires a fundamental revision of our understanding of what a corporation is. It requires a systemic shift.

The central contention of this chapter is that the primary value of life is in the living of it. All social institutions should ultimately serve the value of life as lived. This includes economic institutions. Understanding this is the first step in constructing a human-centred vision of political economy.

Notes

1. I shall employ the expression 'intrinsic value' to indicate non-instrumental value but without implying that such values are non-relational.
2. In this way, the idea that well-being consists in acquiring more benefits of purely instrumental value is mistaken. It is mistaken even if it were true that such benefits always contribute to well-being. However, the condition may not always hold. For instance, a very depressed person, who acquires many instrumental benefits, which he or she cannot appreciate, may not actually live a better life. Possessing or owning is a material relationship that does not suffice for the appreciation of value, which may require a change in the person. Having a benefit cannot constitute the living of a value.
3. These two views don't exhaust the answers to the question 'What is a corporation?' For example, there are contemporary contract theories of the public company. See 'The Financial Theory of the Firm', Wayne Norman, *Finance Ethics*, ed. John Boatright, John Wiley and Sons, 2010.
4. If I own something then I have duties of care that come from ownership; even if these duties are not always legally recognized, they often are.
5. Making directors and top executives shareholders through share bonuses attempts to blur this distinction. The idea that shareholders may need to blur the distinction reinforces the point that, otherwise, the interests of the company and of the shareholders are distinct. Such definite actions are needed to align them because the interests of the company can conflict with those of the shareholders.
6. Which is not to say that this is what they actually do.
7. Wants and needs are not the same. The differences are centrally relevant to the themes we are discussing. See Garrett Thomson, *Needs*, Routledge, 1987.

7. Love, Compassion and Respect in Earth System Governance: The Contribution of Convergence*

JENNETH PARKER

> Informed action for interdependent planetary and human flourishing
> —Schumacher Institute workshop on key objectives, 2015

> ...when one speaks of convergence of humankind, or convergence of religions...(it) is to be thought of as a multi-dimensional process, operating at many different levels...it implies a complex network of relationships amongst many different parts.
> —King, 1989, p. 120

Introduction: The Gathering Begins Before We Arrive

This introduction outlines the genesis of the chapter and sketches the landscape of broader concerns and linked themes/issues within which this discussion is placed. The chapter arose from my participation in the 2014 Spirit of Humanity (SoH) Forum in Reykjavik, Iceland, with its guiding theme of 'Love and Compassion in Governance'. I had been working on an EU funded project called CONVERGE which aimed to 're-think globalisation'

---

* Acknowledgements:
The author has been helped in writing this chapter by conversations with Tom Stedall; Gabor Karsai; Ursula King; Vala Ragnarsdottir and Harald Sverdrup; Sister Serab Tso; and David Cadman. Conversations and reflections at the 'Call of the Time' Brahma Kumaris retreat Spring, 2014, have also been of great assistance. The responsibility for the limitations of the piece is mine alone.

in the light of Earth System science and I was invited to talk about how this was being taken forward in the work of the Schumacher Institute.[1] Once I had arranged to go I began to think more deeply about my contribution and how love and compassion linked to the whole overall purposes of the work in which I and my colleagues are engaged. I found that the whole process of thinking through in advance of the event was itself generative of new insights...the gathering began before we arrived. The experience of discussing the many issues at the conference with a varied group of really great people and the warmth and support at the event renewed the belief that we could share this planet in a cooperative spirit.

One issue that the SoH gathering did highlight for me was the lack of connection between the resources of the western philosophical tradition and some of the more faith-based discussions taking place.[2] Many of the governance issues raised in the workshops have at least begun to be addressed by some normative political philosophers—people who bring questions of ethics and values to inform political questions to do with law and social structures[3]. Therefore, I will refer here to 'traditions' that can contribute to our understanding and practice of love and compassion—including philosophy, debate, and dialogue as a humanistic practice (UNESCO, 2007).[4] One of the key achievements of rational thought is to recognise aspects of its own limitations. Nonetheless, this whole chapter is concerned with the possibilities of something like a 'Faith Alliance for the Future' that can respond to the challenge of evolving a meaningful and ethical response to our global challenges.

Questions of knowledge and power have also been very appropriately raised to hold enlightenment to task. It is in this spirit that I include the term 'respect' in this piece. 'Respect' as understood as that recognition of the 'other', of difference in the sameness of our common humanity and the uniqueness of our flourishing (Cuomo, 1998). This also reflects an orientation towards concerns of equality in governance. It was said in the SoH Forum that we wanted to avoid a top-down concept of love and compassion as being only the movement from the powerful to the dispossessed. 'Respect' for the knowledge, struggles and practices of love and compassion of ordinary people who keep the web of social relations in being, must be a cornerstone of any moves to global sustainability.

Furthermore, to address the concerns of the global Earth System crisis, the relationship of science to 'right action' has to be considered. Here, I will assume that care, love and compassion should be at least consistent with science though in no sense reducible to it (Parker, 2010). These questions fall broadly into the wider discussion of the human sustainable development project as entailing critical analysis of what to keep, both from modernity and from traditional societies and what is in need of transformation. I do here assume that modernity has brought many benefits[5]—but that consumerist modernity is the problem (Badiner, 2002).

What resources of love and compassion are there globally to assist in developing an effective form of local-to-global governance that can meet the needs of the time? Many elements were in evidence at the SoH forum. This event also contributes much in the way of understanding the kinds of dialogue that we will need for moves towards Earth system governance—some other elements will be discussed further below.

The Implications of Earth System Science

Earth System science (ESS) has developed rapidly over the past 30–40 years, aiming to develop dynamic studies of the living and non-living components of this system to provide an integrated understanding of global change (ICSU, 2013). Society is increasingly concerned about human-induced changes to climate, and this has been the main focus of the huge international scientific programme under the lead of the International Panel on Climate Change (IPCC). Research into the ways that climate, ecosystems and landscapes have changed historically can help to provide predictions about future changes. In this way climate science is a part of wider ESS. The models and observational data produced by ESS allow predictions to be made of the likely consequences of different climatic conditions. This understanding has important implications for human society, for example, the potential impact of different degrees of climate warming on key socio-economic sectors (such as agriculture, fisheries, water resources, biodiversity, etc.) (Cornell et al., 2012).

Two very important concepts in any systems discussions are those of 'feedbacks' and of 'tipping points'. Feedbacks can be controlling and useful in a system, helping to maintain its functioning. However, feedbacks can also become pernicious—as in the case of the increase in greenhouse gas methane in the atmosphere as a result of the thawing of tundra—itself due to global warming. This is what is meant by 'runaway climate change'. The concern is that the Earth system may 'tip' into a new state that cannot support life.

In studying the Earth as one interconnected system, ESS is demonstrating beyond all doubt the radical interdependence of planetary living. It also demonstrates our human dependence upon the bio-capacity of the Earth, and our living connections with the wider web of life. In this respect it raises vital concerns of justice and the human future and deeply challenges some of the currently still dominant narratives of human progress. For example, work done on 'Ecosystem services' and the Economic Evaluation of Biodiversity

(TEEB, 2010) project not only demonstrated the gross ecological inefficiency of our current global development model, but also stated that ecosystems are the 'GDP of the poor'. Around the world billions of people depend upon key ecosystems such as coral reefs for their livelihood. These are threatened by climate change.

Earth System science seems at first sight to focus very much on the frailty of human embodiment on this time-bounded and limited planet. The unfolding drama of climate change is revealing the dependence of humanity on biophysical cycles—apparently in direct opposition to human narratives of transcendence and freedom. Certainly those narratives that are based on unending extraction, manufacture and consumption of Earth's resources and living bio-capacity are still in flat denial of the continuously and rapidly emerging real facts of the matter. This has caused a crisis in the relationship between science and development that is still being played out—and played down in many quarters. Human land-use and changes to our planet have led some commentators to propose that we are now living in the Anthropocene age of the Earth, where human impacts are now decisive for our planetary future. Much of the response to 'waking up in the Anthropocene' has been in terms of human guilt for perceived greed and negligence. This traumatic realisation that we are implicated in a system that is undermining our own future and that of others has often led to paralysis and denial.

One key question regards the refocusing of attention on human limitations and vulnerability that the recognition of global limits involves. Will this be accompanied by a return to a more compassionate understanding of ourselves and others (Dalai Lama, 1992)? Is there something essential to compassion that recognises the pathos of some aspects of the human condition and the commonality of these—despite all the attempts by some to paint themselves as above such weaknesses?[6] At present there is a very deep division between the kind of ESS being undertaken and questions of human rights and needs worldwide. One prominent ES scientist told me that he would like to undertake a study of the kinds of climate mitigation strategies that could also maximally deliver on human rights. However, he was not expecting to be funded for this anytime soon as the political and strategic agendas are still dominated by the architecture of state interests and failed traditional economic approaches such as Carbon Markets. An approach to global research informed by ethical commitments seems to be something which a 'Faith Alliance for the Future' could support.

What Is 'Earth System Governance' and Why Do We Need It?

There is a very simple joke that summarises our situation at the current time and the problems of understanding that we confront. A sinking boat is tilting into the water at one end. At the other end one of the occupants congratulates themselves and the others; 'I am glad the hole isn't at our end!'

The recognition of the perilous state of the Earth system and the need for action has inspired the International Human Dimensions (IHDP) programme for Earth System Governance (Biermann et al., 2009). The still growing human population is now in the Anthropocene Era of the Earth where human impacts are the biggest cause of global change—we are now 'in charge' of the planet and its future. So far we are doing a lousy job! If we recognise that we are all now in the same boat we need to work out ways to keep our bit of the boat in good shape, but also to repair the whole boat. This means thinking about others—often at a great distance from ourselves.

Consider further—how are we to make decisions that impact on our planet? One dramatic example is that of 'Geo-engineering' for climate stabilisation (Royal Society, 2009). How might decisions be made? Suppose a realistic proposal for technical intervention to gain us a few more years to respond to climate change is developed—who would make that decision on what grounds? Those scientists who are most concerned with biodiversity and the access of poor people to food and livelihood broadly support 'Eco-geo-engineering' or 'Gardening the Planet' (Parker, 2014) for human well-being and restoration of planetary bio-capacity. We need to engage our global citizens in all their diversity in appreciating the need for global governance for the protection and restoration of our shared inheritance of the bio-capacity of the Earth and the need to use mineral and other resources wisely.

In addition to responding to the Earth system or ecological crisis, the CONVERGE project also considered the situation with regard to certain key resources—and the rate at which they are being depleted. This has implications for many areas of life on which we depend on resource use—the most commonly cited example being oil. However, many key metals, minerals and other more complex resources such as living soils are also in a severe state of depletion. The current rush for global development on last century models is leading to a 'feeding frenzy' for resources and consequent waste and misuse.

Figure 1 shows how important the element of phosphorus is to food production.

The developing food security problem is a global issue in which we are all involved. As the harvests in key exporting countries are affected, this will cause a food crisis in rich and poor countries alike. The accumulation of wealth in some countries will not help as 'we cannot eat money'.

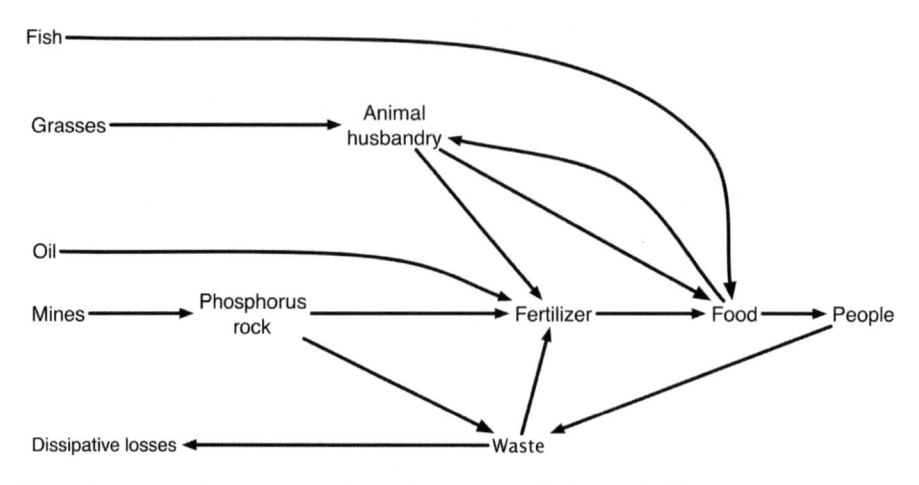

Figure 1. How rocks, oil, fish, and grass lead to people (Koca, 2013).

The question is: Can the need for Earth System Governance help to galvanise effective global dialogue? David Cadman (2014, p. 35) recently expressed: 'To find our way forward…we will have to find our way out of the constraints of separation and disintegration…and find our way into a new realm of reverence, connection, interdependence and wholeness.'

It seems that at the same time as we are challenged to recognise our limits and vulnerability, we are also charged with great responsibility as a species. The globalising narrative of liberal individualism is a very poor preparation for this key moment in human history. We are 'caught on the back foot' with a need to rapidly rediscover and evolve new forms of collective responsibility and decision-making. To date, work on Earth system governance has not centrally included engagement with faith and value traditions (Biermann, 2014). The interdependence of the planet of our well-being may require love and compassion—but these (some would say rediscovered) facts may not necessarily provoke us to feel more loving and compassionate. We could spiral down into more intense competition and violent conflict over the remaining life-supporting resources of the Earth and be overwhelmed by the task confronting us. However, many believe and hope that the recognition of the interdependent nature of the Anthropocene may itself involve an openness to recognition and/or recovery of forms of meaning and significance more sympathetic with unity of humankind.

Convergence

Convergence is seen as a process whereby human well-being, prosperity and consumption across different groups merged to equitable levels—within planetary limits. This means that richer countries and groups need to reduce their use of planetary resources while still supporting developing nations to increase theirs. The aim is to 'Converge' at a sustainable level, reducing inequality across and within nations. Convergence is, itself, the result of applying a concept born of love and respect—that of equality. Contraction and Convergence TM (Meyer, 2000) was a proposal made at the Kyoto climate summit where a standpoint was sought that could be ethically acceptable across nations as a basis for climate governance. The proposal was that all global citizens should be seen as having an equal right to use the global atmosphere and that this would therefore require that rich countries should contract their use, poor countries should develop and we should 'converge' at a sustainable level.

Why Convergence?

The EU FP7 funded CONVERGE project extended this ethical intuition to hold that all global citizens have a right to access the bio-capacity of the planet and its resources for their livelihood and for human development. This project was thus concerned with questions of local-to-global governance, allocation and access to resources and the transition towards greater equity in the world. CONVERGE was based on the latest sciences of the ecology of the Earth, the state of resources and their use and depletion, and information about the great social, political and economic inequalities that exist in the world today.

In the process of 're-thinking globalisation' as set out in the research call from the EU, we did not focus on critique of the current economic system. There is no doubt that the current global financial architecture is still geared to ecologically destructive and socially inequitable forms of development[7]. UN-based attempts to respond to the challenge of the Anthropocene are inevitably opposed and watered-down by the club of states with their limited interests and skewed power relations. Nonetheless, the proposed Sustainable Development Goals are a very welcome development which should be supported and further developed[8].

While we do not know all the details of exactly what a 'sustainable level' of consumption is, there is plenty of evidence that we urgently need to reduce our impacts on the ecological systems of the Earth and to use resources gained from the Earth much more wisely (Wijkman & Rockstrom, 2012). Convergence also refers to a 'Convergence' of the agendas of two broad social movements with global reach that need to be working together more productively—the environmental movement and the human development/social justice movement. Although sustainability aimed to bring these together, there is still much work to do. Convergence as a concept, vision, and strategy can add some additional dynamics to sustainability by focussing much more closely on 'Equity' and governance in the context of our increasing knowledge of planetary interdependence and the limits of the planet to absorb human impacts.

So what is the Convergent Vision? Convergent Globalisation calls for a conscious transformation of social and economic organisation and of human relations—across the scales from local to global. Human development also relies upon finite resources and this means a much greater effort to use resources wisely and to bring in reduction, reuse and recycling of resources. Convergent Globalisation will involve change within all major, global institutions to employ decision making informed by Convergence as a goal for humanity. This involves new forms of action at other levels (such as the city for example) where we propose we can use Convergence decision making.

Kristinsdottir et al. (2013, p. 31) highlight the key principles of Convergence:

1. In a converging society, every global citizen has the right to a fair share of the Earth's bio-capacity and social resources, to enable him or her to live a fulfilling life.
2. A converging society uses its resources efficiently, recognising the critical value of services from natural systems and limiting its harmful impacts upon them. It recognizes interdependence amongst human societies and between human societies and nature.
3. A converging society invests positively in human, social and environmental resources; and cares, maintains and restores them.

From these principles we can see that Convergence for sustainability is the progress towards equal opportunities for all people, within biophysical planetary boundaries. However, to truly integrate Convergence in the Global System will mean that we must overcome several important cultural challenges, to which I will turn next.

Cultural Challenges for Convergence in the Global System

The wider 'global system' is not simply bio-physical but social and cultural. There is now increasing recognition that global sustainability represents a profound cultural challenge (Bokova, 2013) and some elements of that are addressed here.

Current forms of Western-dominated economic globalisation have been guided by self-interest as being the first (and best) rule for decision-making. Whilst we now see the rise of countries such as Brazil, India and China, the fundamentals of the system have not been radically altered. The consequent neglect of the global commons and fellow human needs produces rising inequality, deficit in governance, endemic corruption, and a financial system prone to systemic failure. These emergent properties continue to show that this model cannot address the future of humanity in the Anthropocene era of our planet. There are signs that some global regions are beginning to recoil from some of the destructive aspects of consumer-based individualism and rediscover other, deeper traditions. Convergence challenges us to evolve a new level of global innovation to collaborate for our future.

With its focus on wealth accumulation as an end in itself, the current development model cannot find ways to include the interests of future generations (Adam, 2012). This 'growth at any cost' model has inherent processes that inevitably exaggerate inequalities and that lead to Earth system collapse. Climate change is just one symptom of this collapse—loss of key ecologies and biodiversity of species is another fundamental symptom. Both of these worsening processes affect the world's poor most immediately and directly— but they also sound a warning bell for us all.

The 'religion' of consumerism and accumulation and the model of development and individuation of the human being through consumer choice is being severely challenged. The worry is that the liberal consensus underpinning consumer-based social democracy will be too thin and fragile to survive without the ability to continually distract the populace with consumption. In times of growing scarcity a 'thicker' social project seems to be indicated and that means that a more explicit set of values is required (Palmer & Wagner, 2013; Poole, 1991). In many ways the human polity or public sphere seems to have atrophied and the discourse about the nature of the 'good life' has weakened in the glare of the economic imperative. This capacity for public discourse, debate and development of 'thicker' social values and consensus will need to be reinvented so that the new social order of the Anthropocene can be formulated in a positive way[9]. What is the role of love and compassion in the process and how might our ideas about these dispositions and virtues be changed and challenged by the current 'Call of the Time'?

Here let's examine four ideas.

Resources of Hope and Connection

One thing we can always take from social movements is that there are always resources that can be re-utilised for positive change. One of our most important global resources for positive human change in the face of the challenge of the Anthropocene is our very diverse, but linked traditions of love and compassion. The challenge for many of these traditions is to enter into dialogue based on respect and love for the 'other'. One very strong argument presented here is that the crisis of the Earth System in the Early Anthropocene provides a hugely strong motivator for these moves to be accelerated. This chapter proposes that the concepts and approaches developed under the heading of 'Convergence' can be of assistance in these processes of dialogue as they form a framework that can be one initial starting point for dialogue.

The Global Public Sphere

Whilst many bemoan the dissolution and degradation of the public sphere under the growth imperative, there has been a huge development of committed global communications taking place in the internet or 'Fourth Estate'. There is a global army of committed, often young, people who are developing an active global citizenship and awareness through forms of social media. Their activities do not stop there; they extend to developing forms of open-source sharing of information and collaborative fora for design and development of products often under the heading of social and ecological business formats (McLurcan & Hinton, 2015). The online community is proving to be politically innovative and influential and will doubtless be a huge factor in the ability of humanity to respond constructively to the huge challenges of the Anthropocene. Can resources supporting love and compassion be more fully mobilised to support and inform these initiatives? Can faith and values traditions in turn learn from these dynamic innovations?

Respect: Difference and Diversity in Convergence

In this process the discoveries of the interconnected Earth System need not and should not imply any loss of appreciation for diversity and difference amongst humanity. Our very different histories and trajectories equally require a systems understanding of the ways in which 'global principles' need to be applied in context and according to more localised understandings of priorities and concerns. The systems approaches underlying Convergence help to outline how we can share a common vision for humanity but understand that this vision will need to work itself out in different strategies and priorities depending upon context.

Compassion and the Inner Landscape

Love for humanity in our fragile and flawed search for development and flourishing dictates critical examination of narratives of guilt and blame for global Earth system crisis. 'Waking up in the Anthropocene' is a shocking experience as connections of cause and effect become more obvious. When we are told 'there is no alternative' to high consumption growth culture we can only believe that we are participating in a doomed civilisation (Jackson, 2009). Can we forgive ourselves for the mess—face up to it together and move on?

Many people resist forgiving as they feel that the full recognition of the harm done should come first. However, we do know that psychologically (and maybe spiritually) people need to feel that they could find a way to forgive themselves *before* they can recognise the harm done. They are terrified that the guilt would overwhelm them. A systems understanding explored in a loving spirit can help us all understand that much of the harm inflicted on the planet has been unintentional. Much of the continuing harm currently in process is the result of us being trapped into a systemic logic that we are finding very hard to escape—or to transition away from. This can help us to have compassion on ourselves and others—which can release energy for love and action.

Conclusion: Dialogue Is Love—But Food Comes First

The real motivation of this piece is to engage the bearers of values other than the recent obsession of humanity with 'stuff'. Can they—we—overcome our competitiveness, hostility, mistrust and inertia to meet the 'call of the times'? In this effort we can engage in informed dialogue as a powerful technique to aid global debate on difficult questions. We can also realise that recognition of the 'other' will often take us out of our comfort zones; if we are to engage in co-evolution, nothing else will do. We can also begin to make amends, to join with others in restoring our shared planet and helping to bring our societies into loving and compassionate dialogue about how we share this Earth. We can contribute to developing Earth System Governance informed by, and worked out through processes of, love and compassion. One urgent example is consideration of food.

Embodied humanity on a limited planet has over-exploited our food systems beyond their limits and we are facing a choice as a species.[10] We can decide to allow the weak and poor to go to the wall and thereby reduce planetary population or we can adopt Convergence approaches to food, shelter and human needs. While we may understand 'love' at many levels in the human being—the manifestations of love in the Early Anthropocene may well be as basic as they have often been: to share; to care more about others' well-being than developing ourselves through consumption; to find and rediscover other ways to celebrate being human together.

Notes

1. www.schumacherinstitute.org.uk
2. The historical trajectory of Western Christianity and philosophy has been one of a parting of the ways—for a while (Tarnas, 1991). But why should we accept this disjunction when we consider the global issues of faith, values and right action at this point of crisis for the Earth?
3. For example, discussing the roles of faith and value traditions in informing governance does not necessarily imply an attack on the 'secular state'—conceived as a non-fundamentalist kind of 'secularism' that underwrites religious and other freedoms. However, the centrality of the state is itself challenged by the recognition of interdependence and the rise of other scales of political agency such as city-regions.
4. This is an important ground for the process solution to the competing demands of 'respect' and 'challenging' of the other. Habermas recognised that one form of practice of equality is the process of challenge whereby I presume that you might change my mind. This is a part of love and respect.
5. It is quite easy to romanticise traditional cultures from the more comfortable position of taking the benefits of modernity for granted. For many poor people in the world these benefits still seem hopelessly out of reach. This is why Convergence recognises the right of the poor to development.
6. The refusal of our vulnerability has gender dimensions as recognised in Val Plumwood's (1993) painting of the 'master' subject who can apparently escape the weaknesses of embodiment by assigning the care of the body to an army of unseen helpers (cleaners, cooks, nurses). One might also add that in highly pressured 'achievement' cultures, the 'care' of the emotional life is often 'outsourced' on a gendered basis with men remaining in a state of emotional incapacity.
7. Global biophysical interdependence and the related governance issues directly challenge absolute property regimes. By way of contrast, Elinor Ostrom won the Nobel Prize precisely for demonstrating the effectiveness of social-ecological approaches to livelihood.

8. http://sustainabledevelopment2015.org/
9. For example as part of the CONVERGE project the Schumacher Institute hosted a European conference on 'A New Social Contract for Sustainability'.
10. See the report of the UN Special Rapporteur Olivier de Schutter on the right to food, '*The transformative potential of the right to food*', De Schutter, O. (2014), 24th January, 2014.

8. Globalisation of Compassion: The Example of Global Health

David G. Addiss

> *Concern for effective action is a way of expressing love for the other.*
> —Fr. Gustavo Gutierrez

Introduction

Global health emerged from the fields of public health and international health during the 1990s, catalyzed by novel infectious disease threats, such as HIV/AIDS; the globalisation of the economy; the environmental movement; and an infusion of funding for public-private global health partnerships (Brown, Cueto & Fee, 2006). Global health seeks to address, transform, and prevent suffering in some of the most marginalized and neglected populations on earth. It does this through extensive multilateral coordination, multidisciplinary collaboration, and an embrace of both prevention and clinical care (Koplan et al., 2009).

The astonishing growth of global health during the past decade reflects an accelerating pace of globalization, not only in culture, trade, and communication, but within health itself. Highly publicized health threats of recent years—the Ebola virus being a particularly poignant example—underscore the fact that health and disease are global issues, beyond the control or purview of any one nation. Global health is therefore inseparable from the other forces of globalization.

Given its global scope and mandate, what exactly *is* global health? Consensus on this point, even among its practitioners, is elusive (Beaglehole & Bonita, 2010). As Koplan and colleagues (2009) have observed, global health can be thought of as a notion, an objective, or a discipline. It has a complex structure. It also can be considered as a particular manifestation of a larger shift in human consciousness toward the globalization of compassion. In this chapter, I first discuss our understanding of global health from these different perspectives. I then describe several important challenges to compassion in global health, review how these challenges can be addressed, and conclude with some reflections on compassionate governance for global health.

Understanding Global Health

Global Health as a Notion

As a notion, global health reflects an emerging consciousness that is also found in concern for the environment (Macy, 1991), religious plurality (Goshen-Gottstein, 2014), and the global economy (Sachs, 2008). The meaning of the term 'global' in this context is crucial. It does not necessarily mean 'international'—affecting two or more nations. Rather, it refers to health problems (and their solutions) that are global in scope, even if they occur locally. Global health embodies a spirit of interconnectedness and it recognizes the need for global cooperation to solve these problems. This principle is illustrated by the story of ivermectin, the only safe and effective drug for onchocerciasis (river blindness), a parasitic disease that causes blindness as well as debilitating itching of the skin. Initially isolated from fungus found on a golf course in Japan, ivermectin was developed as a veterinary drug by researchers in Australia; tested in humans by Dr. Mohammed Aziz, a scientist at Merck & Co, Inc. who was born in Bangladesh but had worked in Sierra Leone, where onchocerciasis is endemic; and evaluated for its potential against onchocerciasis by a global network of scientists organized by the World Health Organization (WHO) (Campbell, 2012). Because those affected by onchocerciasis could not afford ivermectin once it was approved for human use, in 1987, Merck & Co., Inc., in Rahway, New Jersey, USA, pledged to donate ivermectin free of charge for as long as needed to control the disease. Some 1.5 billion treatments have been donated for this purpose, greatly reducing the prevalence of blindness in sub-Saharan Africa and Latin America and leading to the elimination of onchocerciasis in some countries (Mectizan Donation Program, 2014).

Dr. Bill Foege (2012), former director of the US Centers for Disease Control and Prevention, alluded to global health as a notion or a worldview when he said in a speech at the Task Force for Global Health, 'Everything is local and everything is global. Global health is not 'over there'—it's right here'. Onchocerciasis—a local problem in isolated African villages—became a global health issue when a few motivated individuals conceived of it as such and resolved to do something about it. The major social determinants of health—poverty, inequity, lack of education—are similar regardless of locality (Marmot & Wilkinson, 2006). From this perspective, no matter where they live, health care workers and public health officials who provide treatment and work to prevent disease in underserved populations are engaged in global health, even if they do not identify themselves as global health practitioners. The notion of global health, therefore, is not defined or limited by geography. Rather, it is grounded in a deep awareness of the interconnection of all living beings, a global worldview.

Global Health as an Objective

The twin objectives of global health are to improve the health of all people and to achieve health equity (Koplan et al., 2009). The vision of 'health for all' was first articulated and adopted at a 1978 conference on primary health care (WHO, 1978). The Alma-Ata Declaration endorsed the WHO definition of health as 'a state of complete physical, mental, and social wellbeing, and not merely the absence of disease or infirmity,' and further affirmed that health, thus defined, 'is a fundamental human right' (WHO, 1978). Alma-Ata launched a primary health care movement that, despite its challenges, has profoundly altered the global health landscape. In recent years, the circle of concern in global health has extended beyond humans to include other sentient beings and the ecosystems in which they live and on which we all depend for our survival (Nicole, 2014). The inclusivity of this emerging field of 'one health' is breathtaking, its scope the entire planet.

The second objective of global health, that of health equity, is rooted in the principle of 'a preferential option for the poor,' which has been most clearly articulated in Roman Catholic liberation theology (Griffin & Weiss Block, 2014). A preferential option *for* the poor and *against* their poverty is necessary not only for ethical reasons; it is also required for global health to be effective, since, as Dr. Paul Farmer reminds us, 'diseases themselves make a preferential option for the poor' (Farmer, 2013a, p. 36). Global health's urgent insistence on health equity distinguishes it from its predecessor, the field of international health (Farmer, 2013b). In defining health equity as a key objective (Koplan et al., 2009), early global health leaders shared Farmer's observation that 'the more scientific progress achieves, the more scandalous it is that people are excluded from its benefits' (Farmer, 2013b, p. 118). They, too, were scandalized, and oriented the field on a path toward social justice (Gostin, 2012), committing it to overcoming health disparities that were sometimes viewed as 'given' in public health and international health (Brown, 2014). As we shall see, in practice, global health has yet to fully grapple with the implications of this core principle, or to live up to it.

Global Health as an Academic Discipline

Koplan et al. (2009, p. 1993) have noted that 'global health is fashionable,' and indeed it is. As the field of global health grows, a burgeoning academic discipline is emerging to support it, with scholarly journals, conferences, institutes, and departments within schools of public health, medicine, and nursing (Landrigan et al., 2011; Macfarlane, Jacobs & Kaaya, 2008; Merson, 2014). Positions in medical residencies and fellowships that provide opportunities in global health are in great demand (Battat et al., 2010; Kerry et al., 2013), and a recent survey of medical students in 75 countries identified a large unmet need for global health teaching, particularly in maternal and child health (Gopfert et al., 2014). Global health is also popular among undergraduate students; of 50 US liberal arts colleges surveyed in 2010, all offered one or more courses, 42% had a defined track or program, and 30% had student organizations devoted to global or public health (Hill, Ainsworth & Partap, 2012). The tremendous interest in global health as a field of scholarship and training reflects a strong desire among many young people to engage in a meaningful way at a global level and a passion for reducing health disparities (Merson, 2014).

Global Health as a System

Hunter and Fineberg (2014, p. 1755) recently described global public health as 'a global tapestry of influences' within which 'the individual patient encounter is a local event.' This tapestry of influences has many threads: government agencies, both civilian and military; multilateral institutions such as WHO and the World Bank; and private sector organizations, including foundations (most notably, the Bill & Melinda Gates Foundation), for-profit corporations, religious institutions, and thousands of non-governmental organizations (NGOs), as well as a host of public-private partnerships and alliances focused on particular health issues (Frenk & Moon, 2013; McCoy, Chand & Sridhar, 2009).

Numerous attempts have been made to organize global health. Many of these efforts have been confounded by the complex, rapidly evolving nature of the field and the multiplicity of interests and perspectives represented within it. For example, in 2010, WHO grouped together 17 disparate diseases that affect marginalized populations under the rubric of neglected tropical diseases. The intent was to draw attention to, and advocate for, resources to address these diseases. This strategy has been spectacularly successful (WHO, 2010); in 2013, more than 1 billion people at risk of neglected tropical diseases received treatment, largely through drugs donated by pharmaceutical companies (Uniting to Combat Neglected Tropical Diseases, 2014). In 2012 and again in 2014, a diverse range of public and private partners pledged additional resources in support of WHO's targets for eradication, elimination, or control of these diseases by 2020.

Given the multiplicity of interests represented by these partners, managing and coordinating this new *uber*-alliance has proved challenging. In addition to the governing 'stakeholder's working group' (comprised of 10 members representing bilateral and private donors, multilateral agencies such as The World Bank, and various coalitions and partnerships), the operating structure for the alliance includes a 'disease-specific' work group (comprised of representatives from alliances or partnerships working on 10 diseases); an 'extended donors' work group; an advocacy and resource mobilization work group; and an 'industry engagement' work group (Uniting to Combat Neglected Tropical Diseases, 2014). This system, along with a 'scorecard' to track progress, is layered over existing structures and relationships that define and link its many constituents.

Neglected tropical diseases represent a relatively small segment of global health activity. The structure of global health as a whole is infinitely more complex; any attempt to succinctly describe it would be incomplete. To extend the poetic description by Hunter and Fineberg (2014), that of a 'global tapestry of influences' within which 'the individual patient encounter is a local event,' I suggest that global health is constituted by all *acts* of health care and disease prevention everywhere; by the estimated 59 million *people* who perform them (WHO, 2006); and by the *organizations* in which they work. The vast majority of the actions that comprise global health take place at the local level—expressions of a fundamental human impulse to care and to relieve suffering. In the end, the global-level organizations and systems remain relevant insofar as they improve health at the local level. Thus, the structure of global health is not monolithic or centralized, but rather emergent, comprised of an astonishing array of actions, people, and organizations.

Global Health as a Manifestation of Compassion

We have explored global health as a notion, an objective (or aspiration), and a discipline, and have examined its complex structure. At a more fundamental level, I would suggest that global health can be viewed, in the words of the late performance artist Ben Israel, as 'a mass uprising of compassion' (Vitello, 2012, p. A22; Addiss, 2013b). The remainder of this section explores the evidence for such an assertion as well as factors that undermine or threaten compassion in global health.

First and foremost, global health is an expression of compassion because it is dedicated to relieving suffering. Toward this end, global health mobilizes vast human resources (McCoy, Chand & Sridhar, 2009) and has developed extensive infrastructures. It is unequivocally action-oriented. Global health, then, is entirely consistent with a description of compassion offered by His Holiness the Dalai Lama: 'not just a wish to see sentient beings free from suffering, but an immediate need to intervene and actively engage, to try to help' (Dalai Lama, 2002, p. 225).

Second, global health extends this wish, as well as immense effort, to alleviate the suffering of *all* people. One of the great challenges in our times is that we reserve our compassion for those who are close to us, or who seem worthy of it (Goetz, Keltner & Simon-Thomas, 2010). As Mother Teresa has said, 'The problem with the world is that we draw the circle of our family too small' (Reifenberg, 2013, pp. 194–195). Great spiritual and religious teachers throughout time and space have emphasized the need to extend our circle of compassion. As a human species, we have not yet done very well at this. In tangible and practical ways, though, the secular field global health embodies what is essentially a spiritual call to universal compassion: health for *all*.

The authority of WHO, generally considered the lead agency for global health, is invested in it by national governments, so-called member states, which, quite naturally, are motivated by national self-interest. Once, when asked about compassion in politics, US Vice President Hubert Humphrey picked up a pencil and said,

> Just as an eraser is only a very small part of this pencil and is used only when you make a mistake, so compassion is only called upon when things get out of hand. The main part of life is competition; only the eraser is compassion…in politics compassion is just part of the competition (McNeill, Morrison and Nouwen, 1982, p. 6).

In this light, it seems surprising that secular global health should articulate and put into practice a compassionate response to suffering that transcends national boundaries and self-interest to include all people. To what can this be attributed?

Peter Brown (2014, p. 273) argues that 'religious motivations of individuals and institutions' have played an important role in the evolution of global health. We have already noted the moral voice of liberation theology in grounding global health in a preferential option for the poor. A spiritual call to compassion, combined with deep theological reflection, also shaped the primary health care agenda of the 1960s and 1970s (Bersagel Braley, 2014). As the post-colonial era unfolded, the World Council of Churches was revising its understanding of healing and rethinking the role of medical missions. It established the Christian Medical Commission in 1968 to study 'the most appropriate ways in which the churches might express their concern for *total* health care [emphasis added]' (Patterson, 1998, p. 3). The Commission worked closely with WHO to advocate and prepare the international health community for the Alma-Ata Declaration and to champion the cause of health for all through primary health care (Bersagel Braley, 2014).

The WHO definition of health—a state of complete physical, mental, and social well-being—reflects a holistic perspective that, I suggest, is grounded in spiritual awareness. It is spectacularly broad and far-reaching, and, for this reason, has been criticized as being both unattainable and impossible to measure (Larson, 1996). But in a world where health 'care' has become mechanical and reductionistic, the WHO definition serves as a crucial reminder that the health that we all desire is much more than 'merely the absence of disease or infirmity.' It is this broader, deeper vision of health that the emerging field of global health has embraced. For many reasons, the spiritual awareness that undergirds this vision remains implicit. Indeed, proposals to include spiritual well-being in the WHO definition have been repeatedly considered, but never approved by the World Health Assembly (Nagase, 2012). However, the debates on this topic cut to the heart of what is meant by human health, well-being, and spirituality.

The contribution of faith communities in providing health care across the globe also testifies to the spiritual and religious underpinnings of global health. Faith-based organizations provide 30–50% of health services in many African countries (Mwenda, 2011), and communities of faith deploy a wide range of health assets, both tangible and intangible (Kiser, Jones & Gunderson 2006). Thus, although global health, on its surface, is primarily secular, governed and funded largely by WHO member states, its embrace of universal compassion and its insistence on health equity indicate a profound influence of religious and spiritual values.

A third reason that global health can be viewed as a 'mass uprising of compassion' is that compassion is a significant source of motivation for many individuals who enter this field. Those who work in large international organizations or national Ministries of Health labor tirelessly on behalf of people they will never meet, often separated by great geographic, cultural, and economic distances. They have drawn 'the circle of family' very widely indeed. In the past several years, I have become interested in what motivates and sustains such an effort. In unguarded moments, many of my colleagues will point to compassion as an underlying—if unspoken—core value. To explore this theme, a small group of global health leaders gathered at The Carter Center in 2010 (Task Force for Global Health, 2011). They concluded that global health is rooted in the value of compassion, grounded in an awareness of our interconnectedness and a concern with the whole.

Lastly, I suggest that global health's core concern with social justice and human rights is further evidence of its being grounded in compassion—even though the word 'compassion' is rarely mentioned in global health training, conferences, or professional journals. Compassion and social justice are not in conflict. Rather, the quest for social justice is ultimately rooted in compassion, particularly in an age of globalization (O'Connell, 2009). True healing and reconciliation require both justice and compassion (Lederach, 2005); such healing is only possible when, in the words of the Psalmist, 'Truth and Mercy have met together; Justice and Peace have kissed' (Psalm 85:10). Liberation theology offers global health a compelling framework and model for infusing its social justice and health equity with the power and sustenance of compassion.

Challenges to Compassion in Global Health

The language of global health, from the WHO definition of health to the principles put forward by global health leaders (Beaglehole & Bonita, 2010; Koplan et al., 2009), is intentionally aspirational. Yet in practice, global health priorities are driven by concerns that are distinctly more partisan than health equity and health for all. The field is influenced by foreign policy, military strategy, institutional advancement, and, at times, personal ambition (Gow, 2002). Tropical medicine, from which global health emerged, originated during the late 1800s primarily to protect European soldiers and colonists, rather than to improve the health of those they colonized (Farley, 1991). The historical role of faith-based health and development charities in Africa has been particularly complex (Manji and O'Coill, 2002).

There is no question that US military-funded research has significantly advanced the fields of tropical medicine and global health (Beaumier et al., 2013). However, this research is ultimately driven by military and national security priorities, not by the fundamental principle of health equity. The title of a recent publication from the Center for Strategic and International

Studies is telling: 'Global Health Engagement: Sharpening a Key Tool for the Department of Defense' (Daniel & Hicks, 2014). Do we really want global health to be a tool—especially a sharp one—of the military? Such a notion is completely at odds with global health's commitment to health equity and social justice. Indeed, it threatens to hijack and distort global health, making it merely the 'eraser' on the back end of a military and foreign policy 'pencil.' A particularly egregious example of the adverse potential inherent in such views came in 2011, when the US Central Intelligence Agency, operating under the cover of a hepatitis vaccination program, collected blood from family members of Al Qaeda leader Osama bin Laden—a ruse to identify his whereabouts (Gostin, 2014). The distrust generated by this breach of public health integrity seriously undermined efforts to control polio in Pakistan and still threatens to undo decades of work to eradicate the disease globally.

In addition to substantial institutional and geopolitical challenges, global health practitioners face personal challenges, on a day-to-day basis, remaining connected to the compassionate impulse that led them into the field. What does it mean to have compassion for entire populations, from whom one is separated by great geographic or cultural distances? For those who work in large institutions, especially, the instruments of global public health, the means through which compassion is expressed and suffering relieved, are not direct and personal, as with clinical health care. Rather, the instruments of compassion in this setting are organizational and bureaucratic—even mechanical—in nature: proposals, budgets, logistics, and the like. In such an environment, the empathic signal, the faces behind the numbers, can quickly fade. This challenge, compassion at a distance, is a particular concern for young global health professionals.

The overriding challenge to global health is fear—regardless of whether the perceived threat is to individual well-being or national security. The 2014 outbreak of Ebola in West Africa highlighted both the paralyzing effects of fear and inspiring examples of extraordinary compassion. On August 3, 2014, Dr. Thomas Frieden, Director of the US Centers for Disease Control and Prevention, called on the compassionate impulse of the US public when the climate of fear threatened to derail sound and sensible public health measures to address the Ebola crisis. He said, 'I hope that our understandable fear of the unfamiliar does not trump our compassion when ill Americans return to the US for care' (Henry, R. & Stobbe, M. 2014). His address underscored both the power of fear to undermine the compassionate impulse as well as the power of compassion to overcome fear.

Addressing These Challenges

A central hypothesis of this chapter is that global health is a radical proposition—both actively facilitating, and itself a manifestation of, a fundamental shift in human consciousness toward a global ethic of compassion. Clearly there is much unfinished business. The potential and vision of global health remain largely unrealized. Yet the very fact that global health has emerged to give voice to its radical goal—that of alleviating suffering for *all* people—is a remarkable embodiment of the spiritual value of universal compassion. The fact that this endeavour is supported, and made possible, by such a range of governments, corporations, private foundations, and NGOs, among others, is even more remarkable.

The crucial question for the future of global health is whether it will fully connect with and grow into its prophetic voice or allow itself to be manipulated as a tool of its most powerful constituents. To realize its potential, global health will have to further align with its core principles of health equity and universal compassion, which lie at the heart of its prophetic voice. As we have seen, putting these principles into practice is not easy, and there are significant internal and external challenges to doing so. To what extent does the principle of health equity apply to people that my government—or yours—considers as enemies?

Global health can draw on several key resources to further transform and realize its vision. Courageous, compassionate, and skillful global health leadership will be absolutely essential. The career of Jim Grant, the executive director of UNICEF from 1980 to 1995, provides a remarkable example of such leadership. At the time of Grant's death, it was estimated that some 25 million children were alive who otherwise would have died (Jolly, 2001). Through his personal example, indefatigable spirit, compassionate presence, and persistent engagement of world leaders, he transformed the culture within UNICEF. Dr. Bill Foege, a contemporary of Grant, remarked that 'there was a feeling of compassion in that organization that one didn't see before or after' (Task Force for Global Health, 2011). Compassionate organizations—and global health—will require capable, effective, and compassionate leaders.

For global health to achieve its vision, it must reconnect with its spiritual roots. By spirituality, I refer to a definition developed in 2009 at a consensus conference on palliative care: 'that aspect of humanity that refers to the way individuals seek and express meaning and purpose and experience their connectedness to the moment, to self, to others, to nature, and to the significant or sacred' (Puchalski et al., 2009, p. 887). Hospitals and medical centers actively promote their core values of compassion and service, but within global health, a curious conspiracy of silence is pervasive on matters that concern us most deeply, both individually and collectively. The reasons for this silence are undoubtedly complex, but, when given the opportunity, global health practitioners are eager to speak of the compassion that motivates them, to tell the stories of the personal encounters that inspired them to join the field and continue to provide sustenance.[1]

The collaboration between physician Paul Farmer and theologian Gustavo Gutierrez has opened up a rich dialogue, a model for how global health might connect more intentionally and deeply with its spiritual foundations. In the words of Fr. Gutierrez, we must 'drink from our own wells' of spirituality if we are to sustain effective action (Gutierrez, 2003). The choice is not between effective action on the one hand and spiritual or contemplative practice on the other. Aligning one's spirituality with one's work in the world is central to authentic living (Palmer, 1990). Spirituality is also essential for sustained, effective action in global health and for the compassion and accompaniment that such work requires (Gutierrez, 2013). Along these lines, Joanna Macy writes,

> To heal our society, our psyches must heal as well. The military, social, and environmental dangers that threaten us do not come from sources outside the human heart; they are reflections of it, mirroring the fears, greeds, and hostilities that separate us from ourselves and from each other. For our sanity and our survival, therefore, it appears necessary to engage in spiritual as well as social change, to merge the inner with the outer paths (Macy, 1988, p. 203).

What sources do global health practitioners and leaders draw on to inspire and sustain them? Little is known about this, in part because of our conspiracy of silence. Certainly, for those whose jobs are primarily administrative or who work in large organizations, trips to the field to literally see the faces restore a sense of connection and purpose. Some draw on religious faith to give meaning to their work and some make time for meditation, reflection, or daily personal rituals as ways of grounding and renewing themselves.

Compassionate Governance for Global Health

As we have seen, the question of governance in global health is problematic, given the fragmented and complex nature of the field. The most established and well-recognized governance structures, based on the power of national governments, lack inclusiveness and have significant limitations (Frenk and Moon, 2013). Private foundations (most notably the Bill & Melinda Gates Foundation), NGOs, and a host of public-private partnerships have stepped forward in an attempt to bring greater coordination and more efficient governance to the field. To a certain extent, these efforts challenge the authority of the old order, even while infusing the field with new resources and energy. However, they, too, have limitations (*Lancet*, 2009). It seems unlikely that a unified or monolithic global health governance structure or processes will be established any time soon. The field is too diverse—there are 'too many cooks in the kitchen.' Rather, most relevant and crucial levels of governance will remain at the level of the health district, state, or organization. For all of these, one of the most critical challenges to good governance is how to represent and engage with local communities.

This in no way negates the essential need for good governance and visionary leadership within existing institutions, coalitions, and partnerships that operate at the global level and which, to a large extent, govern and direct the field of global health. Across this complex environment, we need more leaders like Jim Grant, who can persuade constituents to act in accordance with what Abraham Lincoln called the 'better angels of our nature.' The ivermectin story provides a compelling model of what can be accomplished in the absence of centralized governance. In this case, researchers and top management at Merck, the leaders of the Task Force for Global Health, the African Program for Onchocerciasis Control, and others combined their unique gifts and talents to address a specific health problem, guided by a fundamental desire to alleviate suffering and grounded in an understanding that the health of all humans is interdependent.

One of the key principles of global health that distinguishes it from international health and medicine is its commitment to trans-disciplinary collaboration (Koplan et al., 2009). Global health as an academic discipline has lived up to this principle more fully than global health practice. For the field to mature and find the full measure of its prophetic voice, it needs to draw on a much broader range of disciplines and constituents and to include them in its governance and its programming.

The need for cross-sectoral linkages and collaboration in global health is increasingly obvious (Frenk and Moon, 2013). Indeed, new ways of envisioning and implementing global health programs is required. To cite one example, some 14 years ago, WHO called for a global effort to control intestinal worm infections, which affect the health and well-being of an estimated 1 billion people worldwide. A targeted approach, periodic treatment of school-age children, was adopted. Significant progress in scaling up school-based deworming has been made, with pharmaceutical companies donating up to 600 million doses of deworming per year, enough to treat all school-age children at risk. However, to stop transmission of intestinal worms and achieve a more lasting impact, improved access to clean water, sanitation, and effective hygiene education is necessary, as is expansion of treatment to younger children and adults (Addiss, 2013a; Anderson et al., 2013). This more comprehensive approach has captured the imagination of a new generation, since intestinal worms affect virtually every aspect of human development—public health, nutrition, education, human rights, agriculture, gender equity, and economic development, to name a few. A broad multi-sectoral effort is required, in which the goal is not just reducing worm burden, but rather enabling children and communities to reach their full human potential. Given the magnitude and complexity of the challenge, the perspective of multiple sectors is not only welcome, but also necessary (Addiss, 2014). Such a program cannot be contained within any single government ministry; its structure will be more of a matrix, its processes and methods highly relational.

Conclusion

At its best, global health is a compassionate, coordinated response to human suffering on a global scale. Its core values mirror those of the great religious and spiritual traditions: interconnection, compassion, justice, and interdependence. Global health is eminently practical and universal in scope, but lives and breathes in a complex political and social environment. Its vision and purpose can be thwarted and distorted by the forces of fear, conflict, extremism, and insecurity. These forces cause us to draw our circle of family too narrowly. The need to extend compassion beyond our usual circles has never been greater. Fields such as global health, dedicated to improving the well-being of all, represent a vanguard in the human journey toward the globalization of compassion. Rediscovery of compassion and other spiritual values at the core of global health could provide a renewed sense of meaning for those who work in this field and empower them to connect more deeply with those they seek to serve. It could also animate and solidify the field itself, serving to drive effective global health policy and hastening human flourishing.

Note

1. The Centre for Compassion and Global Health is in Atlanta, Georgia, co-founded by David G. Addis.

9. Communities and Freedom: Transforming Governance

MOHAMMED H. MOHAMMED AND KURIAN THOMAS

A strong community helps people develop a sense of true self, for only in community can the self exercise and fulfill its nature: giving and taking, listening and speaking, being and doing.

— Parker Palmer

Introduction

Set within the consideration of values and governance lies the matter of community and freedom and the ways in which these two may be brought together in governance. This chapter discusses freedom in the context of value-based, inclusive communities that not only enable a release from external constraints, but also the internal struggle of becoming who we want to be. However, we recognise that creating such communities requires commitment and is often hobbled by the demands of our everyday priorities.

Increased globalization and communication, arguably, have created a lifestyle that requires spending more time generating material value and less time for social connections, which are increasingly routed in virtual forms such as Facebook. In the rush for more material well-being, people often spend more and more time at work, commuting rather than communing, and secluding rather than socializing. However, the debate on social connections is not settled and some firmly argue that electronic social networking platforms have in fact maximized the opportunity to forge relations (Dunbar, 2010; Kornikova, 2014). Nevertheless, in the last quarter century, the generation of material value has seen unprecedented growth, whereas we cannot say the same about what is called social capital, that is communal value created by durable networks of reciprocity.

On a macro level, there have been a few attempts to challenge the measurement of human growth purely on the basis of economic performance pegged to GDP.[1] Trends during the last 25–50 years on redefining human well-being and happiness stress the need for a different kind of personhood, group identity and nationhood as demonstrated, for instance, in the Gross National Happiness Index of Bhutan. However, such efforts remain limited. Robin Dunbar, renowned evolutionary anthropologist specializing in communities, explains how highly individual pursuits have heavy social and personal costs of losing social cohesion. In a 2010 article published by *Wired*, a leading technology magazine, he gives a warning: 'We become less committed to our neighbours and each other. If we are to survive in the global village, we must somehow find a way to recreate that sense of community' (Dunbar, 2010).

One response to this comes from the renowned sociologist Robert Putnam who, in his book *Bowling Alone* (2000), expresses a hope that Americans will deeply engage in what he calls 'spiritual communities of meaning':

> Faith-based communities remain such a crucial reservoir of social capital in America that it is hard to see how we could redress the erosion of the last several decades without a major religious contribution… I challenge America's clergy, lay leaders, theologians, and ordinary worshippers: Let us spur a new, pluralistic, socially responsible 'great awakening'. (pp. 408–409).

In a general context, communities are not limited by geography, demographics or beliefs. The boundary between work and personal life is less Goffmanesque—in the sense of scripted and socially as well as professionally 'accredited' roles that are neatly separated from each other to the extent possible—in the twenty-first century workplace (Goffman, 1959). Our private lives are now closely connected with our professional ones through ubiquitous technology, healthcare, retirement, and even social life. Despite some visible downsides, workplace communities provide a highly exciting opportunity to bring a sense of integrated life (Laloux, 2014). It is not uncommon to find organizations that provide on-site child care, nap rooms, fitness centres, healthy food choices, meditation space, and more. Thus, workplace settings are ripe for, as technologists say in the context of reinventing old industries, 'disrupting' in order to extend our capacities as whole humans by leveraging particular communities that build integrity from the ground up and ensure the highest standards of ethical practices are embodied (Mohammed & Thomas, 2014). In this context, transformative communities, whose essence is one of freedom (or what might be described as communities of freedom), are social groups formed for the purpose of cultivating individual and collective capacities for transformation of consciousness from ego-centeredness towards a vision of deep interconnectedness that shatters the illusions of separation from others as well as the natural world around us. It is important to make it clear at the outset that the reference in this chapter to communities of freedom, however, is not intended as a directive concept or blueprint of any kind. Each community is unique, and, through sustained search for meaning, it will find its own path to true freedom.

This chapter explores the literature on how such communities provide an essential sense of belonging and a framework for governance (Block, 2009; Pinker, 2014; Putnam, 2000; Vanier, 1989). It also makes a case for practical approaches to form and conserve communities that nurture fuller human flourishing. We start with some thoughts on how a community of freedom might be established and then discuss the sacred bond of community.

Community of Freedom and Its Characteristics

In considering the characteristics of a community of freedom, we note that Peter Block (2009) highlights modern society as plagued by fragmentation and alienation. Realizing this real threat, some groups have opted to take proactive steps to create their own communities complete with a local economic system. Some of these communities have also scaled up to an international network. One example of this are Ecovillages,[2] which are intentional communities that uphold social, economic, and ecological self-sufficiency, often sharing cultural and spiritual values. Another and older example that combines economic and shared values is the credit union movement, which started in nineteenth-century Europe and which valued communal cooperation before it gave birth to big financial institutions such as the Bank N.V. Then there is the Grameen Bank started by the Nobel Prize winner Muhammad Yunus. Recognizing that banks would not lend money to people in poor communities, he tapped into social capital, trust, and peer reputation rather than material assets as the basis for collateral, and in this way lifted millions out of poverty. Parallel examples that have focused on spirituality at the centre of community include: Eco-Spirituality, Spirit of Humanity Forum, Council for a Parliament of the World's Religions, en+theos and others.

We reiterate that our true selves can only be unveiled through freedom and through an environment that encourages authentic exploration. Whether that represents the tackling of external barriers or dealing with one's own inner blockages, a journey of self-discovery requires freedom to confront a complex reality. Being in a nurturing and patient community provides a powerful transformative opportunity for such a positive shift in worldview; it provides an environment for human flourishing that helps us become what David

Brooks calls 'a person of deep character' (2014): '[In] the realm of intellect, she has permanent convictions about fundamental things; in the realm of emotions, she has a web of unconditional loves; in the realm of action, she has permanent commitments to transcendent projects that cannot be completed in a single lifetime.'

We do not posit, therefore, that communities are a fusion of individual/ family values or a way to confound differences in worldviews. We suggest that in the sharing of ideals within community there must be room for respect for individual identity. Conformity is not expected as a condition; in fact, differences in opinions can contribute to the richness of communal identity. Being together is not an indication of groupthink; community consists of 'relationships that are neither invasive nor evasive. In this space, we neither invade the mystery of another's true self nor evade another's struggle' (Palmer, 2004, p. 64). Similarly, as stated by renowned American psychiatrist M. Scott Peck: '[A] real community is, by definition, immune to mob psychology because of its encouragement of individuality, its inclusion of a variety of points of view' (1987, p. 64).

Community takes on many roles: it provides care, facilitates cooperation, enables healing and growth, fosters sympathy, and builds mutual trust. In the words of well-known theoretical physicist David Bohm, a 'stream of meaning' emerges as people engage in dialogue as equals, which is one of the key features of community, leading to shared meaning that is 'the 'glue' or 'cement' that holds people and societies together' (1990, p. 1).

Beyond the material realm of the everyday, a feeling of relatedness is important for our growth into inner freedom and maturity. In other words, a transcendent capacity helps us collapse the constraints of individualism and self-centeredness by focusing on things other than our immediate needs or even our very existence in this world.

Communities of freedom represent strategic dimensions of being in a field of action that, for instance, play a pivotal role in deepening our sense of the sacred by: providing safe space, fostering capacity for relatedness, furthering self-development and personal/group transformation, exploring one's purpose and meaning in life, and establishing profound connections.

In considering this possibility for an organisation, we want to mention the Fetzer Institute in Michigan, USA that has adapted a collaborative approach to leadership throughout its history. Changes in mission, strategy, and context led to the current model, which has an actively engaged community at its centre (Mohammed & Thomas, 2014).

Let us look at the key characteristics of communities of freedom grounded in freedom and at the questions that they pose.

First, providing a safe space. Fear is not an uncommon characteristic of many work environments where anxiety about relationships, customer satisfaction, peer judgment and job security affect employee morale. By contrast, a community rooted in a sense of freedom welcomes diverse points of views in an open, respectful dialogue. It acknowledges fear and addresses unproductive elements that result from it. Fear cannot be eliminated, but through the process of dialogue in community, one can hope to minimize its negative effects. In this regard, deep listening[3] plays a vital role in boosting confidence in the process and outcome. The key questions to consider include: How do such spaces create mutual trust? How does deep listening become an integral part of the organizational DNA and, therefore, of its governance?

Secondly, fostering a capacity for relatedness. In a paper titled 'Community, Conflict, and Ways of Knowing,' Parker Palmer (1987) conceptualizes community as the capacity for relatedness not only to other humans, but also to events in the past, nature, ideas and 'the spirit'. Communities and the networks to which we belong shape our individual selves in very important ways (Lieberman, 2013); they calibrate our actions and regulate selfish impulses in service of a larger group. According to recent epigenetic studies (Goleman, 2007), our daily interactions leave lasting marks in our bodies. In this way, the qualities of our relations have consequences on who we are and our actions. The key questions to consider include: How do we productively transcend the tension between personal passion and the pulls of 'tribal' mentality? How can science help in analysing the long-term impacts of belonging to an inclusive community?

Furthering self-development and personal/group transformation. When working in community, we are also to be active agents in choosing who we would like to become, we must be aware that such conscious choices can be triggered both by profound personal experience or thoughtful reflections, and by frequently participating in communal activities. The key questions to consider include: What factors augment our agency to transform as individuals within a community? How do our collective actions shape our community?

To explore one's purpose and meaning in life requires the space and opportunity to question as well as analyse without judgment. A community of freedom offers that unique space that is not dictated by doctrine and imposing structures; it welcomes and consists of its members' subjective perspectives on purpose and meaning. The key questions to consider include: What are the best mechanisms that encourage members to openly surface subjective experiences related to meaning and purpose? How do we ensure that such overtures are not subjected to judgement?

Finally, a community of freedom establishes profound relationships. Through regular practice and within a community, a deeper sense of connection with others and a transcendent reality is nurtured. Over time, some of the practices can inform and shape shared values. The key questions to consider include: How can a range of practices be the basis of deep connections without risking endorsing or excluding specific approaches?

Community as Sacred Bond: Some Key Issues

In addition to ensuring a form of social equity, communities of freedom serve as containers of deep affinity. These bonds are sacred, primarily expressed as the experience of participating in something transcendent beyond the drudgeries of the everyday. Romanian philosopher Mircea Eliade (1959) argues that, 'by manifesting the sacred, any object becomes something else, yet it continues to remain itself, for it continues to participate in its surrounding cosmic milieu' (p. 12).

This means that delving into the sacred does not mean a disconnect with material reality occurs; rather, it signifies the quality of our relationship with reality. Encyclopaedia Britannica goes even further and defines the sacred as 'the core of existence' that has a transformative effect on everyone's lives. Describing its accessibility, Roger Walsh (1999) states that 'the sacred can be experienced directly through practice,' which deepens with sustained commitment.

While it is hard to find communities of freedom that serve as ideal role models especially in organisational settings, there are, however, some examples such as Heiligenfeld, a medical service company in Germany; Resources for Human Development (RHD), a human services non-profit serving people of all abilities; Patagonia, a high-end outdoor clothing company; and FAVI, a metal manufacturing company (Laloux, 2014). This, therefore, calls for a focused articulation and prototyping of such communities based on the experience from the Fetzer Institute and others including those mentioned earlier. Things to examine include: shared values, practical numbers, experience of community, facilitation format, practices and symbols, forms of leadership, and consideration of the necessary stages in building community.

Let us consider each one of these.

Shared Values

In seeking to define models of community that can be tested more widely, we have to build on the values shared in small communities. Shared meaning is not about statements and elegantly articulated phrases; it is about coming to an embodied understanding through a process of listening, reflecting, and dialogue (Sandow & Allen, 2005). Working in community can be an important channel to build integrity from the ground up, and instilling a sense of personal responsibility that translates to the highest standards of ethical practices. Rather than the pressure to comply with externally articulated ethical guidelines, or 'exoskeletons' that 'we can slip...off as easily as we can don them' (Palmer, 2004, p. 8), we need an inner force that guides our action from the centre of who we truly are. And when such authentic ways of being become collective, we can hope for a flourishing community that lives fully up to its shared values. A model that can provide strong comparison is the famous twelve-step program, which is also adapted by Karen Armstrong in her book titled *Twelve Steps to a Compassionate Life* (2011), as a practical guide to help people become more compassionate.

Practical Numbers for a Community of Freedom

Social scientists suggest that the maximum number of relations one can manage is around 150. Robin Dunbar of the University of Oxford, who studied the brain's capacity to effectively manage relationships, has made a powerful case that overly extended relationships are simply not possible for the human brain to handle (2010). Others acknowledge this theory and endorse the design of work environments based on this insight (Gladwell, 2000; Kornikova, 2014; NPR, 2011 Pinker, 2014;), which among engineers, in reference to frequency of place-based communication among individuals and teams, is known as Allen's Curve (Allen & Henn, 2006). Companies like Gore-Tex and Steelcase have applied this theory to limit the number of people working in a building at 150, a number that is true for Amish settlements, hunter-gatherer communities, as well as for military units. Dunbar has proposed a formula, 'a rule of three,'[4] which reflects the depth and quality of relationships that can be maintained: a third of 150, which is 50, is a figure for close friends, who are seen often, and considered to be good friends, and once in a while are invited to a 'group dinner' (Kornikova, 2014). The next number, 15, which is about a third of 50, consists of close support groups that provide emotional support and can be trusted with personal matters. It is likely that members of this group could share common values and background; their relationships could have depth and frequency. The last set of 5 people is the most intimate group that involves family members and best friends.

Despite critiques of this theory, it is clear that number matters in maintaining deep and meaningful relationships. Considering the level of trust that we need in expressing our most intimate spiritual experiences, our initial assessment is that the ideal number for a supportive nuclear community of freedom should be in the range of 5 to 15. However, although this represents a smaller social unit, dynamically connecting with larger communities (of about 150) is also important for enlarging the network. Such nimbleness allows people to exercise freedom and adaptability. In practical terms, it is much easier for smaller groups to meet without the necessity to work around complicated schedules and logistical limitations.

Experience of Community

If we compare the experience of community online and face-to-face, we see that online tools make available the ability to reach larger networks of people. In addition to increasing our social capital, they bridge geographical divides and enable a quick filtering of likeminded people. However, such communities cannot be a substitute for face-to-face communities. Susan Pinker in her book *The Village Effect* (2014) argues that online exchanges are less transformative than face-to-face interaction, as many elements of everyday communication are lost. It is true that we can initiate relations online, remain connected and locate old friends. We argue, however, that the role of technology here could be rather complementary.

The reality of our time is such that we are surrounded by technology that permits people to connect remotely and convene when they want. The role of technology is so obvious considering members of a community may not always find the time or resources to be physically present at the same location. Some may prefer to mix face-to-face gatherings with electronic communication. Regardless, although convenient and much cheaper, electronic communications come with their own downsides. For example, among online communities, there is always the fear of misunderstanding and misrepresentation, and above all, serious concerns about privacy. Another real-world issue is levels of proficiency, comfort and access to technology.

Although electronic communication helps transcend geographical and temporal limitations, we frequently choose to connect even electronically with people whom we see face-to-face in our everyday lives (Allen & Henn, 2006). But considering the practical challenges of coordination and availability, technology can play an auxiliary role in helping the community stay together. Indeed, as Parker Palmer says, it is about 'the awareness that we are connected with each other. It is not about the [physical] presence of other people—it is about being fully open to the reality of relationship' (2004, p. 55).

Still, face-to-face seems to be the best interaction method for communities of freedom. Although the minimum ideal number is 15, going higher could be more efficiently managed through technology, as could interconnection across a constellation of communities. Technology allows us to manage our relationships using different modes such as video conferencing, text messaging, voice calls, emails, social networking sites and so on. To an extent, the method we choose to communicate reflects the depth and quality of relationships.

Facilitation Format

In communities of freedom, meeting spaces could be arranged in such a way that they do not burden anyone. Comfortable, yet simple arrangements in natural settings should be adequate. Depending on the size of the group, such communities can meet at work, quiet coffee shops, in apartments, homes, or parks. The norms for being fully present in such communities are important and limiting the use of communication devices and other distractions is crucial. As the late Stanford technologist Clifford Nass said, 'We've got to make face-to-face time sacred' (Yardley, 2013).

Simple and open rules of engagement and the manners of being together are key for the success of a community, as complex and elaborate modalities can have negative effects that may endanger the health of relationships. The following are elements of participatory facilitation that enhance the sense of community and belonging.

First, there is dialogue, which is a means by which we can name and map issues in personal and communal relations. Moreover, it can be a way to gain a sense of direction and pave the way for a breakthrough when necessary[5]. According to leading thinkers, conversations within a community can be sacred, and there is an aspect of holiness in relationships (Buber, 1970; Millis, 2013). Dialogue is not a discussion or debate, and it is important to stress that silence is a crucial part of it, too.

Next comes openness. Authentic communities acknowledge and surface culturally and psychologically entrenched assumptions that stand in the way of positive relationships. Openness entails a conscious effort towards a non-judgmental frame of mind and courage. As much as possible, the use of 'I' statements gives voice to individual participants without leading to unnecessary generalizations. Suspending roles and status is also important because it involves making attempts to keep social and organizational hierarchies out of the communal time together.

Then there is the matter of outcomes. The purpose of communal meetings and dialogue should not always be driven by a desire for specific results or products.

Finally, there is the need for full presence and deep listening. Honouring the time and goodwill of the members of the community is demonstrated by making the effort to be fully present in the moment. It involves letting go of inner distractions and listening with respect.

Practices and Symbols

Working with communities of freedom requires practices that enable the nurturing of a deeper sense of connection with self, others, the natural world and a transcendent reality. It requires sustained exploratory engagements that refresh the commitments of the members of a community to the values that have brought them together, which are essential to keep the community alive. Such reflective practices focusing on the big questions of life are likely to consist of a range of activities such as mindfulness meditation, journaling, silence and so on that support personal and collective growth, which over time, can shape the shared values of the community.

Unlike dogmatic institutions that are built on creating uniformity regardless of the plurality of their members' experiences, one defining characteristic of such a community is 'experimentation' of practices, as one size does not necessarily fit all. Principles of deep listening and dialogue encourage the surfacing of many gifts and interests of members. For example, individual preferences may vary from quiet time to guided meditation, or from silent nature walks to doodling. Other activities may include photography, glass art, collage, journaling and a myriad of others.

Keeping in mind that communities often do not have the opportunity to gather as regularly as is optimal, signs and symbols play an important role in reminding members about the values and meaning they share with the community. Examples include the fleur-de-lis of the scouting organizations and Greek letters used by fraternities and sororities. This may not be limited to just symbols, however. Architecture, clothes, slogans, mottos, sculptures, paintings, and so forth can serve the same purpose.

Form of Leadership

It is difficult to recommend a particular type of leadership, vertical or horizontal or a combination thereof, that suits communities that are motivated by a higher sense of freedom. However, there are some experiences that have proved to be effective. For example, sociocracy refers to a form of leadership of equals that facilitates decision-making based on consent. Popular among Ecovillage communities, this model connects layers of groups to a central body that is representative of all circles. Leadership within such small circles is dynamic, that is every member gets a chance to provide leadership as roles rotate. This kind of leadership resonates with various theories of governance that talk about 'power with' rather than 'power over' (Elworthy, 2014; Green, 2012; Pascale et al., 2010).

Stages in Building Community

Developing authentic relationships among people is not an easy process. It requires good leadership, patience, trust, open-mindedness, and a good dose of curiosity. There may be stages of euphoria or even polite accommodation of each other at the beginning. One should not assume, however, that the work is done because a group of people has decided to come together. As very well described by M. Scott Peck, many communities go through a stage of crisis as they get to know each other better and differences of opinion and methods of accomplishing certain goals surface (1987). Despite the fact there can be phases of detachment along the way, successful communities are those that are able to find ways to capitalize on these differences and still remain committed to their shared values and purpose. The role of leadership in navigating through each phase of building community is conceptualized in the sociocracy model described above.

Conclusion

Communities of freedom are humble realms where we recognize and act upon our interdependence. They are milieus where we welcome and are welcomed by strangers through 'hospitality and generosity' (Block, 2009); a setting where 'sacred conversations' take place (Millis, 2013). From an inner perspective, our actions and relations enable us to realize a 'hidden wholeness' (Palmer, 2009). Such group connections conserve our true nature, which is love, and which often gets eroded in the midst of ego-driven approaches to life (Romesin & Verden-Zöller, 2012).

Like any other human enterprise, community has its struggles. Comfort and trust do not come readily, as members plough through clouds of politeness, chaos, and feelings of disconnection. There is also the shadow side of community that occurs when exclusion is emphasized and boundaries are strictly enforced by tapping into fear, suspicion, antipathy, and hate. Many examples abound across the world where communities are defined by fortresses of exclusion, intent to destroy everyone who disagrees with them. Examples include religious fanatics and bands of credulous minds gathering around ideological demagogues.

Of course, it is naive to say community is the be-all and end-all magic bullet that shatters the disconnection or alienation we experience every day. Individual commitment and sustained practices are important cornerstones that make community possible. Communities evolve constantly as their members and circumstances change. These metamorphoses also shape the practices and purposes communities serve.

However, although they are fluid and depend on ever-changing factors, communities are crucial not only for our survival, but also as being one of the few paths we have to flourish and live undivided lives. They catapult the transformation of consciousness from fragmentation to a realization that we are connected by an intricate web of sacred bonds.

This discussion of community, therefore, offers some insights into the kinds of values that may need to be present if such governance is to reflect values of love, compassion and care of one for another.

Notes

1. Such examples include the Happy Planet Index, Social Progress Index and many others.
2. With number of members ranging from 50 to 150, the approximate number of inhabitants in traditional villages across the world, Ecovillages were the brain child of Georgia Institute of Technology professor George Ramsey. These communities are built on ecological and communitarian ideals with significant spiritual grounding. Currently, such carbon-free communities are spread across more than 70 countries.
3. Deep listening is an intentional practice that encourages individuals to be fully present in the moment and minimize judgment. It includes a respectful engagement without trying to control the interaction or its outcomes.
4. Numbers between ten to fifteen have different symbolic significance in many cultures. For example, the number of people in an American jury is twelve; the number of Jesus's disciples is also twelve.
5. Details can be found on The International Institute for Sustained Dialogue's website. Additionally, David Bohm's work provides insights on dialogue.

10. Pillars of Peace

STEVE KILLELEA

Introduction

This chapter will start by highlighting the urgent need to change the way in which we govern and build the resilience of our societies, simply because the issues we face are global in nature and without a world that is basically peaceful we will be unable to get the levels of trust necessary to solve these problems. This underscores the need for a paradigm shift in the way we solve social problems. I argue that such a shift starts from a new way of understanding peace. Indeed, this chapter proposes that by focusing on Positive Peace, an environment can be created which is optimal for achieving sustainable peace as well as providing the conditions for humans and the planet to thrive together.

The main thrust of this chapter is to outline the current research into Positive Peace, which looks at, in particular, the attitudes, institutions and structures that contribute to creating and sustaining peaceful societies. It argues that these aspects of peaceful societies can act as a system that provides structures, or architectonics, in the words of Johan Galtung, for fostering a culture of peace (Galtung, 1981). We term the eight societal structures and attitudes associated with peaceful societies *Pillars of Peace*. The Pillars include a well-functioning government, low levels of corruption, the free flow of information through society, the acceptance of the rights of others, strong business environment, good relations with neighbouring countries, high levels of human capital as well as an equitable distribution of resources through society.

The chapter also discusses the need for humanity to develop a global set of values and the importance of considering both values and competencies when selecting our leaders.

Pillars of Peace are important but so is the development of all individuals. As a society focuses on strengthening its peace architectonics, individuals will become more knowledgeable, be less distressed, have more access to resources and experience less fear. This creates a virtuous cycle in which members of society have the freedom to become better human beings and the society becomes more compassionate and more 'human'. In other words, peace is no longer just in the domain of the altruistic, it is also in everyone's self-interest.

The Importance of Peace

The 21st century is the dawning of a new epoch unlike anything humanity has ever experienced. In prior millennia, history could be defined as a battle for survival where there appeared to be a need to *conquer* a world in which resources seemed to be boundless and infinite. Humanity's view of its relationship to the world could have been best summarized by the Darwinian expression that dominated the 20th century, 'the survival of the fittest'; where the strongest and most aggressive gained the lion's share of the resources whereas the weaker struggled to exist. This was epitomized by our historical understanding of the progression of *Homo erectus* to Neanderthal and finally to *Homo sapiens*. Humanity survived the other species because we were *the fittest to survive*.

However, such a worldview will not prevail in the 21st century as humans have now discovered that it is not only flawed but also dangerous and could lead to the possible demise of the human race. Indeed we have come to realise that our world which had previously given the impression of having unlimited resources is finite and in fact is *shrinking* daily. This is mainly driven by over-population and over-consumption and expressed as climate change, ever-decreasing bio-diversity, immigration clashes or fast-spreading pathogens. Diseases and pollution do not respect national borders; neither do many conflicts. They often create instability in other countries either directly through armed conflict or indirectly with the movement of peoples escaping the conflict. All of which highlights a level of interconnectedness that didn't exist even one hundred years ago when Darwin was attempting to understand why species change and evolve.

Underlying this is a growing lack of belief in many of our systems (Endelman, 2014). As a result, it has been observed that the number of people turning out to vote is falling (International Institute for Democracy and Electoral Assistance, 2004); and many in advanced democracies perceive their politicians to be corrupt (Rose-Ackerman, 2013). This in many ways has been influenced by 'money in politics' and ineffectual political outcomes since the Global Financial Crisis (Hardin, 2013).

Consequently, unless humanity can change its approach to governance so that it becomes more mature and forward-thinking in the way it oversees the use of the planet's resources, has a more inclusive and equitable approach to distributing these resources and is more unifying in the values it represents, we will face a bleak future.

It appears that doing business as usual will no longer be feasible. The falling levels of belief and trust in our institutions highlight the need for a new approach. A number of important questions need to be addressed; they include: why does only a small minority of political leaders act from unifying values and with ethics? What can be done to restructure and refresh our institutions and restore their vigour and resilience?

It appears that too many of our leaders' worldviews are trapped in the prior age—they are Darwinian at heart and miss to recognize just how strongly we are all interconnected and how limited our resources really are. In other words, few leaders have the capacity to lead from the awareness that human's interconnectedness determines that we are all in it together and that only solidarity can engender abundance rather than competition and opposition.

Another reading of the current phenomenon of political ineffectiveness is that, at its core, lie the criteria upon which we elect our leaders, our expectations and our ability to hold them to account. We do not seem to choose our leaders based on their ethics not on their compassion. Rather we seem to select them based on their economic success and on their ability to prevail upon others. It is imperative that we develop a set of values to guide the choice of our leaders.

Values, however, differ from culture to culture as well as within cultures. To engage with pressing global issues such as those mentioned above, it is necessary that humanity consolidate a set of global values. These values need to be universal, and transversal in a sense that they transcend cultural and religious borders, the secular and spiritual divide and cannot offend. Conceptually, peace is a good starting position to explore global values as it is at the core in the concerns of all regions, cultures and societies and when lost, becomes the major need of all people.

This leads us to explore what are the fundamental values connected to peace? These could be simply expressed as compassion and the caring for the unprivileged. However, although *compassion* on its own is of extraordinary value it is not enough for effective action, therefore competence is also needed. Competence can be seen as knowledge gained both formally and informally and then successfully applied to solve problems or issues. For action to be effective and of most benefit it must be guided by a high level of competence coupled with compassionate motivation. Basically, the heart and mind need to be combined to create dynamic effective action. These are the qualities we need to develop in ourselves and seek in our leaders.

All too often, we seek to promote those individuals/leaders with competence regardless of their motivation. What is needed is a combination of the two, good motivation based on global values and a high level of competence. When selecting our leaders we need to understand what motivates them. They need to be compassionate and inclusive individuals with the appropriate high level of competence to enable them to achieve their tasks. Without the appropriate level of competence the best motivation in the world will not be effective.

As such, a simple core set of values which most people on the planet would agree with are compassion, relevant domain knowledge (competence) and a good work ethic. Compassion could be expressed as 'better caring for the under-privileged and inclusive policies'.

Compassion and knowledge combined with a strong work ethic produce the best outcome. Research by the Institute for Economics and Peace has isolated eight factors that create a peaceful society. The aforementioned values are represented by two of the factors that create peaceful societies, these being *equitable distribution of resources* and *high levels of human capital*. These factors relate to leadership in the above model, however for peace to truly thrive all eight factors need to be strong (Institute for Economics and Peace, 2013).

Global challenges call for global solutions and these solutions require cooperation on a scale unprecedented in human history. Peace is an essential prerequisite because without peace we will never be able to achieve the levels of cooperation, trust, inclusiveness and social equity necessary to solve these challenges, let alone empower the international institutions necessary to address them.

Peace lies at the centre of being able to manage the transition, simply because peace creates the optimum environment in which the other activities that contribute to human growth can take place. In this sense, peace is a facilitator making it easier for workers to produce, businesses to sell, entrepreneurs and scientists to innovate and governments to serve the interests of people.

But if peace is an essential prerequisite for meeting our sustainability challenges and improving our economic and social well-being then having a good understanding of peace is essential. This poses the question: 'How well do we understand peace?' Fifty years ago peace studies were virtually nonexistent. Today there are thriving Peace & Conflict Centers in numerous universities around the world. But most of these are centred on the study of conflict rather than on the understanding of peace.

A parallel can be drawn here with medical science. The study of pathology has led to numerous breakthroughs in our understanding of how to treat and cure disease. However, there is more than that to health. It was only when medical science turned its focus to the study of healthy human beings that we began to understand what we need to do to stay healthy: the right physical exercise, a good mental disposition and a healthy diet. This could only be learnt by studying what was working. Hence the World Health Organization defines health as 'Health is a state of complete physical, mental and social well-being and not merely the absence of disease or infirmity' (WHO, 1946). In the same ways, the study of peace is fundamentally different than the study of conflict, and the definition of peace is more than the absence of war and violence.

Over the last century we have moved from having departments of war to departments of defense and we are now seeing the emergence of organizations that are lobbying for the creation of departments of peace within governments. While these changes are beneficial in improving our understanding of peace, peace is not yet seen as germane to the major academic disciplines, nor is there a methodological approach to the cross-disciplinary study of peace. As an example, there is no university Chair of Peace Economics in any major Economic faculty, yet most business people believe that their markets grow in peace and that their costs decrease with increasing peacefulness.

The simplest way of approaching the definition of peace is in terms of harmony achieved by the absence of war, conflict or violent crime. Applied to states, this would suggest that the measurement of internal states of peace is as important as those external factors involving other states or neighbours. This is what Johan Galtung defined as 'negative peace'—an absence of violence. The concept of negative peace is immediately intuitive and empirically measurable and can be used as a starting point to elaborate its counterpart concept, 'positive peace'. Having established what constitutes an absence of violence, is it possible through statistical analysis to identify which attitudes, institutions and structures create and maintain peace? This is what I will turn to next.

Measuring Peace

Measurement is the key to understanding any human endeavour. We use economic measurements to guide our business strategies, and student examinations to determine our educational targets. Peace is no different. If we do not measure peace, then how can we know whether our actions are either helping or hindering us in the achievement of a more peaceful world? Only by measuring peace can we move to a better understanding of the drivers of peace and how these can be supported.

Let's take the Global Peace Index (GPI) as an example. The GPI was developed in 2007 by the Institute for Economics and Peace (IEP) as one of the first rigorous attempts to measure the relative levels of the peacefulness of nations. By aggregating and generating a comprehensive and reliable dataset which measures direct violence, the GPI adds to the current stock of harmonized cross-country data. Since 2007 it has informed policymakers, academics, and civil society organizations about the objective state of direct violence in countries, covering over 99% of the world's population. The purpose of this research is to move beyond a crude measure of peacefulness and better understand the cultural, economic, and political conditions associated with peaceful environments.

The GPI focuses on measuring 'negative peace', which was described by Johan Galtung as the 'absence of violence' and the 'absence of the fear of violence'. Hence the GPI utilizes 22 indicators of safety and security in society, militarization, and ongoing domestic and international conflict to determine the multidimensional nature of negative peace in 162 countries. This means nations with a high ranking in the GPI are considered more peaceful because they are relatively safer and more secure than countries lower in the rankings.

In contrast to negative peace, Galtung described a second dimension called positive peace. Broadly understood, positive peace is derived from preventative solutions which are optimistic and facilitate a more integrated society. According to Galtung, this results in 'cooperation for mutual benefit, and where individuals and society are in harmony.' From this conceptual basis, IEP defines positive peace as 'the set of attitudes, institutions and structures which when strengthened, lead to a more peaceful society' (Institute for Economics and Peace, 2013).

This work resulted in the development of the Pillars of Peace which consist of eight pillars which when functioning well support and sustain peaceful societies. This body of work was derived empirically through using statistical analysis to isolate the most statistically significant factors. It is important to realise that these factors work as a system, therefore strength in all Pillars is important as the causality between the pillars varies depending on individual circumstances. Therefore it's important to understand the inter-dependent nature amongst all the pillars and focus on supporting all of them at the same time. This could be described as a holistic systemic approach to building lasting peace.

The Pillars of Peace describe the key attitudes, institutions and structures that underpin peaceful societies. In developing the Pillars of Peace, IEP drew on a range of research and data sources including over 4,700 different indices, datasets and attitudinal surveys in conjunction with current thinking about what drives peace, resilience and conflict. From this analysis it was determined that more peaceful societies tend to share eight key characteristics or 'Pillars', including: (1). A well-functioning government; (2). A sound business environment; (3). An equitable distribution of resources; (4). The acceptance of the rights of others; (5). Good relations with neighbours; (6). High levels of human capital; (7). Free flow of information; and (8). Low levels of corruption. Figure 1 illustrates the interdependence amongst these pillars.

Figure 1. The Pillars of Peace.

Let's examine each of these pillars.

Well-Functioning Government

Well-functioning government can be broken down into three key domains. These include a government's effectiveness, the rule of law and voice and accountability. A government's effectiveness refers to the ability of government to provide public goods and services, including the implementation of policy, the overall political culture and management of the natural environment. The concept of the rule of law relates to the functioning of formal and informal justice. This includes the legal regulation of the press, the extent of due process and extent to which government powers are constrained by the legal system. Finally, voice and accountability focuses on the connection of government with the wider population and includes factors such as the extent of civil liberties and a government's accountability to the wider society.

A Sound Business Environment

A sound business environment is crucial to peace. Business provides employment, which is instrumental in providing a viable taxation base, the productive use of human capital as well as providing individuals with access to financial capital. Communities which are prosperous also tend to have lower levels of social tension and a greater capacity to help others.

An Equitable Distribution of Resources

Equity describes the extent to which individuals and groups are treated fairly, regardless of their personal characteristics such as their social position, race, religion or gender. How equitable resources and opportunities are distributed throughout a society may define how easily an individual or group accesses a range of vital goods and services such as land, water, education, health care and justice, all of which are important contributors to human development.

An Acceptance of the Rights of Others

Acceptance of the rights of others is a Pillar encompassing both the formal institutions that ensure basic rights and freedoms as well as the informal social and cultural norms that relate to the behaviors of citizens. These factors relate to tolerance between different genders and ethnic, linguistic, religious, and socio-economic groups within a country.

Good Relations with Neighbours

The Pillar of Good Relations with Neighbours not only refers to the relationship between states, but also encapsulates relations between ethnicities, religious groups and others. The Pillar measures the quality of relationships between the constituent groups within the country and also the quality of the relations with its neighbouring countries.

Together, these eight Pillars were found to be associated with peaceful environments and are both interdependent and mutually reinforcing, such that improvements in one factor tend to strengthen others and vice versa. Therefore the relative strength of any one Pillar has the potential to positively or negatively influence the others, thereby influencing and enhancing the country's resilience.

A Wide definition of Human Capital

Human capital describes a country's stock of skills, knowledge and behaviours. Whilst the concept of human capital is often narrowly defined as the economic benefits associated with education, IEP's approach considers the definition in its wider context to not only include education but also an individuals' health, as both factors play an important role in determining a person's economic and social contribution.

A Free Flow of Information

The free flow of information is essential to a well-informed society. Accurate and well-distributed information underpins the free market, improves human capital, provides transparency of government decisions and improves judicial and government decisions (Brunettia and Wederb, 2003). This Pillar describes how easily citizens can gain access to information, including whether the media is free and independent, the extent to which citizens are informed and engaged in the political process and the diversity of access to information, such as measured through internet access or simply the ability to express political views.

Low Levels of Corruption

Corruption describes the abuse of a position to gain undue advantage. This might occur through a range of channels, such as through government, business or community relationships. Corruption may also result in the generation of wider community tensions, thereby undermining peaceful relations. Corruption within the police, judiciary and military is particularly impactful on peace.

As mentioned earlier, these Pillars are viewed as a system and individual causality is very difficult to predict; consequently to build peace and resilience it is necessary to strengthen the overall system.

Peaceful nations are also better equipped through their attitudes, institutions and structures to respond to external shocks. In fact, analysis by IEP has clearly suggested that the strength of a country's Pillars also has lasting implications for a country's chance of achieving peace in the future. This has been illustrated in Figure 2, where it can be seen that countries with stronger Pillars also experienced more peaceful outcomes over time.

Change in GPI score since 2008

Pillar	Countries with Strong Pillars	Countries with Weaker Pillars
Low Levels of Corruption	~2.5%	~4%
High levels of Human Capital	~4.5%	~5%
Free Flow of Information	~2.5%	~3.5%
Good relations with Neighbours	~3.5%	~5.5%
Acceptance of the Rights of Others	~2.5%	~4%
Equitable Distribution of Resources	~3.5%	~4.5%

Figure 2. Stronger Pillars Lead to More Peaceful Outcomes.

As can be seen, since 2008 those countries which experienced the largest deteriorations in their GPI scores are also those which had the weakest pillars.

The Pillars of Peace were found to be both interdependent and mutually reinforcing, such that strengthening one Pillar would help reinforce the others. These Pillars also create resilient societies, ones that are able to absorb shocks such as Iceland during the Global Financial Crisis and Japan after the 2011 Tsunami. The successful recovery programs would have been much more difficult in societies that didn't have common values and respect for human dignity.

Although societies which are peaceful, socially cohesive, stable and safe are undeniably worthwhile in and of themselves, they also make economic sense, with research by IEP consistently finding that more peaceful societies are also more prosperous. In fact, when the economic impact of violence and the fear of violence are considered on a global scale they are equivalent to at least US$9.8 trillion. Basically, 11.3 percent of GDP is lost to violence every year.

The pivotal role of peace in encouraging prosperity extends to broader social outcomes such as education, health and overall well-being. This has been amply demonstrated as part of IEP's engagement with discussions around the Post-2015 Development Agenda (UNGA, 2013), with there being clear evidence that those countries that have been most successful in achieving development goals are those who were more peaceful, providing a clear indication that peace is not just an end, but a prerequisite, for development.

The attitudes, institutions and structures outlined by the Pillars of Peace can also help promote resilience in society, enabling nations to overcome adversity and resolve internal economic, cultural, and political conflict through peaceful means. It is sufficient to compare the way in which two European countries have been able to deal with their economic crises over the past few years, to demonstrate how a country with strong Pillars, Iceland (Schippa, 2012), was much more resilient than Greece, which is lagging behind on a number of the Pillars. Or in the case of natural disasters, compare the resilience of Japan in the face of the 2011 tsunami, to that of Haiti after the 2010 earthquake.

The Pillars can be seen as interconnected and interacting in varied and complex ways, forming either virtuous circles of peace creation or vicious circles of destruction, with causality running in either direction depending on individual circumstances. Although it is a utopian vision to expect a world free of violence, as we have seen, peace clearly makes economic sense.

Values and Motivation

Political processes are always intriguing and probably no other human activity is covered as much by the media. In some parts of the world the media is relatively free and also without too much bias while in other parts of the world it is tightly controlled and supportive of small elites. In the latter societies it's often hard to distinguish truth from hype and to understand the underlying motivations of the leaders.

In the advanced democracies support for democratic institutions is slipping (Edelman, 2014). This is evidenced by the growing democratic deficit and the falling attendances at elections. The explanation that I would like to put forward to understand this trend is very simple: citizens do not assess the motivation of the leaders they elect and only focus on their political skill set in making a choice. Some elected politicians pass reams of legislation that they were never elected to do and within months recant on the major policy platforms that they were elected to implement.

The moral issues that generally receive the most attention by the media include gender balances, same sex rights, religious orientation, free market philosophies or socialist ideals. All of these moral causes can be impactful and worthwhile in themselves but at the same time, they can also create conflict and strong disagreement. Additionally, individuals ascribing to these values can be either well or poorly motivated; in other words, they are acting either for the common good or in self-interest. We should therefore ask ourselves what are the most overarching values that can unite humanity and equally what should we look for in our leaders?

Values need to be thought of in more fundamental ways. For instance, we could easily ask questions such as: what personal traits do we desire from those who serve as our leaders? Individuals who are both compassionate and care about others or those who are greedy, power seeking and interested in pursuing their own needs? Indeed, the motivation of our leaders is a key, if we consider motivation as part of their characteristics or personal traits.

Similarly, we can ask such questions as: What qualities in the person that helps bring about better leadership and outcome for our society? An individual who is intelligent, generous and inclusive in their decision making or a fractious person who is selfish and lacking the basic skills in what they are doing?

What is needed is a careful consideration of what we believe are the appropriate motivation, qualities and skills needed for leadership. Here the qualities and motivation of the leader merge with the values they live by.

In helping to redefine these values, Figure 3 outlines a very simple model of the relationships and interactions between skills, motivation and outcomes so as to conceptualize a model of leadership that transcends those values that are divergent and looks at those values that are convergent and hopefully can unite.

Effective governance

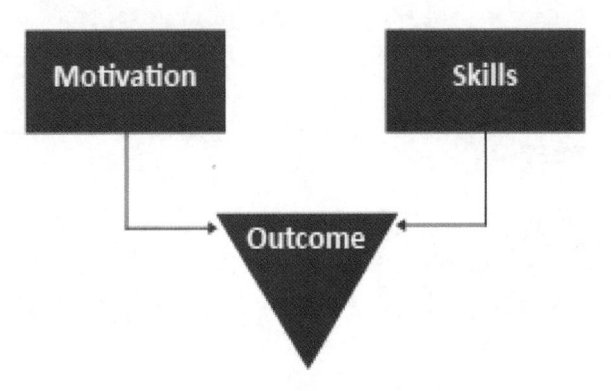

Optimum outcomes can only be achieved through maximising motivation and skills

Figure 3. Effective Governance.

Simply put, effective leadership has two basic components: the first is motivation—why do leaders do what they are doing—and the second is competency—what do they bring to the tasks they are responsible for.

If individuals have the best possible motivation but lack competency in what they are aiming at managing then the outcome in all likelihood will be ineffective. On the other hand, highly competent and skilled individuals can be effective, but without the right motivation they can also be very dangerous as their end goal will be something other than the common good. This could be expressed as a concentration of personal power or pushing the agenda of small vested interest groups.

If we are honest with ourselves, other than a few exceptional individuals, most people carry a mixture of aspects, being well-motivated while also being self-serving and/or fearful. The key question is how much of each.

Individuals also have varying skill levels. In leadership most often there are a number of skills which may be needed. But all too often when we select our leaders we focus on skills to the detriment of motivation.

What is needed is a combination of the two. When selecting our leaders we need to understand what motivates them. Are they compassionate and inclusive individuals with the right level of skills for the task they set out to accomplish?

The best way to determine how a future leader may perform is to look at their past as future actions will most likely follow the pattern of past actions (Ligon, Hunter & Mumford, 2008).

Relationship of Individuals to Society

One of the most important questions regarding governance is whether the sum of the individuals creates the system or whether the system creates the individuals within it.

Causality?

Individual → Collective

Individual:
- ✓ Compassion
- ✓ Empathy
- ✓ Skills
- ✓ Motivation
- ✓ Fear
- ✓ Greed

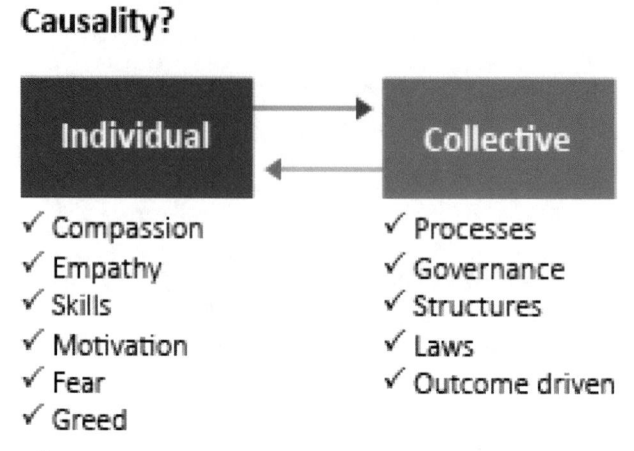

Collective:
- ✓ Processes
- ✓ Governance
- ✓ Structures
- ✓ Laws
- ✓ Outcome driven

Figure 4. Causality.

Likely neither of these propositions is correct; rather what is occurring is a systemic effect where the individuals shape the system and the system then feeds back to shape the individual. Therefore there is not a concept of simplistic causality; the two are reciprocally interacting and creating continual changes in each other.

Figure 4 outlines this very simple model. I do believe that expressing it simply is important as it does give the opportunity to better grasp and understand the effects of the collective on the individual and vice versa.

The collective can simply be described as the formal institutions that govern our societies coupled with the informal institutions within the society. A starting point in explaining this is education. From a young age we go to school; what we learn there does shape our view of the world and our education systems generally aim at reflecting societal norms, thereby causing us to adopt these beliefs. Therefore the system does influence the individual.

Similarly individuals are capable of making independent judgments and will react to society and its institutions based on a myriad of reasons. These factors are as diverse as genetic predisposition, peer group influences, moral outrage or how safe they feel, to name a few. When these influences are shared by many individuals within a society then new views are formed which in some cases lead to altering the status quo.

Individuals do react to laws and where laws are seen as repressive they may respond on a group basis which then alters the laws going forward. Similarly, in democracies, elections can be seen as individuals within society determining the collective. And once the collective, in this case the government, has been established, it in turn creates structures that govern the individuals. In this way government shapes the behaviour of individuals and influences their values, hopefully according to what they have been elected to do.

As previously mentioned this is a simplistic approach to understanding highly complex phenomena. Other effects are also at play such as neighbouring countries' influences, the role of powerful vested interest groups or the impact of the media.

What is important is the concept that individuals' values help to shape the system and the system in turn helps to shape the values of the individuals. Therefore if individuals focus on choosing leaders with the correct motivation along with the appropriate skills the system will reflect these values and reinforce them in their citizens. This then creates what can be termed a virtuous cycle, as shown in Figure 5.

Peace as a guiding principle

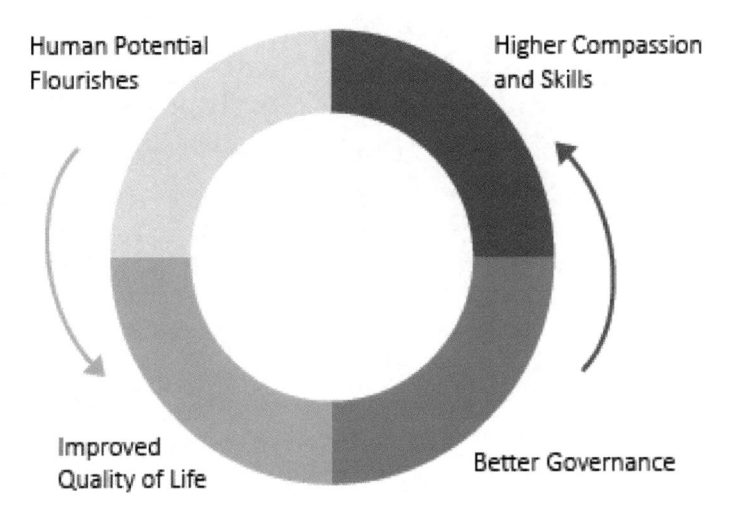

Virtuous and Vicious Cycles – everything is a continuum

Figure 5. Peace as a Guiding Principle.

Conclusion

The key question we should ask ourselves is *how do we create the optimal environment for human potential to flourish?* In other words, how can we achieve an environment that is peaceful, prosperous, inclusive and sustainable, both in environmental and economic terms?

The best outcomes for society would be achieved when the individuals within the society focus on electing and following leaders who have the highest levels of good motivation, combined with strong skills in the area in which they wish to lead. This will instigate ethical governance, better-framed laws and more effective policies as well as a caring society which is more likely to nurture long-term sustainability and productivity.

This will result in a society that cherishes the values which have been outlined in this chapter such as compassion, inclusiveness, knowledge and a good work ethic while focusing on holistic development as expressed through the Pillars of Peace. This, in turn, will create an environment where the individuals will have more opportunities to pursue their passions, resulting in higher levels of achievement for themselves as well as for the overall society.

A virtuous cycle which feeds upon itself.

11. A New Form of Global Governance[1]

POLLY HIGGINS

Introduction

How we choose to align our laws is in part a reflection of collective intent: do we stay as we are in a state of conflict or do we shift to a state of conscious transformation? What I propose here is a new form of global governance based on one simple premise which is, in itself, a distillation of a triumvirate of intrinsic values. The values themselves are an explicit statement of intent. They are, you could say, a summation of that which we are now only beginning to fully understand. What we are beginning to have a glimpse is that life is sacred, we are all one and love is all. It's a shorthand for much of what we are grappling with, and which in the simplest of terms resonates deeply. Some may say these are the words of love not law, and that I speak of soft not hard law, a seeking of harmony not harm. And that would be right. Our laws as they stand no longer reflect our collective intent. Humanity is already transforming.

The particular law that this chapter is concerned with is the Law of Ecocide.

Ecocide law proposals date back to 1972. Olof Palme, the then Prime Minister of Sweden, in his opening speech at the Stockholm Conference for the Human Environment, spoke explicitly of the Vietnam War as an 'ecocide'. The Stockholm Conference focused international attention on environmental issues for the first time, especially those relating to environmental degradation and transboundary pollution. Others, including Indira Gandhi from India and the leader of the Chinese delegation Tang Ke, also denounced the war on human and environmental terms. They too called for ecocide to be an international crime. A Working Group on Crimes Against the Environment was formed at that conference, and a draft Ecocide Convention was submitted into the United Nations in 1973. An international Crime of

Ecocide was included into the drafting of the Rome Statute (1985–1996) and had the support of many countries, but was removed despite objections at the 11th hour.

So this chapter is also a celebration that for over 40 years humanity has finally developed the means to bring ecocide to an end.

Legal Duty of Care

Law, which is of course intent made manifest, is out of step. No longer does humanity (on the whole) intend to cause mass damage and destruction (or wish to be reckless). However, there is a cognitive dissonance: our laws as they stand put profit first without consequence. An imposed value, if you like, has taken precedence—over and above any intrinsic values. For instance, our planet earth's ecosystem is valuable in itself, and should not be merely treated as a means to human consumption end. When laws put human interests over the integrity of our ecosystem, the outcome is ecocide.[2] What is missing is one simple premise: first do no harm. Start from a *first do no harm* principle and everything shifts, and new laws are required to bring to an end significant harm. Indeed, laws create a legal duty of care.

Business, as it is set up today in legal terms, has, through the use of ownership laws, sidestepped an overriding legal duty of care. Instead, the number one duty has been to put the interests of the shareholders first. Thus demand for profit takes precedence over considerations for health and well-being of human and non-human interests. The consequences of there being no international laws to stop companies from putting profit over people and planet are enormous. In addition to human-caused ecocide, the increase of catastrophic events (as a result of global warming for instance) highlights the lack of a fiduciary duty of care not only in business but also in politics.

There is a world of a difference in law between an owner of a property and a trustee. Put simply, an owner can destroy or cause harm to his property without being held to account. A trustee, however, holds in trust—often land—that which he or she has been entrusted to take care of on behalf of beneficiaries for both current and future generations.

A trustee must by law put the interests of the beneficiaries first. When the beneficiaries do not benefit, then the trustee has failed in his or her fiduciary duty and can be held to account. Should a trustee destroy what is the life-form of the trust (e.g., the land), thereby bringing to an end the benefit, he or she has in law failed in their duty of care. A business, however, can destroy the life-form of the contract (e.g., the land) and thereby bring to an end the benefit, yet where there is no legal duty of care, little can be done.

A New Form of Global Governance

Trusteeship is very different from ownership; it carries with it a duty of care for the health and well-being of the given community, not just for the here and now, but also for its future. Whereas corporations who have contracts assigning land to them to use have an explicit duty to put the interests of their shareholders first, which means—for most—to put profit over and above any other interests. How does this work? The legal relationship determines the outcome. As an owner one has very little responsibility to that which one owns and even less to any others; as a trustee, however, one has a legal duty of care, often to others one may not even meet in a lifetime.

In business, under old governance structures, ownership prevails. And so, where a company has contractual rights over a territory and destroys it as a result of pursuit of profit (such as for fossil fuel energy), there are virtually no rules in place to stop the damage, destruction to or loss of ecosystems. At an international level at the moment, it is not a crime during peacetime to destroy vast tracts of land—and yet, during wartime it can be a crime.

Compare this with community land projects, which are set up on trusteeship rules. Unlike business which is driven by the legal requirement to put the interests of shareholders first (which means in most cases to make profit), community land projects have a legal duty of care, which means that health and well-being principles take primacy. So, in legal terms, broadly we have been running business on ownership rules rather than trusteeship rules, which in turn has led to lack of duty of care for the community affected and a lack of responsibility for current and future adverse consequences. Moreover, business, like politics, is run on short-term returns, thereby mitigating against planning for the longer term. Neither politics nor business has an overarching legal duty of care to put the interests of the wider Earth community[3] first before profit. Very different laws exist for business: they are not governed first and foremost by a legal duty of care. As a result, communities across the world suffer significant harm on a daily basis for want of fast-gained financial returns.

Thus, our laws have, in part, locked us in. We have become chained by a system of our own creation that has failed to value the sacredness of life (ours and others), a system that has allowed us to sever our deep affinity with the natural world and has commoditized and instrumentalized that which we love.

Daring to Be Great

All chains can be broken or unlocked. The recognition that we are restricted by the very system we as humans have created can equally open up the possibility to unchain us. This is a space, an opportunity, to put in place a new form of governance, something greater and more ethical than before. Great laws based on the principle of first do no harm. But take note: as we aspire to something greater, we invite greatness into our lives.

There is great power that can be harnessed through the pursuit of greatness. I talk here of the power to effect greatness within our lives which in turn contributes to a greater world, a world that is ecocide-free, free from cultural, ecological and our inner ecocides. Power brings with it the responsibility to use, not abuse, for the greatest good. By taking responsibility for the most powerful state of being, we cultivate the most powerful state of doing.

Self- and global governance, when operating from the same 'first do no harm' premise, is no longer misaligned. It becomes embedded in the collective psyche. No longer is profit put before people and planet. Our priorities are flipped to a newfound power—that of being empowered.

When we dare to be great, when we ask 'what is my legacy to be?' when we look two thousand years hence, our vision of what is possible expands. We shift our sense of what's possible and we step outside of ourselves for just a moment in time to explore a far bigger picture. What that picture looks like arises from our preconceptions of what is possible and what is not. By parking our preconceptions for even just a moment to allow ourselves the space to explore without restriction, our vision can be truly big—unfettered by the inner critic that says 'that's not possible'.

Creating enabling frameworks through the creation of law or the setting of intent (for creation of law is one form of setting of intent made manifest) is an essential aspect of how we move forward. What are the enabling conditions each and every one of us requires to flourish? Put a group of people in a camp surrounded by barbed wire and withdraw their right to their land and you will find that those people very soon begin to suffer. The community can no longer live in greater freedom and as a result begins to break down. The same thing happens when we surround ourselves with barriers that prevent our freedom to think big—the voice that says 'you have no right, who are you to speak?' These are barbed words indeed and in accepting them we no longer allow our being to be free, in greater expansion in thought and action. We become imprisoned in our own smallness.

Just as in law we have Enabling Acts—acts of law that cut through the chains that hold progress back—so is it sometimes necessary to break with convention so that a greater freedom can operate. We too have our own enabling actions, or practices, that empower us to move forward. More than that: when we break our own chains that bind our mind, we create a greater freedom not only for ourselves but also for others around us. When we shift our own terms of agreement, those who do not agree tend to move away, creating more space for others to radiate in who are aligned with our new state of being. In turn, our world begins to operate on a different level; one where we choose what happens next. Our world begins to constellate events and circumstances that meet our intent. Now all that is required is for us to take action.

The Sacred Trust of Civilization

There is in law an ancient tenet that dates back in writings to the 16th century. Oft overlooked, it nonetheless is encoded in the first charter for the United Nations. The original wording makes explicit our overriding duty of care to all beings—not just human beings. It is the language of trusteeship law. By 1945 the wording had been narrowed down to a limited remit, applying only to territories that were officially designated to be former colonies now named Non-Self Governing Territories (NSGTs). Nevertheless the principle here, of putting first the well-being of all beings, remains.

Set out in Article 73 of the United Nations Charter:

> Members of the United Nations which have or assume responsibilities for the administration of territories whose peoples have not yet attained a full measure of self government recognise the principle that the interests of the inhabitants of these territories are paramount, and accept as a sacred trust the obligation to promote to the utmost, *within the system of international peace and security established by the p*resent Charter, the well-being of the inhabitants of these territories...

In law, trustees' duties are based on the equitable notion of conscience and conscionable conduct. Prioritising of personal, professional and business interests are improper; what comes first are the duties of service to ensure the well-being of all beneficiaries. The trustee therefore, must act on behalf of the interests of the beneficiary, not for their own interest. Therefore, for the purposes of the sacred trust of civilisation, it is us who are the trustees who are bestowed with the position of responsibility, who have what is termed as a 'fiduciary duty', to the beneficiaries of the trust asset. The asset to be administered by the trustees is the territory, and the beneficiaries are the inhabitants.

Thus a sacred trust is both a state of *being* and of *doing*, which when adhered to it prevents the abrogation of the universal value of the sacredness of life. The very use of the word 'sacred' underlines the importance such a trust is accorded, reinforcing the moral as well as the legal obligation it imposes on all.

A sacred trust is premised on two values: the sacredness of life and our interconnectedness. I believe we can bring the sacred trust to the fore by placing it firmly at the center of our world. Written law is one thing; what we adhere to within ourselves is another. Can we put at the heart of all we do a sacred trust? I believe we can. When we value life as an end itself, something fundamental shifts. Our ability to embrace a world of peace is suddenly attainable.

Article 73 of the UN Charter has wider implications for how we engage with civilization as a whole; a sacred trust need not only be for the few—at the heart of it lies the belief in the supremacy of a duty of care that applies to everyone. Each of us counts, and how we choose to action a duty of care for humanity and for the Earth is up to each of us.

Holding to Account

Holding to account sets in place something that acts as a check and balance. To be counted is to matter, to be valued. Accountability is the ability to be included, to be answerable. The notion of answering for our actions arises from the origins of the word accountability—answering for money held in trust. The basic premise is a trusting one and where the trust is broken, we are held to account for our actions.

To simply overlook a harm is to remain complicit; however to hold to account is to stand fully in our belief that we all count and the actions that cause harm, or the lack of action to prevent a harm, are no longer lawful.

Criminal law flips the burden of proof. But it goes further than that: creating a law of ecocide means that it is no longer acceptable to say that ecocide is needed (for profit, jobs, etc.). It is not a defence to say a harm is a good harm. In the eyes of criminal law, what is determining is whether a harm is occurring. When evidence is brought to the court, it matters not that it is justified on economic reasons; what matters is whether the harm is so significant as to amount to an ecocide. Fines are not applicable to international criminal law (remember it is individuals who are held to account first and foremost, not the company or corporation). By way of analogy, take the example of a CEO of a publishing business running the defence against pornography and trafficking charges, that he should not be convicted because many people's jobs depend on it. His counsel would advise his client he has no defence in law. Apply this same situation to a CEO of a company running the defence against ecocide charges—likewise his counsel would advise the same.

Criminal law in effect changes the story of our times. No longer do we buy into the justification of Ecocide as a valid harm. Instead we choose a greater story—one free from harm.

Law of Ecocide

Most commonly understood as ecocide is ecological harm—often it is visible, such as the destruction of the Amazon. Cultural ecocide refers to the damage, destruction to or loss of a community's way of life—both ecocides are premised on a wider expansion of concern for the Earth community and our relationship with all beings. It is the consequences that occur, or could occur, that are prohibited. Why is this so? Because most ecocides are in fact not deliberate. Most CEOs do not wilfully decide to destroy; profit is the driver. Where there is intent, it counts as an aggravating feature.

To bring to an end the occurrence of ecocide—the absence of care and the causing of significant harm of our Earth community—is dependent upon the creation of law that names ecocide as a crime, as opposed to a mere civil breach. There is a difference: civil laws seek to give remedy for a harm (by way of pay-out) whereas criminal law seeks to break the pattern of harm by prohibiting it. Civil law does not necessarily remedy the wrong caused at source (the company can continue as usual), whereas criminal law can (a person is held to account in a criminal court of law). The power of criminal law is the power to prohibit, prevent and pre-empt certain acts that are no longer acceptable.

In 2010, I submitted the proposal to amend the Rome Statute to include an international crime of ecocide into the International Law Commission (ILC).[4] ILC is the UN body mandated to promote the progressive development of international law and its codification.

The purpose for creating the offence of ecocide as the 5th international Crime Against Peace is to put in place at the very top level an international law. One hundred and twenty-two nations are (as of 2014) signatories of the Rome Statute. International Crime (which is codified in the Rome Statute) applies not only to the signatory states. If and when a person commits a Crime Against Peace, the International Criminal Court has powers to intervene in certain circumstances even if the person or state involved is a non-signatory. The Rome Statute is one of the most powerful documents in the world, assigning 'the most serious crimes of concern to the international community as a whole' over and above all other laws. In addition, I have drafted primary legislation to be used at a national level, called the Ecocide Act. Section 6 of the Ecocide Act sets out the explicit right that is given recognition by the crime of ecocide:

> The right to life is a universal right and where a person, company organisation, partnership, or any other legal entity causes extensive damage to, destruction of or loss of human and or non-human life of the inhabitants of a territory... is guilty of the crime of Ecocide.

Crimes that already exist within the jurisdiction of the International Criminal Court under Article 5 of the Rome Statute are known collectively as Crime Against Peace. They are the most serious crimes of concern to the international community as a whole, including: (a) Crime of Genocide; (b) Crimes Against Humanity; (c) War Crimes; and (d) Crimes of Aggression. To be added, (e) Crime of Ecocide.

The inclusion of ecocide law as international law prohibits mass damage and destruction of the Earth and, as defined above, creates a legal duty of care for all inhabitants that have been or are at risk of being significantly harmed due to ecocide. The duty of care applies to prevent, prohibit and pre-empt both human-caused ecocide and natural catastrophes. Where ecocide occurs as a crime, remedy can be sought through national courts and the International Criminal Court (ICC) or a similar body. Proposals for a new court exist, such as The Brussels Charter 14 and the Coalition for the International Court for the Environment 15. Ecocide law has both criminal and civil law application.

Trusteeship and Ecocide Act

A law of ecocide also imputes a legal duty of care in the event of natural catastrophe (e.g., rising sea-levels, droughts, earthquakes). The United Nations Trusteeship Council's purpose (as one of the founding pillars of the UN Charter) was to assist territories that were unable to self-govern; it is proposed that the Trusteeship Council reopen its doors and be put to use again to assist non-self-governing territories that have been or are at risk of being harmed by Ecocide 16. It can be used to assist territories suffering from ecological ecocide as well as cultural ecocide.

By reopening the UN Trusteeship Council chamber (closed in 1994), Member states have a ready-made forum in which to determine what support and aid to put in place for non-self-governing territories facing ecocide.

It has been acknowledged that damage to or destruction of or loss of ecosystem(s) leads to crimes against humanity, nature and future generations; conflict; diminution in quality of life for all inhabitants in the territory affected; diminution of health and well-being for all inhabitants; catastrophic disasters leading to food loss, poverty, water pollution and shortages, unnatural climate change, deforestation and more. Ecocide law creates an international and transboundary duty of care which is preventative, pre-emptive and prohibitive in nature ('First do no harm' principle); ecocide law breaks cycles of harm.

In 2010, after I submitted the proposed amendment into the United Nations Law Commission, I and a group of lawyers co-drafted the Ecocide Act in draft form, which was then used in the UK Supreme Court, where the law was tested in a mock trial. It proved to be a success[5]. The Ecocide Act was then mirrored in the draft European Parliament Ecocide Directive proposed by the social movement End Ecocide on Earth.

The Bigger Picture: Claim, Name and Frame

How we claim the space and frame the narrative shapes the outcome. Often when it comes to contested issues, it becomes a war-like zone: does peak oil exist? Is fracking safe? Is GM harmless? Depending on whether you listen to the companies with a vested interest and much money to pay PR companies and commission reports that back their claims or whether you choose to undertake some due diligence yourself, either way you may end up completely confused.

Who to listen to? Well, maybe you do not need to be an expert to determine where you personally stand. Ask yourself: is this for the best? Is it for the best to continue drilling for oil with ever more adverse consequences? Is it for the best to drill underground and pump down vast quantities of chemicals? Is it for the best to modify genes?

There is a common thread here: does X cause harm? If so, it makes sense to stop. You need not be an expert to determine whether a significant harm has occurred. Just look at images of ecocides across the world, such as the Athabasca Tar Sands, mountain-top removal, deforestation of the Amazon—the harm is visible to the human eye in these instances. This means that abuses on a major scale have become accepted as our norm. Just as slavery was accepted as a norm because it was not a crime for a long time, so too is ecocide.

But also like slavery, public disapproval is escalating; communities adversely impacted by their ecocide are speaking out. People across the world are becoming increasingly proactive to show their support and where local communities are not being heard, their stories are being shared across social media in real time. It becomes harder and harder to hide. Individuals are taking it upon themselves to connect into an alternative media that portrays a very different story; proper reportage, rather than repeat-age. Choosing to discern our news-feeds, rather than accepting the norm, is in itself an opening into a whole new story. Often the new story reports directly counter what the mass media says. Which takes us back to our starting point: does X cause harm? And if so, is it a significant harm?

A law of ecocide sets out parameters of size, duration or impact. They are guidelines only, as every ecocide is unique. Just as we do not have checklists to determine whether a human has suffered grievous bodily harm (GBH) or actual bodily harm (ABH), there are some cases that are clear cut and others that fall into the grey area. Case law builds and is used to help a court determine whether the harm is so significant to be a GBH or the lesser harm of ABH.

We do not yet have an international crime of ecocide—whether or not we choose ecocide law is up to we the people. Do we choose to end the era of ecocide? To stand up to what seems an enormous weight of force that keeps an existing system in place seems to be a great challenge. This is why I believe it shall take greatness to put in place ecocide law and if we are to call on our political leaders to be great, then surely it becomes our duty to be great too. Those leaders with a strong moral compass have already seeded in them the kernel of greatness. As do each of you reading this book. So, let's lead by example—name our ecocides.

This is our land. It's up to us what happens next. How we choose to claim the space is up to us. View the Earth as a thing and it simply becomes a commodity that can be bought and sold without care for the consequences. But view the Earth as a living being and we embrace its intrinsic value, not the imposed value—the very sacredness of life. Instead of 'I own', we shift to 'we owe a duty of care'. It becomes a collective responsibility, not just for here and now, but for the lives of future generations too. Care replaces commodity. Costing nature tells us that it possesses no inherent value; that it is worthy of protection only when it performs services for us; that it is replaceable. In one fell swoop, we demoralise and alienate those who love the natural world while reinforcing the values of those who don't. We remain stuck in the cycle of harm.

Claim the space. Not as an owner of your patch of the Earth, but as something far greater instead: as a trustee, a guardian, a steward. Instead of ecocide (harming of our home), let's put in place a duty of care.

Give it name. Harm with no name remains hidden. Often law plays catch-up with where civilization is; it took the aftermath of World War II for genocide to be given name; this time round it has taken much more for us to get the point where we say—this is ecocide.

Frame the narrative. How we choose to call in support for ecocide law is important. We can be raging bitter, fighting against—or we can come from a place of deep care, seeking restorative justice and a better way of preventing future harm. Ours can be a vision of a world where we have ended the era of ecocide—a world where we harness the power of the sun, water and air to provide the alternative to unconventional fossil fuel, a world where we no longer cause significant harm to the Earth, culturally and ecologically. A world where we are protectors (not protesters), speaking from a place of care and upholding a system of decision-making where a 'first do no harm' principle is prioritised.

By framing the narrative in terms of a better world that adopts a law of ecocide, investors shift their perspective: mining and extraction of oil becomes a risky venture—looming laws that will prohibit dangerous industrial activity, such as mining operations/pipeline proposals/deep sea drilling, mean that what was previously the norm is no longer viewed as a secure financial investment or trading commodity. Long-term investment signals flip: with ecocide law, it no longer makes sense to put money into what is soon to become an illegal activity.

This is our legacy. What we choose to do next opens up a space for something greater to emerge. It's up to us—together we can claim, name and frame.

Conclusion

I have argued elsewhere that ecocide is a law to stem the flow of destruction from the outset. It is an upstream solution and is far more cost effective to implement such preventative measures than punishment, e.g., paying fines and restoration costs after the damage has been caused. Moreover, it is a law that will create a level playing field for business across the world.

To continue business as usual will jeopardise not only human but all life on Earth. It is time to change our course of action through creating the legislative framework to ensure a rapid and smooth transition.

To move forward, what is needed is leadership and governance structured around values; and leaders who can act from duty of care and who can live the values they aspire for. After all, this work requires collective and individual endeavour and a commitment both in our professional and personal lives.

Indeed, what we choose eat, to use, how we choose to live and in what manner we choose to do business matter a great deal. So by daring to be great, we will rediscover how to use the creativity, passion and power that lie within us; by daring to be great, we can find freedom and inspiration to break the cycles of harm playing out in our world, together.

Notes

1. This work is licensed under a Creative Commons Attribution-NonCommercial 4.0 International License. For more information please visit: www.creativecommons.org/licences/by-nc/4.0/
2. I have proposed to define ecocide as 'the extensive damage to, destruction of or loss of ecosystem(s) of a given territory, whether by human agency or by other causes, to such an extent that peaceful enjoyment by the inhabitants of that territory has been or will be severely diminished.'
3. By the wider Earth community I include not only humans but also all who live and are inhabitants of our Earth.
4. The submission was published as Chapters 5 and 6 in my first book entitled *Eradicating Ecocide: Laws and Governance to Stop the Destruction of the Planet*, published by Shepheard-Walwyn in 2010.
5. Read the transcripts, download the documents, watch excerpts and the full trial online at www.eradicatingecocide.com/overview/mock-trial

Part III:
Governance in Action

Introduction to Part Three

The third part of this book is a collection of narratives providing both principles and practical examples of governance models at different levels and of different scales. Situated within a variety of contexts, these 'stories' all have as an explicit aim to enable the work of Love. They thus introduce to the reader some realistic and concrete passages into what might, perhaps, seem to be the impossible voyage described in the previous parts of the book.

Four overlapping topics emerge from these narratives:

The first is that the purpose of governance must be aligned with the noble aim of 'flourishing of all'. This means that all decisions are to be informed by genuine care and compassion and to ensure the interests and well-being of all (people, communities and planet).

The second is that governance and politics are intertwined and form a fundamentally human enterprise. To support the 'flourishing of all' agenda, as our contributors illustrate, requires an imaginative and innovative structure (social, political and institutional), which is the fruit of political endeavours at local, national, international and global levels.

The third topic is that at the heart of governance lies 'servant leadership'. This means the primary task of leaders is to serve, a conscious choice made with the deepest belief in altruism. Through such a serving mentality comes the authentic 'power' of leading, which is not reflected in the leader's personal gain, but rather in the growth and well-being of those being served. In this way, authentic power is distributed power, as servant leadership ultimately encourages people to serve each other.

The fourth topic suggests that leadership is about embodying values. Returning to some of the insights developed in both Part One and Part Two of the book, Part Three points out that leaders who proactively live out the values they and their community hold can further strengthen individual caring and moral values. This is authentic leadership. Through context-specific narratives, the chapters in Part Three illustrate with force and clarity how principles and values can be integrated in governance and decision-making.

The story begins with Chapter Twelve by Thabo Makgoba, Archbishop of Cape Town, who draws on his theological background as well as South Africa's constitutional values to critique the state of democratic South Africa. He points out that governance is fundamentally about relationship, where elected leaders must consider people as citizens with and for whom they are to develop relationships of trust and sharing while leaders work out and live their personal and public destinies, which are the well-being of all in a society.

The archbishop believes there is a false dichotomy between religion and politics. Although religions tend to support the moral regeneration of a society, the real essence of religion is to enable people to pursue a truly spiritual life, which includes amongst other things, ensuring a duty of care and instilling moral sensibility amongst people. Religions thus can potentially support politics in many ways, but they must also provide a constructive critique to any system of governance that drives the nation, institution or community away from the core vision of democracy and values. Referring to the impact of political corruption, the biggest challenge confronting South Africa's democracy, the archbishop suggests that honesty and truthfulness are fundamental principles that not only apply to our religious or private lives, but also should underlie all our relationships with one another, across society, including politics. He calls for a return to Mandela's example: leading through caring and serving.

In Chapter Thirteen, South Africa's challenges are placed next to other post-conflict countries' effort for peacebuilding by Ervin Staub, Professor of Psychology, Emeritus, University of Massachusetts at Amherst. Drawing on his rich experiences working in countries traumatised by violent outbreaks, Ervin's main concern is with reconciliation, restoring positive relationships between peoples and groups. He argues that reconciliation is the foundation for acceptance, trust, compassion and a desire to address or prevent suffering. In other words, reconciliation can generate love, a key to peace.

Ervin distinguishes two kinds of peace—cold peace, or coexistence without mutual acceptance and caring, and a more resilient warm peace. Warm peace has more trust in the other and more positive psychological orientations in individuals and groups towards members of other groups. There are organisations and institutions in place that can address both the root causes of violence and emerging issues and problems. But most importantly, Ervin stresses the points already highlighted in Part One and Part Two: that there

Introduction to Part Three

needs to be humanising systems and structures in place that are governed by caring and compassionate principles. There also needs to be leaders who embody these principles, which in turn can strengthen individual caring and moral values and generate compassion. Reflecting on reconciliation and healing work in Rwanda, Cambodia, Palestine, Israel and other countries, Ervin further suggests that compassion, forgiveness and altruism can be born out of suffering. Care for others thus strengthens the self, and is humanising both for the sufferer and the one who offers help. Lastly, he proposes that education is a key to cultivating a compassionate and harmonious society.

Post-conflict healing work is contrasted with healing through compassionate care in health in Chapter Fourteen by Jean Watson, Founder/Director Watson Caring Science Institute and Distinguished Professor Emerita, University of Colorado. Jean maintains that human caring can only be effective and serve the end of healing when it is demonstrated and practised interpersonally. This integrated process keeps alive a common sense of humanity, as the humanity of one person is reflected in an other. In Other words, only mutually humanising care is healing, which is conceived as becoming whole (physically, emotionally, cognitively and spiritually) and as being liberated from suffering. Narrating and analysing her experiences in creating and managing Colorado Center for Human Caring and the Denver Nursing Project in Human Caring, Jean is able to demonstrate that governance is about systematically facilitating relationships, collaboration and partnership amongst institutions, agencies, organisations and individuals under a shared vision. In this way, leaders must invite human spirit to emerge, thrive and be the guiding light that harmonises relations with self, other and planet. Jean terms this 'reflective leadership', a form of loving surrender and mystical connection.

Servant leadership and reflective leadership are further explored in Chapter Fifteen by two storytellers: Heiða Kristín Helgadóttir, TV Presenter of the 365 Broadcasting Corporation and former National Committee Chairman for the Bright Future Party, Iceland, and Derek Masselink, Canadian ecologist, designer, educator and community animator. Through the tale of two islands and their political initiatives occurring on opposite sides of the Northern Hemisphere, one was inspired by the other. Seeking and exploring a creative and hopeful approach to transforming systems of governance, these two stories put forward yet another approach to governance—authentic leadership.

Recounting the story of the birth and evolution of the Best Party (later to become the Bright Future Party) of Iceland, whose founder Jón Gnarr was elected the Mayor of Reykjavik in 2010–2014, Heiða reflects on the importance of incorporating humour, openness, authenticity, trust and engagement in the system of governance. This Icelandic story highlights the necessity of the leaders' own voice—the authentic voice of who we truly are. Describing the founding of the Best Future Party on a tiny Island in British Columbia, Canada, and inspired by the Icelandic experience, Derek discusses the necessity for leaders to stay true to the principles, values, approaches and friendships that enabled them to set foot on the political path, winning the election and being entrusted with the welfare of the communities.

The very last chapter of the book comes from Saudi Arabia. In the context of Islamic phobia plaguing the West, violent conflicts breaking the borders in the Middle East and the recent death of Saudi Arabia's King Abdullah bin Abdulaziz, Amal y. al-Moallimi, Director of King Abdulaziz Center for National Dialogue (KACND) and Fatima M. Al-Bishri, Interpreter and Programme Supervisor at KACND, bring the message of peace from the depth of Islam through the story of the KACND effort for national and international dialogue.

Amal and Fatima use the KACND's programmes as a case study to illustrate that human values, such as tolerance, understanding, moderation and dialogue, can be cultivated and integrated in the citizens' life through political and grassroots effort. Their experiences also show that educational programmes can play a huge part in enabling young people to learn to be caring and compassionate towards the Other, and to appreciate human diversity. Such training can be a powerful way to prepare young people to become ambassadors of peace, helping them to spread seeds of love and understanding among the people of the world.

Together, the contributors in Part Three have used different narratives to show that the plea of 'daring to be great' put forward by authors in Part One and Part Two has been responded to in different corners of the world. By daring to be great, the authors critique corruption and demand leaders to be serving; by daring to be great, leaders are rediscovering creativity, imagination and authentic power; by daring to be great, those who have suffered are reaching out their hands to the needy, the vulnerable; by daring to be great, our stories take wings, and those who catch them hear them as they know they are told with love, compassion and care.

12. Governance and Politics

THABO MAKGOBA

> *No one is born a good citizen; no nation is born a democracy. Rather, both are processes that continue to evolve over a lifetime.*
>
> —Former UN Secretary-General, Kofi Annan (Annan, 1998)

This chapter contributes to critical debate around compassion and governance, more specifically the theme of governance and politics within contemporary South Africa. Governance and politics go together and, coupled with values-based systems, they can be instrumental to serving society in a caring and compassionate manner. Essentially, governance is about relationships. As the saying in my mother tongue, Sepedi, goes: *kgoši ke kgoši ka batho* (A king is a king because of his people). Most importantly, as Latour and Weibel set out in their book *Making Things Public: Atmospheres of Democracy* (Latour and Weibel, 2005), governance is how we assume and carry out the responsibility of providing leadership, while politics is defined as activities associated with the governance of a country or an area, and especially the debate between parties that have power.

These writers add that politics is not just an arena, a profession, or a system, but a concern for that which is brought to the attention of the fluid and expansive constituency of the public. The Greek root of the word further implies that politics is about the affairs of the citizens—their care and welfare and the sense of their own agency.

The way that leaders negotiate and exercise political power matters. The DNA of governance should be around how leaders make decisions. Drawing on this brief conceptualisation of governance and politics, one can conclude therefore that values are critical in guiding decisions taken by leaders. Public leaders are to be servant leaders or, in theological terms, God's servants for the good of all. In this chapter I will, therefore, draw on my biblical and theological background as well as South Africa's constitutional values to critique the state of democratic South Africa, mainly relying on my public speeches, sermons, previous articles and the oral tradition which is a significant identity of our community.

Nelson Mandela said in 2000 that 'The single most demeaning feature of our modern world is the persistence of massive poverty' (Mandela, 2000). In similar vein, U.S. President Franklin D. Roosevelt, in his second inaugural address, said, 'The test of our progress is not whether we add more to the abundance of those who have much; it is whether we provide enough for those who have too little' (Roosevelt, 1937).

Locally, as a faith leader, in the present-day South Africa, I am drawn to Roosevelt's observation. I also firmly believe it when God says that people matter. God cares that his beloved children should all have adequate food, shelter, clothing and so forth. God cares that everyone should be treated with complete respect by everyone else, with no one marginalised, excluded or voiceless in the ordering of our common lives. This is what democracy is all about (Makgoba, 2011). The Anglican Church has aspired since the seventeenth century to be in the forefront globally in speaking for the voiceless. As Anglicans today we have kept that tradition: we try to act in solidarity with the needs of the poorest, the most vulnerable, and the most marginalised; including the strangers, the foreigners, in our midst. We are in solidarity with available, affordable health-care for all. We are in solidarity with effective rural development. We are in solidarity with education for all that truly equips our young people to be responsible citizens, able to face the challenges of adulthood (ibid.). In South Africa we support the country's National Development Plan, as conceived by the government, as consonant with what we advocate. We are concerned with honour and respect, with freedom, with unity and diversity, with healing, with democratic values and social justice; with human rights, with quality of life and liberating potential, for every single one of us.

I have argued elsewhere that in South Africa we need to breathe life into these commitments to one another, arguing that all those, in all sectors of society, who have influence and power, should return to Nelson Mandela's way of governance and leadership: governance that was not threatened by healthy social discourse; governance that was always mindful of the plight of the poor and the marginalised; governance that took seriously its responsibility to all people who have given leaders their trust (Makgoba, 2014).

People of faith and of no faith subscribe to the prescription: 'In everything do to others as you would have them do to you' (Matthew 7:12). The Golden Rule, as we describe it, calls us all to care for others as we would like to be cared for ourselves. It seems so simple and yet we find it difficult to practise. Indeed, the history of South Africa would have been quite different had we begun long ago to live by this rule, especially during the eras of colonialism and apartheid, and our current condition would be different if democratic South Africa observed it now. Yet there is nothing to stop us from making the 'golden rule' our baseline in addressing our governance and political issues.

When I raise these issues in South Africa, the question always arises, why is an Anglican archbishop 'meddling' in issues of governance and politics? Anyone who thinks that Christians and churches ought to 'stick to religion' and not involve themselves in the public sphere, let alone become involved in questions of governance and accountability (politics), has clearly never read the Bible with their eyes open to what it really says! From one end to the other, it carries the clear message that we are called to be involved in and make a positive difference at every level of society, acting as the 'salt of the earth' of which Jesus spoke (Matthew 5:13). Our task is to attempt to hold the centre for an open society intact (Makgoba, 2011) by calling upon all people of good will to become active citizens within South Africa—to put away the false dichotomy of politics and religion, which feeds complacency.

When I address South Africans, I urge them to see that governance is another application, perhaps one of our most critical applications, of value-based decision-making. Governance is as much about human guidance as it is about institutional guidance. We exercise our responsibility for our future through the kind of leaders we put in charge. It is not about lording it over others; it is an expression of our care for others. This goes back to what I intimated earlier, that governance and politics seen together are really about servant leadership, value-based leadership and agency.

Before addressing the current situation in South Africa, let me locate my reflections on politics and governance within the context of the sacred texts which guide Christians. I have already referred to the exhortation in the Gospel of Matthew that we should do to others as we would have them do to us. Other biblical injunctions tell us to love our neighbours as ourselves, and require those elected to political office to be good stewards, to show mercy and yearn for justice. The ninth of the Ten Commandments, in its instruction that 'you shall not bear false witness against your neighbour', calls for honesty and truthfulness, not only in personal or religious matters but, as is clear from elsewhere in the Law of Moses, in everything—including issues of business. Every aspect of trade and employment must be conducted honestly, and with compassion extended particularly to workers and those in positions of weakness. This includes injunctions that proper rest must be granted, the cloak of a poor person (which doubles as a blanket) cannot be kept overnight as surety, and special provision must be made for widows, orphans and other vulnerable or needy individuals. The values-based framework which these guidelines provide requires from those in political leadership that they see citizens not as pawns to be manipulated, but as people with and for whom they are obliged to build relationships of trust and sharing as they work out and live their own destinies.

South Africans regard theirs as a religious country, in which even many members of the Communist Party see no contradiction between their political allegiance and going to church, reading the Bible and reciting the Lord's Prayer. It is particularly appropriate, therefore, for me to critique South Africa through a religious lens. The Christian Old Testament tells us how it did not take long after the establishment of the monarchy for a succession of prophets to arise who felt obliged to condemn the ruling elites for extensive corrupt practices across economic, legal and political sectors, through which the poor and honest suffered. Prophets such as Amos were moved to exhort: 'Let justice roll down like waters, and righteousness like an ever-flowing stream' (Amos, Chapter 5:24).

In the South Africa of today, there are times during which I feel like the prophet Amos. Twenty years after liberation and the inauguration of Nelson Mandela as the founding president of our democracy, we are experiencing an alarming decay in public morality. I wrote recently:

> Corruption is ruining our South Africa. Crooked leaders are betraying every South African. Valueless leaders are pocketing unearned monies, diverting resources from our communities and treating South Africans like a herd of sheep.
>
> And everywhere I travel, more and more South Africans are saying: "We are tired of hearing the promises that are never kept. When will our leaders wake up?" (Makgoba, 2015)

This article, and a speech I made at the end of a protest march to the South African Parliament last Easter—protesting against the treatment of our Public Protector, or ombudsman, for her handling of corruption issues surrounding our president—were not popular with those in power (Makgoba, 2014). However I am encouraged by the fact that I can appeal to the national values we espouse—established during our transition to democracy—to guide us in how we speak, act and react in the church, business, politics, education and society in general. These values should be the spinal cord of our daily living. It is only when our values are in place that we get to do the right thing at the right time. They are embodied particularly in our country's Constitution. In the Preamble of this founding document, adopted in 1996, we begin by recognising the injustices of the past, then commit ourselves to

Governance and Politics

healing the divisions of the past and to establishing an open society based on democratic values, social justice and human rights and to free the potential of every South African. It concludes this section by boldly stating 'May God protect our People' (Constitution of the Republic of South Africa, 1996. In this way, our constitution enjoins all South Africans to ensure that its vision becomes a growing reality for all. It reminds South Africans using openly biblical language that at the heart of who we are and of a true state is the ability to care for one another, to protect one another, to heal one another and to respect one another.

How, then do we view our current democratic system in the light of these values and against the background of the past hurtful, bad governance and corrupt politics? Our new circumstances raise new questions about the interpretation and application of the Bible's teaching. If we believe that constitutional democracy is—or has the potential to be—'God's servant for the good', does this mean that government has the right to expect Christians to support whatever they do unreservedly? And is this true especially of the ruling African National Congress and its partners, given that they were the ones who played a leading role in ushering in this new political era? Furthermore, if this is the case, does this reinforce the view held by some, including within the ruling party, that faith communities should indeed 'be subject' to those in power, and let politicians get on with concentrating on 'politics', and instead focus their engagement in areas of so-called 'moral regeneration' of the country, coming into the public arena only to denounce crime? Are Christians bound to submit in the face of government, observing the admonition of St. Paul in his letter to the Romans in the New Testament: 'Let every person be subject to the governing authorities' (Romans 13: 1–7).

To accept such constraints on Christians—or on anyone, of whatever faith or none—would be to give a naïve and superficial interpretation to St Paul's words. For we must be careful not to confuse the system of government that we enjoy under South Africa's Constitution, with the way in which it is implemented by whichever party holds power. Importantly, the Constitution is not at the service of this or that political grouping, but instead, politicians and their parties must operate as servants of the Constitution for the good of the entire nation. And Christians, churches, and all citizens, have the right—and, indeed, the duty—both to offer critique of the Constitution itself, and to assess how faithfully those holding elected office and the public servants who support them in this, are abiding by its provisions and pursuing the vision it offers.

Outside the churches, there are other prophets too who hold a mirror before our political leadership for them to readjust their moral compass. One such prophet is the poet, Antjie Krog, who expresses my sentiment eloquently and differently in her poem 'Like Death in my Arms' (Krog, 2011) where she says in the last stanza:

> One thing I'm learning
> the more I destroy you the more
> I myself am run into the ground.

This is apt indeed, for the more our leaders govern badly, the more they run themselves and the country down. It is thus imperative to have citizens who speak out and hold to account those in servant leadership, insisting that they indeed serve.

We in South Africa are, as Kofi Annan says about any democracy, evolving: we are still learning how to become a democracy, and still feeling our ways into the new relationships appropriate to constitutional democracy. Government, political parties, the private sector, academia, the media, civil society, faith communities, now each have our distinctive contributions to make to the life of the nation as a whole. We are still learning where we should stand in solidarity with other elements in society, and where we should be critical; what it means to hold and to exchange legitimately diverse perspectives; and how to deliver and receive criticism that is constructive. At the core of these questions is how we guide those in political power and governance by holding them to our national values, their institutional values and even their personal values. How can they serve with these values in mind and use them to transform all into being loving and compassionate, interacting and interdependent communities sharing common interests, common goals and shared value?

Justice, particularly towards the most vulnerable in society, is clearly intrinsic to God's intended good, as described in the opening paragraphs of this essay. Hand-in-hand with justice comes peace, godly peace, which is far more than mere lack of active conflict or noisy disturbance. Rather, it is encapsulated by the Hebrew word of the Old Testament, 'Shalom', which conveys the sense that 'all is right with the world'. The prophets Jeremiah and Ezekiel have shalom in mind, when they denounce political and religious leaders for speaking of 'Peace, peace' when 'there is no peace' (Jeremiah 6:14, 8:11; Ezekiel 13:10). Superficial peace is hypocrisy and worse, when it is not allied with justice. So bad is the situation, says Jeremiah, that society from top to bottom is consumed with greed for unjust gain, by bribery and immorality, with such a total lack of shame. We have every right to expect our political leaders to pursue and deliver genuine shalom. This does not rest upon external appearances of quiescence. It entails comprehensive well-being, through and through, that comes from everything being truly 'all right'. It comes with healing, wholeness, redemption, reconciliation, and abundant, flourishing, life.

Abundant life must involve, as our Constitution puts it, improving 'the quality of life of all citizens', by working diligently to overcome the enormous backlogs in the provision of health, housing, education and other services which apartheid has bequeathed us. The challenge which the Constitution presents to those in politics and governance to fulfil the expectations of the Constitution is matched by that presented to Christians, who are enjoined to feed the hungry, shelter the homeless and tend the sick. In the past two decades, our government has made great strides in improving people's lives by building houses, clinics and schools, and in providing social grants for the poorest of the poor. But we have to summon up the courage to speak out wherever leaders shirk their responsibilities and people are needlessly left in situations of unjustifiable want, short of food, shelter, clothing, health care and a good education. It is this which has led us as religious leaders, as I alluded to earlier, to say that we must stand in solidarity with the needs of the poorest, the vulnerable, the marginalised, the excluded, the voiceless, the stigmatised, and also with the strangers in our midst—the migrants from other parts of Africa who at times have been so cruelly targeted in xenophobic attacks in poor communities resentful of their relative success.

One of the biggest challenges to those of us who were brought up in the apartheid era is how to speak to authority. Under the previous government, the issues were straightforward: apartheid was wrong and there was no need for nuance in our condemnation of the evils of the system. But now the debates involve more subtle arguments than in the past. Rarely are issues so clearly fully right or fully wrong as they were in the apartheid days. Thus churches may work closely with the government in promoting primary health care, our understanding of what is good for people coinciding closely with that of the health department. Yet we have also voiced our concerns about the injustice and lack of cost-effectiveness of the health care system as a whole: while the one the one hand, there is a public health sector which is under-staffed, under-skilled and under-resourced, and so provides inadequate services to most people, on the other there is a private health care system which is getting more and more expensive as funds increasingly answer to shareholders, not to members.

This example illustrates the importance of recognising that to engage constructively in debate means we have to take seriously the complexities of much of contemporary democratic life. Often we are confronted with situations to which there are no easy answers, where every possible option has both positive and negative consequences. The stands that we take must always be rooted in realistic assessments of the situation and of the choices that governments face. Achievements must be acknowledged, and strengths promoted, and it is not going to help to demand unachievable outcomes. It is far easier to be negative and break down, than it is to offer contributions to positive rebuilding. Criticising and undermining, without offering plausible alternatives, is not going to improve the quality of life of citizens. At the same time, we expect politicians to be realistic in their presentations to the public, since neither will it help for them to make promises that cannot be delivered.

Our outspokenness on the question of corruption, to which I referred earlier, is of course an exception to this. Here is there no room for nuance: most South Africans believe that corruption—in government, in business and in our communities, even in churches—is endemic and is eating at the very moral fibre of our nation and its democratic values. Corruption threatens the dream of rooting out 'residues' of apartheid and creating the South Africa the Constitution envisages. Beyond being illegal and immoral, when money is misused, its potential to be used in constructive and helpful ways is lost. Housing, education, health services and social development cry out as obvious examples where we can least afford this. Corruption also causes costs (Omar, 2013) to escalate and often new programmes are sidelined. Money to employ badly needed personnel 'disappears,' and resultant under-staffing leads to poor services, worsening results, and a continuing downward spiral. Corruption at this level is the point at which many people get most upset, but it does not happen only on the scale of national government and big business; many South Africans acknowledge having offered or having been offered a bribe at some point in their lives, whether to escape a traffic ticket or secure quicker access to a government service. Corruption at that level has an insidious effect on the type of society we are building, which seriously concerns me as a person of faith. The ability of us all, especially those who are most disadvantaged by society's injustices, to always 'do the right thing' is further undermined when it seems that dishonesty by those in positions of power and influence goes unchecked and unpunished.

In a recent lecture (Makgoba, 2014), I expressed my puzzlement by what South Africa's president and his lawyers reportedly argued in representations to prosecutors who were considering bringing corruption charges against him. According to a newspaper which saw a prosecution analysis of their reasoning:

> One of the reasons President...Zuma believed criminal charges against him relating to the arms deal should be dropped was because corruption is only a

crime in a "Western paradigm". And even if it was a crime, [Mr] Zuma's lawyers apparently argued, it was a crime where there are "no victims". City Press, Johannesburg, October 12, 2014

The President and his lawyers have never responded to the newspaper's report, which led me to ask what values—whether they be cultural, constitutional or faith-based values—they used to come to that conclusion. Moreover, I added:

> And what can they be talking about if they are saying corruption is a Western paradigm? Presumably, this means that cracking down on corruption is somehow a Western phenomenon which is not appropriate in Africa. Actually, I think it's the other way around. Corruption is a two-way street, a two-way transaction. For corruption to happen, you have to have a corrupter, someone willing to pay the bribe, and what I will call a "corruptee", someone willing to take a bribe. For Africans, over the 50 or 60 years since liberation, the Western paradigm—if indeed there can be said to be one—is one in which Westerners have been the corrupters, and African elites the corruptees.

Drawing from the Ten Commandments, I have said that honesty and truthfulness are fundamental biblical principles that apply not only to our religious or private lives, but which should underlie all our relationships with one another, across society. It seems to me that dishonesty and the concealment of the truth are perhaps the greatest threats to constitutional democracy we currently face. We have to demand that our leaders abide by these principles and the principles of the Constitution. Of course not all of them are corrupt but all are complicit in corruption. They only need to turn to the examples of our founding fathers to learn how to lead, through caring and serving. For example, one of Nelson Mandela's greatest characteristics was his ability to revisit his positions and decisions and to change course when it seemed right to do so, not in his own personal interests but in the interests of building and holding the nation together. Our political leaders are challenged now to reset their moral compasses and to follow his example.

No country can flourish where truth is distorted, suppressed, or subordinated to any interests other than the genuine common good, the abundant life of freedom and shalom. When those who ought to be leading by example instead engage in, or turn a blind eye to, misconduct by those in authority, or become embroiled in untruths and cover-ups, the rot spreads. When those whose lives are most difficult because of joblessness, homelessness and long histories of being disadvantaged, see and read about corruption on the part of those who are in positions of power and influence and wealth, from those who claim that they are leading the country in overcoming the legacies of the past, why should they not draw the conclusion that this is the way forward for all citizens?

Conclusion

Those who have the privilege of exercising authority, especially elected authority, must know themselves as servants of the nation, especially of the poorest, the weakest, the neediest. The world's greatest icons are those who were prepared to risk their own well-being, and if necessary, suffer hardship, so that the rights of the disenfranchised, of families, of women, of children, of all who were oppressed, might be realised.

As a Christian leader, I say to my own constituency that churches have a particular responsibility for inculcating an understanding of what such servant leadership might entail, since we are followers of Jesus Christ, who, insisted that he came 'not to be served, but to serve' (Mark 10:45). Here I can boldly also state that Jesus embodies the best that those in governance and politics can aspire to be.

Let me end by quoting Thomas Paine, who offered the following description of effective constitutional government: 'When it can be said in any country in the world, my poor are happy; neither ignorance nor distress is to be found among them; my jails are empty of prisoners, my streets of beggars; the aged are not in want, the taxes are not oppressive; the rational world is my friend, because I am the friend of its happiness: when these things can be said, then may that country boast of its constitution and its government' (Paine, 1856). We still have a long way to go before we achieve this. It is utopian but we must keep its ideals before us, and keep striving to attain them. Sometimes we weep that they have not been realised, and that there are too many who see democracy as providing access to power, influence and authority merely to enrich themselves, their families and friends and so betray the legacy for which so many strove, and which in South Africa is enshrined within our Constitution.

We cannot and must not lose courage. The God who plants in our hearts a vision and a longing for a society where the well-being of all is found, is the God who will encourage and strengthen us. He will help us hold fast to all that is good, and right and true, so that we can dedicate our lives to following the paths of justice, of honesty, of truth. He will help us overcome complacency, and confront all that threatens the exercise of good governance and accountability.

I hope I have been able to argue for governance and politics as human enterprises which require all of us and especially our leaders to be motivated by doing the right thing, taking responsibility and serving. The South African context, though we are a secular state, cannot escape the fact that more than 80 percent of its citizens are said to be religious and so I have in this chapter repudiated the artificial divide between religion and politics and juxtaposed the constitutional and religious values to which we aspire. While my argument may affect different nation states in unique ways, the principles underlying good governance and the ethical practice of politics are global and extend beyond geo-political boundaries.

13. Reconciliation: From Hostility and Violence to Valuing the Other, Compassion and Altruism Born of Suffering

Ervin Staub

Hostility and violence between groups, as well as individuals, is tragically common. There is genocide, mass killing as in the disappearances in Argentina, persistent violent conflict as between Israelis and Palestinians, or Tamils and Sinhalese in Sri Lanka, terrorism by members of one group aimed at members of other groups. There are wars that supposedly aim at preventing harm done by violent groups or nations but create great destruction, as the U.S. war in Iraq. On the individual level there can be persistent hostility between people, violence, physical and sexual abuse of children and adults. After victimization by one party of another, or mutual victimization, even if it stops, without reconciliation it is likely to start again. Reconciliation changes the relationship between parties. By helping each party heal and feel more secure, it enables people to be constructive members of their communities, have constructive relationships to others, and lead better lives.

I define reconciliation as mutual acceptance by members of hostile groups of each other and the societal structures and processes directly involved in the development and maintenance of such acceptance. Genuine acceptance means trust in and positive attitude toward the other, and sensitivity to and consideration of the other party's needs and interests (Staub & Bar-Tal, 2003). Reconciliation also means that in people's minds the past does not define the future. It means that members of previously hostile groups engage in actions that represent and further create positive attitudes and peaceful coexistence (Staub, 2006, 2011, 2014a; Staub & Bar-Tal, 2003; Staub & Pearlman, 2001). These views of reconciliation are consistent with those of others. For example, Everett Worthington and Dewitt Drinkard define reconciliation between individuals as the "restoration of trust in an interpersonal relationship through mutual trustworthy behaviours" (Worthington & Drinkard, 2000).

There is a long road from the psychological wounds, pain, fear, anger and sometimes desire for revenge that often result from great harm to acceptance, compassion and even love for others, potentially even members of the group that has harmed one's group, oneself, or the people one loved. As individuals and groups engage in processes of reconciliation, they change. People learn by doing, change as a result of their own actions. This is the case when they engage in harmful actions—or positive actions (Staub, 1989, 2011, 2015). But the path toward reconciliation, if it is travelled, is anything but straightforward. It usually has setbacks, generated internally as people revisit their pain and suffering and what has happened to themselves, or those they loved, or the group they identify with, or externally by new threat, real or imagined.

In this chapter, I will write about some principles and practices necessary for reconciliation. Central to the great transformation from hostility and violence to reconciliation and living in harmony and peace is a change from the usually extreme negative views of the other to acceptance of the other group and its members and ultimately empathy and compassion with them. This requires more than individual change; it requires changes in the structures and the cultures of groups. Most of the principles and practices I will discuss are also relevant to reconciliation between individuals.

Reconciliation as a concept and practice in the relations between groups usually becomes a goal after substantial violence. But it is also important when there is antagonism, hostility, between groups in a society or nations (or between individuals) which has not yet led to great violence. The component processes of reconciliation—such as healing from past violence or other bad treatment, developing more positive views by members of groups of each other, justice, and others—while challenging, make people's lives and relationships better. These processes substantially overlap with what is required for preventing violence (Staub, 2011). Reconciliation after violence is a way of preventing new violence, and before it is a way of preventing significant violence to occur. It needs to be a mutual process, an increasing mutual acceptance. Without mutuality even healing is difficult, since people who have been victimized will continue to feel insecure, in danger. Reconciliation makes it more possible to accept the past, to hold it as one's history, tragic as it may be, that does not define the present and the future.

Reconciliation builds peace. Scholars have talked about cold peace, which is really coexistence without mutual acceptance and caring. But coexistence can break down in the face of conflicts and problems within and between groups. A warm peace is more resilient, with more trust in the other, more positive psychological orientations in individuals and groups toward members of other groups, and more organizations and systems in place that can address emerging issues and problems. Beyond acceptance and trust, reconciliation can generate compassion, an understanding and feeling with others' suffering, with a desire to address or prevent suffering. If so, ultimately it may also generate love.

Understanding the Roots of Violence, Its Impact, and Avenues to Reconciliation

Crucial to reconciliation and peace is including another group, its members, in the human realm, so that moral and caring values become applicable to them. When there has been past violence, this can be helped in part by understanding the other, how the other got to the point that led to violence by them. Between 1999 and 2006, my associate Laurie Anne Pearlman, a clinical psychologist, and I conducted workshops/training in Rwanda, with at first a focus on understanding the influences that lead to genocide, as well as its traumatic impact on survivors. We presented a conception of how genocide comes about, with examples from other countries, based on past research (Staub, 1989). The participants then themselves applied this information to Rwanda. By doing the latter, the training seemed to create an "experiential understanding." An informal evaluation showed significant changes in participants. A more formal experimental study showed that Hutu and Tutsi members of newly created groups, led by some of our workshop participants, had more positive attitudes toward the other group than people in control groups, had lower trauma symptoms, and showed other positive effects (Staub, 2011, 2014b; Staub, Pearlman, Gubin and Hagengimana, 2005). Participants in the training themselves originated discussions of what might prevent violence between groups. In later trainings with members of the media, national leaders, and others, we included information about and extensive discussion of what is required for reconciliation and what can prevent violence (Staub, 2011; Staub & Pearlman, 2006).

In workshops with national leaders we used Tables that on one side showed the influences leading to violence, and on the other side influences that can prevent violence, for example, devaluation of the other and humanizing the other, psychological woundedness and healing, or very strong respect for authority versus moderate respect (which allows questioning the leadership by authorities). One of the activities was having leaders discuss, in groups of three, laws or practices they had just introduced or planned to introduce, and whether these would make hostility between groups more or less likely. They did this very effectively.

In my early work, I stressed the importance of followers, since without them potentially destructive leaders will not have influence, and passive bystanders who allow a harmful evolution to unfold. The ideology of leaders and the group matter. The current Tutsi leaders in Rwanda hold an ideology of unity—there are not Hutus and Tutsis, only Rwandans. In our first workshop with leaders when I started to talk about devaluation by one group of another, to our surprise, in 2001, seven years after the genocide, these leaders said that in Rwanda there are no groups. Only after long discussion did we come to a shared understanding that perhaps there are no genetically different groups—as they stressed—but certainly people see themselves as belonging to different groups. A problem with the ideology of unity as a constructive ideology (see below) is that in its name the Rwandan government strongly discourages references to Hutus and Tutsis, which makes it difficult to discuss issues between the groups, and also eliminates political opposition (Staub, 2011, 2014b).

The ideology of a group, and other members of a group can exert powerful influences on individuals—whether a leadership group in a country or a terrorist group. They can create dominance of the values embedded in the ideology, or loyalty to a leader and group, over people's individual moral values. Ideas and environmental influences can shift the hierarchy of a person's values, so that non-moral values take the place of moral ones. Compassionate individuals can lose compassion, especially for devalued others or people identified as ideological enemies. Becoming aware of this, and finding allies in the group who help resist this, can help people to maintain commitment to moral and caring values (Staub, 2011, 2013).

In contrast, caring and compassionate ideologies and leaders can strengthen individuals' caring and moral values and generate compassion. Even as General Lee put down his arms, President Lincoln began to engage in actions that were to create reconciliation—such as having the army band play "Dixie," the anthem of the South, at the ceremony. Nelson Mandela by his words and actions after he left prison and as he became president did the same. In line with the definition of reconciliation I offered earlier, he immediately began to point to a better, shared future (Lieberfeld, 2009).

While the leaders we worked with were deeply engaged, unfortunately, in retrospect, our work with them was limited. Because we were asked by many parties to extend the reach of our work, we started to create educational radio programs, in collaboration with a Dutch NGO La Benevolencija

Humanitarian Tools Foundation which produced the programs, and after two workshops with leaders we did not have the financial and human resources to also continue with workshops. As I proposed in my book *Overcoming Evil* (Staub, 2011) trainings/workshops for leaders that go on for some time, similar to those we have conducted but extended with some additional elements, may help generate constructive and compassionate leadership.

A radio drama, *Musekeweya* (New Dawn) started to broadcast in May 2004 and is still continuing. It is a story of two villages in conflict, with attacks, counterattacks, a bad leader and followers, positive active bystanders. Over time, the villages reconcile and jointly help prevent violence in the region. The educational content is in line with what we did in our workshops, with information about influences that lead to violence, the impact of violence on people, and avenues to reconciliation and prevention. An early evaluation study of this broadcast drama showed a variety of positive effects, including more empathy with victims, survivors, and also bystanders, perpetrators and leaders, greater willingness to say what one believes, and less orientation to authority (Paluck, 2009; Staub, 2011; Staub & Pearlman, 2009). There is other, anecdotal information, for example, a young man inspired by the radio drama persuading members of his village who killed Tutsis in a neighbouring village to go there, work in the field alongside those villagers, and ask for forgiveness. Over time this led to positive relationships (Ziegler, 2010). Because about 90% of the population of Rwanda listens to this radio programme, there is no control group for formal evaluation of its long-term effects. We later expanded to Burundi and the Congo (DRC) the radio dramas and informational programmes, which we began in Rwanda.

As attitudes toward the other change, as the other's behaviour becomes to some degree at least understandable, and as people begin to heal from their psychological (and physical) wounds, caring and compassion can slowly develop. This also depends on the behaviour of the other. Do they acknowledge harm they have done, do they acknowledge their share of the responsibility, do they show regret? These are very difficult to do for groups that have harmed other groups, but are essential for reconciliation.

From Devaluation (and Hate) to Positive Views of the Other

A history of one group devaluing another, or groups mutually devaluating each other, seeing each other in an intensely negative light, is central to harming another group. Devaluation is often intensified by scapegoating, and then by creating visions of a better future for one's group (or all humanity) such as racial superiority, nationalism, or even social equality, the vision of the Khmer

Rouge in Cambodia (Staub, 1989). This is accompanied by identifying the devalued and scapegoated group as an enemy standing in the way of the fulfilment of this vision or ideology. As this group is then harmed, it is justified by further devaluation, and by increasingly excluding the group from the moral and human realm (Fein, 1979; Staub, 1989, 2011). To re-establish the humanity of a victim group and build positive connections is central to reconciliation.

Social psychologists have done a great deal of research on contact between individuals as a way to overcome prejudice, or what I call devaluation, and moving people to a more positive orientation to others. Bringing people together to positively engage with each other has been one practice. Seemingly more powerful is having people participate in joint projects in which they work to fulfil shared goals. These practices have been found to generate more positive views of and interactions with members of a previously devalued group, or even a group that has been seen as an enemy. Such projects range from bringing Israeli and Palestinian children together in summer camps (Hammack, 2011), to cooperative learning procedures in the US in which children in mixed race groups work on shared tasks (Aronson, Stephan, Sikes, Blaney & Snapp, 1978), to providing support for farmers from different groups to work together in the Ivory Coast. In the latter instance, presumably as a result of it, when there was later violence in the region it did not include the area where these farmers lived (Chirot & McCauley, 2006). For contact to work requires that participants have positive experiences in the course of interaction, and in fulfilling goals.

Structures that create persistent positive contact help create deep, lasting change. In India, in three cities where after instigating events there was no violence, Hindus and Muslims closely worked together in various institutions and acted to prevent violence. In three other cities where violence followed there was no such significant contact (Varshney, 2002). Schools as well as workplaces can be environments that support and maintain positive contact.

Being in the same life space is clearly not enough, as it is shown by a long-ago study of New Yorkers living in the same environment (Deutsch, 1973) or by observing the Congress of the United States, where members are in contact, but their attitudes toward each other across party lines have been deteriorating for decades. The unwillingness to identify shared goals, except abstract ones such as making America better, and having concrete goals that are in opposition, makes contact adversarial. There has been little compassion for political opponents and little willingness to work together. Another issue, as shown by Israel and the Palestinians, is that with groups in violent conflict, positive attitudes fostered by contact is difficult to maintain (Hammack,

2011) and may not exert an upward influence on leaders. Helping leaders engage in significant contact may work better (Staub, 2011; Wolpe & McDonald, 2008).

For real change contact and other practices need to work together. One of these is leaders expressing positive views of the other group, by their words and actions humanizing the other group. Of course, for that leaders have to first change. As our work in Rwanda suggests, information of varied kinds that relates to people's experience can change people. Healing is also crucial, increasing openness to other sources of change.

From Victimization/Suffering and "Defensive Violence" to Healing and Altruism Born of Suffering

Being the objects of violence or other significantly harmful behaviour or conditions creates suffering, trauma, and often brings about psychological wounds. People feel vulnerable, insecure, and see other people, especially members of other groups, in particular those that have harmed them—and the world in general—as dangerous. Significant harm directed at people frustrates what I consider, following others (Kelman, 1990; Maslow, 1971), but with specification and elaborations of my own, as universal human psychological needs (Staub, 1989, 2003, 2011). These include the need for security, for a positive identity, for feeling effective and able to control important events in one's life, for connection to other people, for some degree of autonomy, and for an understanding of the world and one's own place in it. These needs can be fulfilled destructively, so that fulfilling one need interferes with the fulfilment of others (for example, exercising control over events becoming so important after experiences of harm that they interfere with one's relationship to others), or harm other people (creating security or a positive identity or control through dominance and aggression).

Victimization creates suffering, but also in some individuals and groups violence. Researchers have found that most violent men have been abused or mistreated (Rhodes, 1999). Many boys who are aggressive have been harshly treated (Dodge, Bates & Pettit, 1990). Group traumas can become a central focus of group life, what Vamik Volkan has called chosen traumas (Volkan, 2001). They shape identity, culture, the perception of events and responses to them (Staub, 2011). Some individuals and groups simply suffer; others may see hostility where others do not, and tend to believe that the right response is what I have called in writing about the behaviour of groups "defensive aggression" (Staub, 1998, 2011). But since often the behaviour they respond to is not hostile, individuals and groups that have been victimized become perpetrators of harm.

How can people be helped to heal their psychological wounds? As in therapy, so in life in general, it is important to be able to talk about painful experiences to empathic others. This can happen in small groups where people support each other (Herman, 1992) or through "testimonies," people talking about their experiences in front of a group of supporting people. Solace ministries in Rwanda have been providing opportunities for people to do the latter. Knowing that others in the group had similar experiences and will understand them can be important in enabling people to talk about what happened to them.

In educational radio dramas, in Rwanda in particular, we encourage people in the population to support each other this way. Characters in the radio drama notice others' distress and encourage them to talk about their feelings and experiences, listening and engaging empathically (Pearlman, 2013; Staub, 2011, 201 2014b). In countries where many people have been affected by great violence, where people have been victimized as members of groups, and where usually there are few professionals to help, people supporting each other this way is crucial (Staub & Pearlman, 2006).

Commemorations can also help in grieving and healing. Usually commemorations focus on the suffering, which may help with grieving but also maintain the wounds. They may contribute to intensely painful events in the life of the group becoming "chosen traumas." Commemorations become truly constructive when they also point to a positive future. Over time, commemorations can include outsiders who support the group, and members of the groups that created the harm, remembering and grieving together already creating a more positive shared future. Commemorating rescuers—members of the perpetrator group who have endangered themselves to save others, some successfully and some killed as a result—can contribute to reconciliation. It shows survivors that some of the members of the perpetrator group deeply cared about what happened to them, and shows members of the group that had perpetrated violence that the other group sees the goodness in them (Staub, 2011).

Altruism Born of Suffering

If many people who are psychologically wounded become hostile and or defensively violent toward people or members of other groups, or even inclined to revenge, or just withdraw from the world, life in that society and relations between groups becomes increasingly challenging. But some people who have suffered greatly become altruists, concerned about others' suffering, wanting to prevent suffering and help those who have been harmed. I have called this "altruism born of suffering." Part of the evidence for this is that many people who have themselves, or whose group has, suffered violence and trauma work on prevention and the healing of others; part of it is from research (Staub, 2005, 2015; Staub & Vollhardt, 2008; Valent, 1998; Vollhardt & Staub, 2011). While some groups that have been victimized are more likely to turn against others, organizations within some previously victimized groups have become active, at a later time, in responding to harm done to others (Brysk & Wehrenfennig, 2010).

I have proposed that certain experiences help transform the psychological wounds that result from victimization and trauma. These include: people receiving help from someone while they are being harmed (which means that helping people who are victimized has long-lasting effects); and/or they are able to act on their own and/or others' behalf at that time; receiving care, support, help afterwards (trauma specialists say that trauma is not only the effects of traumatizing events, but what happens afterwards (Danieli, 1985); healing experiences; and beginning to help other people, which strengthens the self, creates connections to others, and together with having received help and support shapes one's perception of the world. Experiences of love and care before traumatic events can create resilience and also likely to contribute to later altruism.

Truth, Acknowledgment of Harm Done, Justice, and Societal Justice

People who have been harmed deeply yearn for acknowledgment of the harm that was done to them, and for some form of justice. The truth, therefore, is essential—both for them, and for their society so that it is less likely to happen in the future. Establishing what actually happened is also crucial because each group has its own truth, often blaming the other, which makes future violence more likely.

Acknowledgment by the world if a group's suffering contributes to healing is important. But acknowledgment by the group that has inflicted violence—not necessarily the perpetrators, but its members and those who subsequently become its leaders—is especially important. Their expressions of empathy and request for forgiveness can significantly contribute to reconciliation.

Some form of justice is also crucial. Often so many people have been involved in violent actions, that all of them cannot be punished, without creating new resentment and hostility. But punishment of the instigators and the especially violent perpetrators is important. Another form of justice is compensation by the perpetrator group, whether financial, or work in the service of balancing the harm done.

This already has elements of "restorative justice." Another of its forms at the individual level is a perpetrator and a victim meeting, often together with family members and other supporters of each, the perpetrator acknowledging the harm he or she has done, apologizes and asks for forgiveness (Strang et al., 2006). Apologies by leaders of a group can be meaningless, pro forma, or important and meaningful, as in the case of Willy Brandt, the chancellor of Germany, kneeling and crying at Auschwitz.

However, as I have mentioned, perpetrators usually resist acknowledging the harm they have done. An extreme example of this is Turkey's refusal to acknowledge the genocide of the Armenians. Currently there is a movement in Hungary to create a history in which Hungary was a victim of Germany and had no role in the Holocaust there. However, there were only fifty SS soldiers involved in this "task," led by Eichmann. They were helped, according to estimates by historians, by about 200 hundred thousand police and gendarmes, as well as volunteers, in gathering about 450 to 500 hundred thousand Jews and transporting them to Auschwitz (Braham, 2014).

What may enable perpetrators, or at least members of the group that perpetrated violence, to accept responsibility for the harm they have done, or both groups to acknowledge their responsibility if the violence was mutual? One of them is healing. Perpetrators of significant violence may have been psychologically wounded before, and are wounded by their own violent actions (McNair, 2002). Healing can change their attitude toward themselves and others. Another is information about the origins of violence, the social and psychological processes that lead to violence, which I discussed earlier. This can help change the perception of perpetrators and more importantly of their whole group, by others and by themselves, from seeing them as simply evil, to seeing them as people responsible for what they have done, but still human beings who made choices that led to participation in human processes that resulted in terrible violence. Our experience in Rwanda was that such information, and learning how such things have happened in other countries, increased readiness for reconciliation. Research studied have also found that affirming individuals or their group makes it more likely that they acknowledge harm done by their group (Čehajić-Clancy et al., 2001; Noor et al., 2008). Having information about the origins of violence can be a form of affirmation.

For future harmony, another form of justice that is required is social justice. This includes a fair and unbiased justice system, reasonable equality of opportunity and a society that addresses core human needs, material and psychological. Creating this is a long-term project, beyond the immediate specifics of reconciliation. However, it can be built into reconciliation activities from the start. In Rwanda new laws eliminate discrimination in employment and admission to educational institutions (Staub, 2011, 2014b). As this becomes widespread practice, it contributes to reconciliation.

From Destructive Visions/Ideologies to Constructive Visions and Constructive Values

One core reason that a group turns against another is a history of devaluation, which in response to difficult life conditions can lead to scapegoating. Another is a destructive ideology, a vision for the better future of the group combined with identifying an enemy, usually the previously devalued group, that stands in the way. After violence, without reconciliation, groups that have harmed another tend to hold on to devaluation and to some degree their destructive ideology.

An important contributor to healing, reconciliation, and developing positive relations is a constructive ideology, a positive vision of a shared future to which each group can contribute. For example, in the Palestinian Israeli conflict, such a vision could be a shared economic community, which benefits both groups, and contributes to peace in the region (Staub, 2011). In Rwanda it could be a vision of Rwanda as a country of unity and justice, in which everyone's rights and opportunities are protected. I mentioned earlier the ideology of unity, the principle that "we are all Rwandans," rather than Hutu or Tutsi. This ideology is now used by the government to limit free speech—such as discussion of ethnicity and grievances related to it—a free media, and political participation (Staub, 2011, 2014b). The government fostering rather than enforcing such a vision could turn it into a positive ideology.

Raising Inclusively Caring and Morally Courageous Children

Long-term reconciliation and harmony in a society (and in the world) requires that the socialization of children, the experiences they have, promote caring about other people, not only those in their group, but also others beyond their group, including formerly devalued groups and former enemies. Certain practices can do this. They include love and affection; guidance that stresses the humanity and value of other people and caring about others' welfare and helping them; guidance and discipline that stresses reasoning and may be firm but not punitive; what I have called "natural socialization"—since children and adults (and groups) learn by doing, from their own actions, giving children responsibilities and involving them in activities that help other people, including people outside their group (Eisenberg, Fabes, & Spinrad, 2006; Staub, 2013, 2015). In a number of my studies, we had children help other children—by making toys for hospitalized children, or older children teaching younger children, or in other ways, this increasing children's later helpfulness in comparison to children in control groups. Very importantly providing children in families, schools, in the media and literature with positive models is essential. Guiding them to be helpful will not work if they see important people around them not be helpful (Mischel, 2014).

Such socializing of children requires a change in adults. Many of the things I discussed in earlier parts of this chapter need to happen, so that adults develop the motivation and skills to socialize children to be inclusively caring and morally courageous.

Conclusions

Groups that have suffered great violence, and those that have perpetrated it, or groups that have mutually harmed each other, can move from fear, loathing, hostility and their deep wounds to mutual acceptance. But can they also move to love and compassion for each other and people in general? Certainly nations, such as Germany and France, have moved from intense hostility and great violence to friendship. After WWII they have engaged in many joint projects, even before and then after the creation of the European Community. In February 2015, as I write this, the leaders of those two countries are going together on a joint mission to Moscow to promote a political resolution of the war in Ukraine. This is like our educational radio drama, in which after long conflict the people in the two villages join to attempt to stop new violence from a third, outside source. Such joint activities further develop friendship.

In one of my projects, we developed a training for students in schools to be active bystanders who engage when they see harassment, intimidation and harmful actions (bullying) by students against other students. We then trained a group of students as well as adults to be able to teach others and had student trainer and adult pairs train about 700 eighth and tenth grade students, in two schools, to be active bystanders. The evaluation of the effects of this, with control schools, showed a 20% decrease in harmful behaviour by students, several months after the end of the training (Staub, 2015, Chapter 6). Anecdotal information showed further, wide-ranging effects, such as students reporting someone who planned to engage in violence in the school.

Student trainers were only evaluated in interviews, which suggested that they were substantially affected by their experience. They showed compassion for those who were harmed, and some of them said things like 'I used to do such harmful things and never thought about its effects on the other person.' Most likely compassion can develop even after people have done even more harmful things. Perhaps there is "altruism born of harm one has done." But we need research in this realm, both to assess the extent of this and the experiences that contribute to it.

Hostile groups have seemingly never engaged in all the elements of reconciliation I have discussed in this chapter. The more are practiced, the more success they are likely to have over time in creating genuinely positive attitudes and relations, and compassion for other people. I hope that using such practices, introducing them into the functioning of organizations and systems will become common, not only after violence, but before.

14. Caring Science

JEAN WATSON

This chapter offers an overview of Caring Science (Watson, 2005, 2008, 2010) and its influence on nursing and healthcare. This transformational form of caring moves beyond the current, medical-technical, business orientation, moving organizations towards the care of the whole person, whole system approaches to caring, healing and health for all. I provide two personal and professional examples of transformative change from within, which took place at the University of Colorado, whilst I was serving as dean and distinguished professor of nursing in the 1980s and 1990s. These examples reveal new professional educational-practice models whose governance became guided by core human values of care, an ethic and theory of caring. The chapter ends with a brief description of my Theory of Human Caring.

Caring Science

Caring Science is informed by an ethic of universal connections, a unitary view of our world. Its theories and practices in the field of nursing have evolved over the past two to three decades and they now provide a hopeful paradigm for sustaining authentic caring relationships by honouring an evolved human consciousness. This evolved human consciousness, embedded within Caring Science, draws upon the human spirit as the basis for wholeness, true healing and new notions of health care for self and society. Caring science models of nursing practice are happening in nursing education and hospital practices throughout the USA and other parts of the world, bringing caring and love together as mindful approaches to healing our world (Caritas-Watson, 2008; Sitzman & Watson, 2014; Watson, 2005, 2008).

Given the dominant medical-disease hospital system, this maturing of nursing professional practice models is revolutionary and has had a major impact on hospital staff, patients and society alike. However, even with these best practice hospital successes, and even with the maturing of nursing as a distinct discipline and profession, the professional practices of nursing are still surrounded by an outdated scientific Western worldview. This worldview is confined to physical body care, medical-disease, sick-care practices, external technical interventions, and latent and overt norms established by an institutional, industrial hospital culture.

However, a global quantum, scientific, spirit-filled evolved consciousness is now emerging throughout all of humankind. For our very survival, these global shifts are governed by core human values towards sustaining Planet Earth and ourselves as one. These shifts in human consciousness are awakening to energetic models and possibilities of inner healing and mental health; they are oriented towards self-love, self-caring, self-knowledge, self-control and self-healing approaches, addressing individual and collective human suffering. This awakened view for humankind returns us to the heart of our humanity; it invites and requires practices for sustaining a healthy environment and human-environment caring for our shared humanity in one cosmic universal field.

These larger seismic, underlying worldviews are pulling the so-called rug out from under the conventional Westernized hospital model of 'fixing-up' the status quo, placing the public and hospital systems at the fault line for major upheaval, and requiring a new worldview to guide the future.

Everything is change and nothing is the same; our world and our reality is being turned outside in, inside out, and upside down, constantly being deconstructed before our eyes. We are faced with the living paradox of a changing reality: a reality of fear that is now basic to our daily-life world, and which is revealing the good/evil, the shadow/light of humanity, within and without.

What is happening today, demands an expanded, and dramatically different, worldview—a cosmic, unitary, view of our world and Planet Earth, which points us in the opposite direction of the dominant physical treatment-cure model. The new worldview moves us away from what has been defined as Era I (body physical thinking), away from material medicine and external interventions and the physical cure-of-body at all cost mentality. Now the move is into quantum field views, non-local consciousness, an energetic view of all of life, views related to inner-health, inner-healing, healthy communities and environment—Planetary health (Watson, 2010, 2014a; 2014b).

Developments are even occurring in the field of Caring Economics; for example, Eisler (2008) has called for an economics of caring in contrast to the current economics of domination and control, acknowledging that human caring becomes a foundational necessity for the survival of our world, not only economically but in actuality. Richard Layard (2006), a professor at The London School of Economics, has suggested that the big breakthrough in economics was finding out that you can ask people how they feel about their lives as an economic indicator of well-being, rather than wealth. As a consequence, he is now advising governments around the world to focus their economic policies on happiness and well-being rather than on current indices such as gross domestic product (GDP). His work is related to thriving, to addressing widespread depression, anxiety and mental health in the measurement of national economic performance. The small Kingdom of Bhutan, on the borders of China, India, and Nepal, has a Global National Happiness Index (GNHI), and Layard has consulted with, for example, the United Kingdom and the German governments to consider the GNHI model as a substitute for GDP.

This new thinking involves notions of human flourishing, not just control and survival; it is emerging from an evolved consciousness of humanity, and ways of being in right relation with self, other and planet—notions that take us beyond material wealth. We are at a point in human history where we now seek to surrender to our universal, shared, humanity; that is, the stark quantum reality, that everything is connected, reflecting the view that we all "Belong to the infinite field of universal Love" (Levinas, 1969), which is one of the foundations of Caring Science (Watson, 2005).

We can now draw upon this reality in guiding forms of "reflective leadership", attending to health, healing and spiritual harmony with the All (Levinas, 1969; Watson, 2005, 2010, 2014a, 2014ba). This view is not only consistent with new trends for medical science and technology but also with indigenous teachings and wisdom traditions across all time, traditions to which we now have to return and honour for our daily health and our individual and collective survival. If we take reflective leadership seriously, these rhetorical, existential and spiritual questions remain as touchstones for our time. For example: How do we as a society and as a global village learn to give new meaning to living, dying, suffering and human existence? What is nursing in this new world? What will it be when the present systems of medical physical science, are no longer there, defining and dominating the culture of practice? What will nursing and health care become when there is a shared universal world view of health, healing for all? These are questions facing nursing, all health care practitioners, and all of humankind for sustaining human and planetary health.

The good news is that as we face these questions new values are beginning to emerge, and we can look for new symbols for change—signs of rebirth. Ancient global symbols and archetypes exist to remind us of the normal life-death cycles. For example, the Indian divinity, Vishnu, stands as a universal symbol for creation and destruction, ruling all cycles of birth and rebirth, beyond the full control of mankind, but ruled by Nature's universal principles. Other universal symbols are the circle, the mandala, and shamanic visions which see humans as luminous beings connected to all of humanity in a universal cosmic field.

Native and ancient world traditions have always called up a universal spirit world. For example there are the Brazilian healers, *Cueranderos*, and other shamanic indigenous practices, such as distant healing, chanting, drumming, soul retrieval—all are in communication with the broader field of connections with a universal spirit and Source. And all are energetic connections that transcend time, space, and physicality.

These ancient symbols and codes are archetypal reminders that reflect the contemporary scientific propositions emerging in quantum physics and global unitary views of science and human beings. In nursing there is the work of Martha Rogers (1970, 1992, 1994); and there are the deep philosophical starting points for science in the work of Levinas, who posits the 'ethic of belonging' as the first principle of science (Levinas, 1969). These all lead to global unitary views for survival, and require, if not demand, new reflective approaches to humanity and organizations.

These reflective, ancient and converging contemporary mind-sets are located within new discourses identified as Era III thinking (Dossey, 1991, 1993; Newman et al., 1991; Watson, 2008, 2010, 2012) which are consistent with notions of 'unitary science' and 'unitary field'. Concepts such as 'transpersonal', 'trans-disciplinary', 'integrative medicine', 'mindbody medicine', 'mindbodyspirit medicine', 'unitary caring field', 'caritas field', and other similar words, are reflecting a new reality and worldview shift. These words and concepts attempts to capture creative and imaginative images, a new emerging consciousness toward body as energy, life as energy, a spirit filled existence. This shift in worldview invites inner approaches to health, well-being and post-hospital, community-based and home-based care.

With such quantum shifts in front of us, how are we to consider new liberating structures, evolved systems, reflective-learning communities and environments for transformational, front line leadership? How do we move contemporary successes, such as the exemplary Magnet hospitals, toward visions of the future that embrace authentic, creative and spirit-filled change—change that can take us towards the practice of better caring and healing as part of a healthier and more integrated world?

Caring Science: A Personal Story

My work in developing and implementing Caring Science at the University of Colorado and my own Theory of Human Caring in education and practice, together with these views of a global unitary, quantum consciousness field, are part of my own story, a story that embraces and builds upon the reality that humanity as a whole, and educational and healthcare organizations in particular have to move beyond the status quo, with a renewed focus on human and environmental care, healing and health; these are models of caring that take the notion of well-being beyond the narrow confines of medical disease and physical care. As part of my story, I offer two examples of being on the front line of change, changing organizations from inside out to become whole systems. The first example is the creation of the Colorado Center for Human Caring; the second is implementing the Denver Nursing Project in Human Caring.

The Colorado Centre for Human Caring

The 1980s were an interesting time for the University of Colorado School of Nursing on the Health Sciences Campus in Denver, which has a long history of leadership and national standing. The School was one of the early schools offering master's degrees in nursing before such programmes for nurses were really known, and before the health system in the US even knew how to use or benefit from a master's level nurse. The history and origins of the, now international, nurse practitioner model began in 1965 at the University of Colorado under the vision and leadership of Dr. Loretta Ford and of Dr. Henry Silver, a paediatrician in the Medical School. This programme led to what is now considered mainstream Nurse Practitioner programmes offered at both masters and doctoral level, changing the nature of professional nursing. The University of Colorado School of Nursing developed the first public-funded clinical nursing doctorate (the ND degree) as the career professional practice degree, which has evolved to the current Doctor of Nursing Practice Degree (DNP) as national US standard degree for Nurse Practitioners.

However, in spite of the history of innovative leadership and visionary programmes, during the late 1970s and early 1980s the School of Nursing was in throes of chaos and decline. There was even the possibility that the School would be closed down. This chaos and decline was spread throughout the US. After a long history of educating nurses, Boston University abruptly closed its school of nursing, and Duke University closed its undergraduate program, threatening undergraduate nursing programs in other parts of the USA.

It was at this time that, having just completed my PhD in 1978, I joined the faculty at the University of Colorado School of Nursing which had had a series of successive deans, all with brief tenures. After national searches and the School going through a good deal of inner and outer turmoil, I was appointed Dean of Nursing 1983. The hope and expectation was to bring new vision, new life and new directions to nursing at the University. For, in order to survive, the School of Nursing had to ask, and find answers to, two big questions: where would and should the School be in the twenty-first century: and where would and should nursing be in 2000, when the School would be one hundred years old?

These challenges came to me, both from the President of the University, Arnold Weber, and from the Health Science Centre Chancellor, John Cowee. By accepting the challenge, and serving as dean, I had committed myself to setting a path for new philosophical and organizational standards for the faculty, students, colleagues, clinical agencies and the broader health and public community.

During my time as dean, and through the development of the Centre for Human Caring, the School of Nursing became an international centre for practice, research, education and scholarship in Caring Science. The Centre established new relationships with clinical partners, and other departments and faculty within the broader university—for example, within philosophy, arts, humanities, classics, music, drama, and existential studies, religious studies—and with the broader public. These broader relationships and programmes brought new life and new connections, inspired programmes for non-traditional scholarship, methods of research, and explored underdeveloped connections between and among disciplines.

The Centre sponsored monthly open seminars for the university community as well as the general public, seminars on Caring and Art, Caring and Music, Caring in Dance and Movement, Caring in Film and Literature. And the School of Nursing held concert series, inviting faculty in the Boulder Campus College of Music to be on the Health Science Campus. Monthly seminars were offered for faculty scholars in Philosophy, Literature, English studies and religious studies, together with experts in phenomenology, physics, great literature and so on.

Each of these series of seminars and events was framed around Caring Science, identifying and acknowledging how each area programme contributed to understanding human caring as a serious ethical, philosophical, ontological, epistemological, methodological, pedagogical, praxis and policy endeavour, integrating arts and humanities within nursing and health care, beyond conventional thinking. The scholarly notes and opening remarks helped to introduce our faculty, students, clinical colleagues, other disciplines and the larger public to see the connection between Caring Science and arts, literature, philosophy, music, sound, movement and all ways of knowing; all ways of being, doing, becoming, as a foundation for deep dimensions of human caring, healing, health and well-being.

Another specific example was the work of Hazel Barnes, the internationally acclaimed Distinguished University Professor of Classics, known for her translation into English of Jean-Paul Sartre's existential writings and books. She was a visiting professor, coming once a week to offer open noon seminars in the School of Nursing on 'The existential meaning of selected human conditions'. Faculty and graduate students attended her classes as well as professors of medicine and psychiatry. In addition to expanding the pedagogies of our curriculum, we were funded by the University-wide Humanities fund to integrate humanities and the use of literary works into the existing curriculum. We shared nursing arts seminars with a professor of Fine Arts from the Boulder Campus, helping students integrate into nursing art, the artistry of their being and the exploration of subjective human experiences, knowing and learning.

All of these combined efforts, and many, many more occurred under what was now a new vision for nursing and human caring scholarship, education, governance and practice. The nursing curriculum was redefined and reframed with the involvement and commitment of faculty and clinical colleagues. The curriculum was organized within the lines of Caring Science, faculty and students thereby being able to see how everything they were doing was contributing to the larger field of Caring Science. This consistent framework guided nursing and gave voice to its maturing as a distinct discipline and profession, with its own unique standing.

Within this same era, the Centre for Nursing Research was also at work, helping the School to generate substantial research support through federal grants. Indeed, this focus on Caring Science research and its expanded methodologies led to the School of Nursing during my time as Dean to become number 5 in the nation for its research funding.

In conversations and meetings with the University board, with our University president and with members of a newly created School of Nursing National Advisory Visiting Board, I helped others to understand Caring Science more broadly as a science, encompassing the whole human, including values of sustaining humanity beyond medical science. I worked to assist others in understanding nursing as the science, art and practice of human caring, healing and health—helping them to see nursing beyond medical hospital floor duty nursing. As one of the members of the University board said to me: "So you are not preparing floor nurses anymore?" My reply, with a touch of light humour was: "No, didn't you know, nurses do not 'do floors' anymore, now they are going to be 'doing windows'. I am not sure the board member got it, but I loved that moment!

Of course, it is impossible to go into all that happened, but the work included many faculty meetings and retreats. These always included our clinical colleagues and nursing leaders of health-care systems as partners in the transforming and merging of values and cultures for advancing nursing as the science and art of caring, healing and health. Together we developed new Clinical Research faculty, Clinical Teaching Associates, Clinical-Educational Practitioners. We established formal Clinical Teaching Hospital partnerships, whereby the Chief Nursing Officer in our Teaching Hospitals was designated Clinical Associate Dean of Nursing in University School of Nursing, leading to piloting of new professional models of caring and healing within their settings.

These new patterns of curriculum reform, of redefining nursing within a caring science framework, was transformative for staff, faculty of our university and for the larger public. The School's renewed internal faculty relationships, combined with clinical agencies and clinical leaders, led to an evolved and exciting era in the School of Nursing. The creation of the Centre serves as a model of innovative cultural change from within, guided by a core philosophy to expand nursing and caring to serve humanity. By inviting the human spirit to emerge from the people within, by celebrating diversity and by opening new partnerships and new connections where before there were none, this reflective approach opened up new horizons and the advancements of seemingly miraculous changes.

The Denver Nursing Project in Human Caring

In addition to its academic programs, the Centre for Human Caring also housed the 'Denver Nursing Project in Human Caring', which was the site of a nurse-run, interdisciplinary clinical practice centre, serving the health-care of persons with AIDS or who were HIV infected. This 'Caring Centre', as it became known, was guided by my Theory of Human Caring (Watson, 1979) and it served as the cultural norm for the caring–healing relationship between and among the practitioners, the patients, their partners, and the larger public. The centre generated new models of professional practice, allowing for and offering new caring and healing modalities, such as therapeutic touch, intentional touch, music, massage, exercise physiology, counselling, group sessions, psychiatric help and care partnerships with other patients and staff.

Nursing staff undertook education in local bars with patients from the Centre and attended patient funerals as part of their loving continuous-care commitments. New forms of documentation of patient care records were developed and systematically used, documenting what at that time were the original Ten Carative factors from Watson Theory, while adding 'administrating medical treatments' to allow for the respiratory and blood work that was done in the Centre. Every week King Soopers' grocery store donated food for an open lunch time for all staff, patients and their partners. A local Denver florist donated flowers and patients and community members donated piano, artwork, furniture and other furnishings to make the Centre feel non-institutional. This work generated research on outcomes and economics and demonstrated that up to a million dollars annually was saved by keeping people out of the hospital (Leenerts, Koehler and Neil, 1996).

The Caring Centre was federally funded for the maximum number of years possible, and became a destination site for students and practitioners from around the world. It was adopted as a national model at its time for community support and caring community. As one young man said to me: "Why do you have to get AIDS to get this kind of care? It should be available for everyone".

The Watson Theory of Human Caring

As I have said, each one of these initiatives at the University of Colorado was based upon my Theory of Human Caring, and so I end this chapter with a brief outline of what that theory is, since it is governed by the very principles of love and compassion, which are the subject of this book—the practice of loving kindness and equanimity; authentic presence; the cultivation of one's own spiritual practice towards wholeness of mind, body and experience/the practice of "being" in the care and healing environment; and allowing miracles (www.watsoncaringscience.org).

The core concepts of the Theory include: a relational caring for self and others based upon principles of love and compassion; a transpersonal caring relationship that takes us beyond the ego to higher "spiritual" caring; attention to the caring occasion or moment, seen as a heart-centred encounter; the acceptance of multiple ways of knowing though science, art, ethics and cultural and spiritual forms; a reflective and meditational approach to increase consciousness and presence, including an understanding of the patient, client or family member as a person and an understanding of their particular health needs; caring as inclusive, circular and expansive; and recognising that care and caring changes us, others and the culture of groups and environments.

These principles and concepts are set out in the Ten Carative Factors, which I have redefined as Carative Processes, which are guidelines for putting into practice care that is centred on love and compassion. Because these are directly relevant to the subject matter of this book, I list them in full as follows:

1. Practicing loving-kindness and equanimity within the context of caring consciousness
2. Being authentically present and enabling and sustaining the deep belief system and subjective life world of self and the one being cared for.
3. Cultivating one's own spiritual practices and transpersonal self, going beyond ego self.
4. Developing and sustaining a helping, trusting and authentic caring relationship.
5. Being present to, and supportive of, the expression of positive and negative feelings.
6. Creatively using self and all ways of knowing as part of the caring process; engaging in the artistry of caring-healing practices.
7. Engaging in genuine teaching-learning experience that attends to wholeness and meaning, attempting to stay within the other's frame of reference.
8. Creating healing environments at all levels, whereby wholeness, beauty, comfort, dignity, and peace are potentiated.
9. Assisting with basic needs, with an intentional caring consciousness, administering 'human care essentials,' which potentiate alignment of mind-body-spirit, wholeness in all aspects of care.
10. Opening and attending to mysterious dimensions of one's life-death; soul care for self and for the one-being-cared for; "allowing and being open to miracles".

I recognise that as in all times of turmoil and change we face new opportunities and challenges. As we enter into that unknown new space from our depth of values and evolved consciousness, it is here, that we create new possibilities beyond what is and move toward what might be. In our personal lives during crises of illness, tragedy, loss or impending death, we may ponder spiritual questions that go beyond the physical-material world. And it is only when we acknowledge how much pain and suffering there is in our broken hearts and broken human spirit, that we can return to that which is timeless, which can comfort, sustain, inspire and inspirit us. It is here, is reconsidering the basis of health-care and human caring that we can quieten the outer pace, bow down, and surrender to the loving presence of the universe and its infinity, reconnecting with our shared humanity across time and space, and across differences, borders and boundaries.

It is in this loving surrender and reconnection that new and necessary forms of governance in nursing and health-care will be found. This is the matter of Caring Science.

15. Finding the Others: The Re-Imaging of Politics for a Brighter Future in Iceland and Canada

Heiða Kristín Helgadóttir and Derek Masselink

> Who knows what you might learn from taking a chance on a conversation with a stranger? Everyone carries a piece of the puzzle. Nobody comes into your life by mere coincidence. Trust your instincts. Do the unexpected. Find the others.
>
> —Timothy Leary

Introduction

On November 15, 2014 the tiny island community of North Pender, lying just off of the southwest coast of British Columbia, Canada, elected a member of the newly formed Bright Future Party as one of their two local officials. The win was notable as it was the first time in the history of the island that a candidate had run under the banner of a political party and had won! It was also notable because it was the culmination of an 8-month experiment inspired by Iceland's Besti Flokkurinn and Björt Framtíð (Best and Bright Future parties). This chapter tells the tale of two islands and their political initiatives that occurred on opposite sides of the North Hemisphere, one inspired by the other; each seeking and exploring a creative and hopeful approach to transforming systems of governance.

The Story of Bright Future, Iceland

The Origin of Best Party

The economic crash in Iceland in 2008 had an effect: there was a general feeling of fear and panic—people had become accustomed to the easiness. I did, of course, fear for Iceland. The journalists threatened apocalypse, but I knew that things were very serious and yet, oddly, at the same time, that things would be fine. It was important to see through the whole discussion of crisis and understand that we could still build a future without this false money.

In late 2009 I was introduced to Jón Gnarr, a comedian and artist, who at the time thought that he was running for Prime Minister. He was not really sure about government protocols; nevertheless, he did have a very clear idea about what he wanted to do: he wanted to make a mockery out of everything, the whole existing political process in Iceland. He didn't understand where we were heading as a nation and he felt it would lead to something terrible or boring.

Jón has a phenomenal talent, an amazing ability to spread joy, to make people laugh. He loves doing it, and I was immediately drawn to his ideas, especially the notion that we could create a 'Best Party' that would parody the existing political practices in Iceland. I found all of this, the whole project, very entertaining and funny. So Jón Gnarr founded Besti Flokkurinn in late 2009, as a joke. That is to say that we would take part in the 2010 Reykjavik election as an 'anarchy-surrealist' response to the incompetence and short-sightedness of Iceland's governing elite. Indeed, if nothing else we would at least have some fun.

In keeping with political conventions, we promised everybody everything—trips to Disneyland, a polar bear for the zoo, 'sustainable transparency'. It was our attempt to make visible the joke that Iceland's politics and political culture had become. Jón Gnarr had no previous interest or experience in politics, and our party was made up of a handful of inexperienced artists and friends including a couple of avant-garde musicians, a carpenter and a well-known Icelandic architect. I myself was a 27-year-old single mother with two young boys. As I had a keen interest in politics and a degree in Political Science, and I understood where this campaign was going and why it was important. So I was made the campaign manager.[1]

Although it is true that the main agenda and the platform was somewhat a joke, a rather surreal one, the core objective was to infiltrate the system and bring about change in the political landscape, which had always seemed to me rather unappealing and far removed from reality. Indeed, bringing about change from within a system that has been in place for decades should be something every generation aspires to, in my view. However it has become increasingly irrelevant and unthinkable for intelligent and able people to enter politics, especially younger people. This is not just an Icelandic phenomenon; instead, it is a worldwide problem. That's not to say that people care less or are unaware. People choose not to enter this field because it is highly competitive, and the work can seem unrewarding, not to mention that one's life can become very public—at least the mistakes one makes.

So what I saw in the Best Party was a way to describe a huge problem using satire and humour instead of boring facts and figures that tend to be open for debate and interpretation. However, like any good joke, if one tries to explain it, it loses its meaning and magic. Therefore it was a kind of either-you-get-it-or-you-don't type of joke, at the heart of which is the underpinning of our political culture built up in an unsustainable way and which we uphold.

There is inauthenticity or falsehood to the Icelandic political culture that Jón was brilliant at pointing out. He did so by promising the voters everything and at the same time promising to break his promises. We managed to develop a system which allows contradicting promises to be made, like lower taxes, then more jobs, better education and free health care, showing how these things don't add up. For instance, by lowering taxes, it is impossible to pay for the rest of the stuff promised. We thus managed to illustrate that the dialogue between voters and politicians is untrue and the mounting expectations are causing various problems in society where results are necessarily limited, making this realm of work, being in politics, very brutal and inhuman.

Being a messenger with a surreal character, I believe Jón brought a sense of truth to the conversation that had to happen because this 'default' approach to governance is very costly and leads to bad decisions and ineffective policy. It's costing us the quality of life and hope to move forward built on reality.

We ended up winning election with Jón securing the Mayoralty of Reykjavik with 37 percent of the vote and six city council members out of 15.

Building Trust and Being Fearless

On the night of the elections the atmosphere changed dramatically. We had gone from being inside a 'bubble' where anything was possible and we were in control to a situation that was completely new to everyone. Stakes were high and all eyes were on us, especially on Jón to see how he would handle himself and his role as the mayor. It was a mixture of very high expectations from our voters and equally huge scepticism from inside the system—from bureaucrats and other political actors with whom we now needed to work together.

So the main project for the first year was building trust and assuring people of our political sincerity. We also endeavoured to develop a good alliance with our coalition party, the Social Democrats. This focus allowed us to bring about some changes to the system, such as developing a culture of openness and enabling people to say what was on their mind. To us it seemed the only way to do things in politics, but I was amazed to realise just how unthinkable that had been to others. In particular, openness was almost impossible in the relationship between the politicians and the civil servants and government officials often have better knowledge of certain issues than the politicians but they were not always interested in providing input if it didn't agree with their agenda.

To some extent I believe that this is one of the sources of falsehood or lack in openness that have plagued the Icelandic political system for decades. We have a mix of politicians elected by the public, civil servants/officials who are experts in different areas of governance, and special interest groups who represent needs and wants. So the magic of good governance, I believe, lies in some sort of equilibrium between these players. Such equilibrium would ensure a much more balanced approach to power and decision-making.

The relationship between politicians and bureaucrats is complex and as the politicians step into office, and get ready to point their own team to offer civil services, the need for trust and mutual respect is more important than ever in order that the politicians and officials would work together to deal with many immediate challenges confronting us, such as the obvious insolvency of a Geothermal Power Plant (Orkuveitan) that the city owned 97% of. Officials had previously presented this situation to the politicians, yet none was able to act as solving this very difficult problem would make the politicians rather unpopular. That raised a question: what should the politician's core concern, to stay in the office or to serve the communities? Unfortunately, for most politicians, the former becomes the major preoccupation and hence they would do anything to avoid jeopardising their office.

Fear is a powerful controlling mechanism that will ultimately destroy everything that has true value and politics, to me, seems to be often paralysed with fear and hence people would put on a mask to avoid being found out the truths about them, be it their confidence and capacity to lead the table, or their thoughts concerning a particular decision, or their personal stories, breading mistrust and confusion. By contrast, we felt that we had very little to lose and hence we approached our work with a sense of fearlessness as we had no intent to hold on to the power. It has given us some freedom to focus on what is truly important for the city.

Best Party Politics: Openness, Transparency and Engagement

So how did the Best Party, a non-structural anarchy-surrealist act of political performance, end up formulating a proper political party and most importantly why?

Iceland, with a population of 325,000, is very small and Reykjavik, where the Best Party started out, the mother of the Bright Future Party[2], is even smaller with a population of about 120,000 people. Having a real impact on a large number of people is therefore somewhat easier than in a larger society. However I have found that the challenges we face of mobilising the public and raising awareness of our political agenda is pretty much the same all over the globe[3].

The main agenda behind the Best Party (later Bright Future Party) was to infiltrate the political system and try to change it from within. As the Best Party matured into its role as a player in the political world in Iceland, it because clear that we needed to do more. By the end of the first year in office, the public opinion poll showed that we had slipped down from original share of the vote. Our first budget was a very difficult one: two years after the financial crisis, the country's economy hadn't recovered, the revenue was scarce and the demand and need for public service, such as unemployment benefits and other social benefits, were very high. The pressure for public expenditure forced us to down size. Among the most controversial of those downsizing plans was restructuring some of the public schools, when the music teachers and kindergarten teachers nearly went on a strike.

At the heart of all this financial turmoil was the fate of the Geothermal Power Plant (Orkuveitan) that had, up to this point, been the city's 'cash cow'. Ineffective leadership and financial decisions with a political slant had led to the down fall of Orkuveitan. People lost their jobs, my father being one of them who had worked there for nearly 10 years doing marketing and in-house communication. It owed huge amounts in foreign debt that the city was accountable for and, at the same time, had grand plans for expansion that had very little to do with providing the citizens of Reykjavik with hot water and electricity. That situation needed to be dealt with urgently, but it wasn't going to be easy.

Setting up a strategic plan to save Orkuveitan from insolvency took a better part of the first two years. Today the company is on track and is paying back its debts and is now supplying hot water and electricity to the people of Reykjavik who own it.

By being very open and honest about what we were trying to do, however difficult it might be, we managed to see our approval rating go up. Jón was at the forefront of that. He was a sort of shield as he mainly dealt with the emotional relationship between the public and the Party. At the same time, he offered the time and space for other members to get on with what they needed to do. One task of the public relationship was to encourage people's participation in the town hall meetings or in budgetary discussion through a specific online site called Betri Reykjavik (Better Reykjavik). The intention was that we invite others' involvement as much as possible in helping us formulate ideas and engage in a collective action.

From there we started forming a new political party based on values of the Best Party. I was sent out, as I was the youngest on the team (an ongoing joke that I was the only one who had a future here) to try and find others. Bright Future held its first open meeting in February 2012.

Getting people involved was somewhat easier for Bright Future than for the Best Party as the Best Party had proven to be quite successful in running the city of Reykjavík, even after the first difficult years. So when we started out to form the parliamentary party for the elections in 2013, we had a head start and a lot of good will. The fact that we are a small society and the fact that the Best Party's infiltration was a success helped pave the way for a more structured political movement.

Conclusion

Starting as a 'joke', the Best Party's journey transpired to be a worthy pathway towards well-being for the people of Reykjavik. For me, the most important thing is to prepare the ground, pave the way and open up the space and opportunities for others to join us and to be creative.

Keeping with the core notion of fearlessness is crucial. Political voices are multiple, noisy and sometimes very loud. It is therefore really important to stay focused on our own values and avoid from being torn apart by the many different noises. Distinguishing what is truly important and what is background noise is most challenging. So to be able to do so, it is necessary to maintain a shared political consciousness within the team which had helped the Best Party through some really difficult times.

The other point is to have a trusting and supportive team of people who are able to point out truthfully when we were getting caught up in it, and who would be able to catch the balls others throw at us.

Although politics is team work, it is equally important to keep ourselves centred and focused on the main objectives and above all, our own political convictions. Surrounded by the noises of demands, criticism and uncertainty, it is crucial that we are able to hear our own voice—the authentic voice of who we are, from where we know when to let go and when to persist.

Last not least, for me, the challenges are definitely about keeping it interesting and keeping the fire kindled. The political system has a way of pulling us in and taking control of each situation by telling us that things have always been done in a specific way and there is no need to change. At times, we simply have to 'elbow' our way through that 'the computer says no' way of thinking and at the same time, ensuring that it doesn't get to us. It's just the way things are, until proven differently.

Whilst maintaining a forward momentum and keeping it interesting, it is also important to change form—doing the unexpected. If this job gets too comfortable, we need to break it up and challenge ourselves. Politics should never become too familiar, too cosy. When it does, you stop seeing the cracks.

Bright Future, Canada

The Island Trust and Its Preserve-and-Protect Mandate

North Pender is a tiny island 8km wide and 12km long located just off the southwest coast of British Columbia (BC), Canada, in the Salish Sea—an inland sea that separates the much larger Vancouver Island from the North American continent. The Salish Sea—formerly called the Gulf or Strait of Georgia—lies between the urban centers of Vancouver, Victoria and Seattle. It is part of an archipelago of islands known collectively as the Gulf Islands, the ancestral home to the indigenous Strait Salish people for over 10,000 years. Today the Island is home to an aging population of just over 2,000 full-time residents and its economy is mainly dependent on retirement income and seasonal tourism. Access to and from the island is provided by a number of car ferries.

The Mediterranean-like climate, the beauty and warmth of the area coupled with its close proximity to urban centres have made Salish Sea an attractive place to visit and live. In the 1960s, these features resulted in a number of major developments, the largest of which was situated on North Pender Island, and was, at the time, the largest residential development west of Toronto, Canada's largest city.

In an effort to control this perceived unbridled development, the Province of BC stepped in and established a unique local governing body with a mandate to 'preserve and protect' the Southern Gulf Islands for the benefit of the residents of the area and the residents of BC. It works to maintain this mandate through its responsibility for land use decisions for the 13 major Gulf Islands and for over 450 smaller islands found in a 5,200 km^2 area of the Salish Sea. It is understood to be one of the only local government jurisdictions in North America with an explicit conservation mandate.

At its inception in 1974, the population of the Trust area numbered around 8,000 residents. In the past 40 years, it has more than tripled and stands around 25,000. While population growth and associated development in this area have slowed down, the ability to maintain the preserve-and-protect mandate with other agencies has proved challenging. Many residents resent the ever-increasing costs of the Trust along with its restrictive and conservative attitude towards development. Similar to other areas of the world, residents tend to have a negative and cynical view of government and politicians.

As a body with a relatively narrow window of legislative authority and responsibility, the Trust has a very complicated governance structure. The islands of the Trust Area are grouped into twelve Local Trust Areas and one island municipality. This group of thirteen areas is often referred to as the 'Federation'. Every four years, each island group elects two trustees to represent electors and oversee land use decisions on their islands. These twenty-six trustees sit on the Islands Trust Council, which in turn elects four of its members to sit on an Executive Committee. Trust Council holds quarterly public meetings. The Executive Committee meets to conduct the daily business on behalf of the Federation between Trust Council's quarterly meetings. With the exception of the two municipal trustees, all trustees also sit on a local trust committee, a three-person body made up of two local trustees and a member of the Executive Committee appointed as chair. Services such as building inspection, fire, water and waste, are provided by regional governments and provincial agencies, and the one island municipality.

I found myself participating in island politics shortly after moving to the island in 2003. In 2008 I was encouraged to run for the position of Trustee. Like the other candidates, I ran as an independent but was part of an unofficial slate. Unlike Iceland, here, political parties at a local government level are not common. No parties had ever run candidates in an Islands Trust election.

Finding the Others and Re-Imaging New Way to Do Politics

I was fortunate to win in 2008 and served one term in office. At the end of the three-year term I decided not to stand for re-election. I was frustrated by the rigidity and overly bureaucratic nature of the Trust's governance structure. I had been unable to effectively address the many environmental, social

Finding the Others

and economic challenges confronting our community and the Trust area and felt that my time would be better spent engaging my community through other means. I wanted the freedom to work creatively with others on issues and projects that mattered. I wanted to make a difference.

On November 15, 2014, after a three-year absence, my community returned me to the position of Trustee for North Pender Island. What had brought me back?

During my three-year 'sabbatical' I had taught a graduate-level course on governance for sustainability at the Royal Roads University. My students and I were exploring ways in which we could transform governance systems for better outcomes. Because of this work I was invited to participate in the 2014 Spirit of Humanity Forum. In Reykjavik, I came in contact with Jón Gnarr and his Best Party and later the Bright Future Party.

At the time I had an inkling that these alternative approaches to politics, i.e., re-imagining and re-purposing a political party as an attractive non-partisan platform through humor, joy, openness and possibility, might resonate with my community. Iceland and North Pender are both small islands with small populations comprised of high numbers of creative individuals. We both are struggling with the socio-economic challenges associated with small isolated islands with small populations.

In July 2014, shortly after returning from Iceland, with the help of a few close friends we launched our own Bright Future Party—a non-partisan political party boasting a vision for everyone. We thought this offering might expand the relatively narrow and un-interesting political discussion during the upcoming election in the autumn. If nothing else, it would give us an opportunity to do and build something new and creative together with our community—a kind of political performance art project.

We began with all the necessary but practical tasks—designing a logo, drafting a provocative membership pitch[4], building a website and social media platforms, and signing up members. In an effort to focus our limit resources, we decided to only run candidates on North Pender.

Non-Partisan Politics and Radical Trust

Our approach was straightforward. Like our Icelandic counterparts, we believed that our community, especially the young people, desired alternatives to the existing political and governance status quo. Inspired by the Icelandic experience we thought that there might be a way to *do* politics and governance differently on North Pender and perhaps in British Columbia and Canada more generally.

The act of establishing our own non-partisan political party generated a bit of controversy. Many of our residents—particularly those with political experience—did not understand how a political party could be non-partisan. Many questioned the need for a party given the explicit direction of the Trust's preserve-and-protect mandate. Our simple act of re-imagining a political convention and applying it in a different political venue had a ripple effect as people began to examine our new approach to politics and governance on our island. It was akin to throwing a pebble in the pond.

We were purposefully 'cheeky'. Like the Best Party in Iceland, we wanted to attract attention and draw people into the conversation—the performance. We wanted to demonstrate that this could be fun, stimulating and creative. We suggested that the best way for our community to meet the challenges of today and tomorrow was by cultivating an environment of respect, openness, creativity and joy—by practicing radical trust and creating environments that bring out the best in everyone, and that we all do better when we support and expect the best from each other.

The idea of radical trust, being open to others rather than being closed or controlling, was and continues to be difficult for most people to understand and accept. Many worry that this is naïve, and leaves one vulnerable to exploitation. This is a deeply engrained fear—the fear of being taken advantage of. From a young age we are taught not to trust others. We enter into new and different conversations and relationships defensively. So for many, the practice of radical trust could result in an embarrassing or dangerous vulnerability.

Our response to these concerns was to explain that radical trust is not reckless trust. Radical or 'rooted' trust is about expecting the best from others, and from ourselves. It is about being honest and direct with people even when they are not at their best.

We also stated that love and compassion needed to be at the centre of everything that we do on our island—especially in the ways we worked together and govern ourselves. Furthermore, we argued that life was 'far too short to be serious and grumpy' and all of us would benefit from a little more joy and laughter in our lives. This last statement resonated with many people. Over the course of the campaign people shared that our current governance structures and decision-making processes were far too complicated and serious—that they were unattractive and negative and perhaps even resulting in bad decisions. We suspect that this was why our campaign started attracting significant attention and support because like the Best Party in Iceland, we were unlike anything most people had seen or experienced here on our island.

We embodied a new way of doing politics and governance even though it is not yet exactly clear what this *new way* is.

However, it was definitely clear how we differentiated from the other campaigns, by being honest, funny, creative, authentic, hopeful and compassionate. In addition, we were not fixated on winning. Like Jón, we understood ourselves to be an intervention.

Campaigning Differently to Engage, to Understand and Transform

By early September we were in full election mode. Just as we were launching our online presence, a discussion about the election had appeared on a Pender-focused Facebook site. This was a good development as more than half of our community is on Facebook. However like a number of our media 'outlets'—it is an explicitly apolitical space—an example of the measures our community takes to avoid the impacts of discord and disagreement. After all we are a tiny community on a small island and therefore have a strong need for people to get along. Our local paper is also explicitly apolitical and as a result is more like a newsletter or bulletin board than a paper. We avoid debate and discord like a family who wants to maintain the appearance of wanting to get along but at the same time, is totally aware of the skeletons in the closet and the histories lie buried just below the surface.

To keep the peace, the Pender Island Forum (a place to talk about things that matter) Facebook group was quickly established to host political and community-related conversations. The Forum turned out to be an important development. It became a very active space with wide ranging conversations around traditionally contentious issues like housing, waste, economic development, and the Trust. I spent a lot of time actively responding to questions and participating in discussions while the incumbent candidates chose not to participate. Supporters who participated on their behalf suggested that the Facebook environment was too complicated and confusing for them even though both of the other candidates had established websites. It was clear that the incumbents were doing their best to control the conversation and that participation in an online environment was too risky. It was believed that the online audience was too limited and narrow; that most residents would only be reached through traditional campaign approaches such as signs, leaflets, open houses and door knocking and phone calls.

For us, participating in the *Forum* demonstrated a willingness to be vulnerable, available, genuinely interested and responsive. It gave me an open, accessible and somewhat archival platform to develop and share my ideas and thoughts with my community so they could get to know more about me and the Party. My approach was simple: be responsive, positive, honest, helpful, thoughtful, and whenever possible, humorous and self-deprecating.

In the early days of the campaign I tried to find a running mate, after all there were two positions up for grabs. My initial inclination was for a female political 'partner,' preferably a younger mother, as I believe that the world would be a better place if more young mothers like Heiða had more of role in running it. This inclination is not to essentialise women; rather it is a reaction to the overly masculine nature of our political and governance systems. We need more love and compassion—more feminine energy—in positions and systems of leadership and governance.

Wendell Berry (1973) speaks to this notion in his poem "Manifesto: The Mad Farmer Liberation Front":

> So long as women do not go cheap
> for power, please women more than men.
> Ask yourself: Will this satisfy
> a woman satisfied to bear a child?
> Will this disturb the sleep
> of a woman near to giving birth?

Unfortunately, none of the women I approached were willing to become politically involved. They were worried about the impact on their families and on themselves whereas men, like myself, seem to realise that this is only once they've been elected.

On October 11 I registered my candidacy. The Bright Future Party was registered as an elector organisation, officially endorsing my candidacy. Three other candidates were registered running for the two Trustee position: the two incumbents, both men with nine years of experience in local politics, each having been elected, either at a local or regional government level; and Dianne (a woman!), a retired realtor, running because she was tired of the economic and social impact that polarised politics was having on the community.

Now that we were officially registered we now needed to attend to find a way for me to campaign effectively. We had very little resources. I also wasn't able to be on the island for much of October due to my teaching commitments. We needed a different, more effective and efficient way of connecting to the voters and delivering our message of possibility, creativity and joy.

Given my separation from the community I tried to connect via online and social media. I actively participated in the Facebook *Forum*, quickly responding to participants concerns, questions and ideas. I blogged and posted my observations and ideas on my website and our campaign Facebook pages. On weekends I returned to the island to host and participate in a number of events that expressed the attitude and values of the Party. At one such event we hosted a heated 30m-long slip-n-slide to raise money for a local family whose newborn baby was dealing with cancer. The event attracted a lot of people, many of them children. Through this event, people recognised our willingness to put the needs of others ahead of our own and our capacity to do it in a fun way.

In keeping with our efforts to stand out and apart from the other candidates and their campaigns, purple was chosen as the Party's colour. This was done initially out of convenience as it was available and not associated with any particular political or social campaign. It then turned out to be a striking colour that set us visually apart from the other campaigns. I wore something purple all the time. Our four large hand-painted signs were purple, each with a large image of my head pinned to them. We also encouraged our supporters to wear one of our small purple pins or better yet, wear something purple. A wave of purple gradually washed over our island.

While these approaches brought attention to the Party and my candidacy, our biggest impact was made at the island's 'All Candidates' meeting' where each was given an opportunity to share their platform and respond to questions from the audience. Recognising the potential impact of this event, understanding that only about 25% of our island's population would be able to attend it in person, we were successful in seeking permission to video-record it and post it online.

The challenge was now to set our campaign apart from the other candidates. Rather than repeat our platform I took the somewhat unconventional and risky move of telling an allegory in which five aging monks are able to bring back their declining monastery from the point of collapse by bestowing remarkable kindness and respect on one another (Zander & Zander, 2000). As I came to the end of the story, a hush fell over the audience—the point had been made. I was later told that this was the turning point in the campaign. Up until then, our campaign was not necessarily understood or appreciated by the community. The monk's story provided clarity—in a kind and gentle way it brought attention to the interpersonal attitudes and barriers that were preventing us from moving ahead as a community.

Success!

On November 15—Election Day—a few minutes before the polls closed, our team entered the North Pender's polling station to observe the count. Going in we had no idea of the extent of our support, nor what the outcome would be. Within minutes it was clear that Dianne and I had won. This was confirmed an hour and a half later at the conclusion of the count when we were unofficially declared the winners. A few days later, when the official numbers were received Dianne had secured the most votes with me following a close second.

Similarly to Jón and the Best Party, we did not expect to win. The challenge before us now is to prove our approach to governance and politics in practice. We see two aspects to this challenge. The first is the future role of the Party. With a lone Party member operating within an established structure that has no prior experience with electoral organisations, what purpose or value does or can our Party serve? Secondly, as an individual trustee, how do I effectively embody and apply the principles and values of the Bright Future Party in a manner that can have an impact?

These questions still remain. There is certain nervousness about the existence of the Bright Future Party on our island and within the Trust area. Prior to the election and immediately after, a number of disparaging things were said and published about the Party. Much of this fear came from a lack of understanding. The concerns were entirely speculative and were never directly conveyed or discussed with us. Today there is little talk about the Party and like the disputes and arguments our island works hard to avoid, it is not discussed. I still wear the Party pin on my lapel but unless I make a point of talking about it, it is not brought up in conversation.

Conclusion

Our suspicion of party politics here in Canada is indicative of a deeper concern—a certain 'stuckness' and lack of imagination, the challenge we faced trying to establish a political party as a legitimate non-partisan vehicle to re-engage ordinary citizens in politics. That may be good enough reason for us to continue to maintain and further develop the Bright Future Party in Canada.

There are many questions. For instance, with one elected member and limited resources, how will we sustain the attitude and energy that was mustered during our campaign? We will require resources and an ongoing commitment from members beyond our original core team. This will require additional organisational structure. Most importantly it will require an ongoing commitment and investment in this 'experiment'. I'm not sure this commitment exists. With the election behind us and no clear purpose or vision, all Party activities have ceased.

In the past I would have taken this as a kind of failure. To be a success, the Party should be a growing, expanding entity with a staff and resources and a full and active membership. However, I'm now inclined to think that there are other, subtler, and perhaps more powerful and effective ways in which the Party can continue. The idea and experience of the Party is still very much alive in all of us who brought it into being.

Ultimately, it was an idea, an open and generous attitude, a creative stance that brought us together to attract the attention of people and enroll our community in a different way of being and doing together. The challenge now for all of us is to maintain, develop and spread that attitude and stance throughout and beyond our community. Would the continuation of the Party help ensure that this happens? Perhaps. Perhaps it is as simple as maintaining an allegiance to the principles, values, approaches and friendships that put us on this path, which resulted in my election and gave us a platform to propose and model another way of being.

This has been and continues to be a challenging and transformative journey. It was inspired and supported by the ideas and now friendships of people from all over the globe working in their own unique and particular ways of re-imagining and re-shaping politics and governance. These connections and friendships are critical to the initiation and evolution of these ideas.

Heiða and Jón's story from Reykjavik and Iceland has had a major impact on our tiny island community and in ways that are still emerging. Perhaps ours will too.

Notes

1. Later I have learned that people thought Jón was completely lost to have a 'child' for a campaign manager.
2. Björt framtíð or Bright Future is the more serious and somewhat more experienced outgrowth of that initial political offering. In 2013 Björt framtíð was able to secure 6 of the 63 available seats in the Alþingi, the national parliament of Iceland and the oldest parliamentary body in the world.
3. Getting people involved in politics and political debate is one of the greatest challenges we face in modern democratic societies. Social media and internet technologies have definitely transformed our ways to participate in politics, most people remain passive.
4. Our membership form proclaimed: "The Bright Future Party is a new, non-partisan elector organization (a party!)—the first of its kind in the Salish Sea—that supports individuals who believe that a better brighter future is possible together, that we all have the capacity for leadership and that government and politics can be done in a way that is open, attractive and empowering. If you are interested in making this happen, join us. Make history by becoming a member of our Party. It's going to be awesome!"

16. The Efforts of King Abdulaziz Center for National Dialogue to Promote a Culture of Dialogue and Tolerance in the Saudi Society

AMAL Y. AL-MOALLIMI & FATIMA M. AL-BISHRI

Introduction

Saudi Arabia has a unique position due to that the two most sacred cities in the Islamic world; Makkah and Madeena are located on its lands. Moreover, Saudi Arabia has gained political leadership among Arab and Islamic countries due to its increasing economic power as a result of being a leading country in oil production. This being said, it has become a challenge for the Saudi citizen to not only be regarded as a representative for his/her country, but also a representative for a religion and an identity. This has indeed put Saudi Arabia under the spotlight and added more pressure on the Saudi citizen who is expected to be a competent agent for his/her country. At the same time, the government has also realized this pressure and started initiating ambitious programs and projects around the country with an aim to equip the Saudis with the required social, educational, political and economic skills. One of the most prominent projects within the national effort to cultivate citizenship was establishing the King Abdulaziz Center for National Dialogue (KACND), which aims at spreading the culture of dialogue and common human values such as tolerance, understanding, moderation, and communication. Throughout 11 years, KACND has been successful in addressing untapped areas in intercultural dialogue within the country and became a pioneer in opening up channels of communication between different cultures, which resulted in achieving understanding and tolerance among Saudis themselves and among all nationalities living in the same country, and sharing the same grounds.

The Saudi context

Most regions around Saudi Arabia have been already exposed to other cultures due to occupation. These countries attracted foreign attention for a variety of reasons such as interests in natural resources; the strategic significance of geographical locations, historical connections, and so on. However, the Arab Peninsula (known later as KSA) was isolated from any opportunity of forging communication with other cultures or intercultural encounter and experience. Thus it mainly consisted of tribes that had conflicts with each other due to the need to compete for limited natural resources.

This isolation excludes "Hejaz" region (west Saudi Arabia), in which Makkah and Madina are located as they were open for people from all around the world whether as pilgrims or inhabitants. These two holy cities have a spiritual significance for Muslims; Makkah being the prayer direction for more than 1 billion Muslims five times a day from around the world, and Madina being the place in which the prophet Mohammad mosque is located.

The nature of Saudi Arabia's existence of thousands of years of isolation has imposed certain psychological features and characteristics on the Saudis, such as fearing any foreigner presence, defensiveness and over-protectiveness of their tribe or family name.

In 1932 and within this context, King Abdulaziz Al Saud was able to successfully unify all conflicting tribes into one country that he named "the Kingdom of Saudi Arabia". It was the first official state created after one thousand years of political isolation. King Abdulaziz faced the challenge of establishing a political entity for the country while it lacked natural resources and suffered from poor economic conditions.

The first foreign encounter was when King Abdulaziz cooperated with an American oil company called the Arabian American Oil Company (known now as Saudi ARAMCO). This company had a social and cultural impact on the Saudis as it introduced them to the American culture, American people and their way of life. ARAMCO also trained Saudis from all over the Kingdom, some of who couldn't even read or write but had the chance to learn to speak English through ARAMCO's training. This has started a gradual openness to the other and the opportunity of encountering different cultures set forth a promising future for the Saudis and a new era of wealth and prosperity thus began. Ministries, universities, hospitals, and roads were established as the country started implementing continuous development projects and building its infrastructure.

However, the 9/11 attacks were a setback to all this cultural and civil development. It was only after the events of September 2001 it became clear that there was a weakness in communicating Saudi Arabia's cultural characteristics and orientation and conveying its identities to the international community. The Saudis were as surprised as the whole world when terrorists attacked the World Trade Centre in New York, and were shocked when 15 of the attackers were announced to be Saudis! This was clear evidence to the Saudis that there was something wrong and that they needed to assess the past period in order to get things back on the right track.

Saudis not only suffered from extremism themselves, but they also suffered from being portrayed as extremists by westerns, which led to what is known today as Islamphobia adding even more pressure on Saudis as Muslims. It became then obvious that Muslims and westerns are in desperate need for opening up channels of intercultural and interfaith dialogue. Muslims were obligated to clarify the true principles and values of Islam which were distorted by some people who cited wrong verses of Quran or Hadith[1] and was used for political and religious reasons. This portrayed Islam as a religion that encourages violence and killing others with opposing views or religions. This is definitely a misinterpretation of Islam, which actually calls for love, peace, respect, tolerance, and preserving human dignity.

Within this context, the role played by King Abdulaziz Center for National Dialogue (KACND) was crucial. The Center's mission is to spread tolerance and promote dialogue nationally and regionally, and to reinforce national unity and moderation. KACND also seeks to protect Islam from distortion and misinterpretations, and to spread the values of love, respecting the others, peace, tolerance, and dialogue; which are actually values that are derived from the core of Islam. This is achieved by providing citizens with the correct tools and skills to represent themselves as Saudis and Muslims nationally and internationally through training programs and conferences.

Since then, Saudi Arabia has been keen to communicate to the world about its willingness to shift its own cultural orientations and to adopt moderation and tolerance. Indeed, one of the most prominent features of the current Saudi dialogue is to stress the rejection of terrorism in the name of religion, to renounce violence and criminal operations targeting innocent people anywhere, and to refuse using religion as an excuse for committing these crimes.

To explore the concepts of moderation, the country is following two parallel tracks: an internal path that aims at working with Saudi nationals and foreigners living in the Kingdom, and an external path aiming at connecting with people around the world and the Saudis living abroad for different reasons.

Therefore, channels of dialogue and communication were built and many debates among scholars and strict religious leaders took place to establish common grounds for shared understanding and at the same time, to look into the roots of the problem of terrorism. In addition, many seminars were held in which religious leaders and scholars gathered to discuss topics related to citizenship, globalisation, dialogue and other issues that preoccupied the public opinion after the 9:11 attacks, which were followed by terrorist attacks in local sites targeting Saudi authorities. That means that the Saudis were also a victim of terrorism and their identity was highjacked by those perceiving themselves as 'real' Muslims and the guardians of Arabs and the two holy mosques.

The country woke up to a process focusing on dismantling terrorist cells, containing promoters of radical ideologies and violence, and at the same time adopting counseling, debate and open discussion as methods, which are actually reflection, the true essence of Islam.

In addition to placing a new brick in the edifice of world peace, the Kingdom of Saudi Arabia, and in particular the city of Makkah, launched the King Abdullah bin Abdulaziz initiative for interfaith and intercultural dialogue, which has been embraced by the international community. In July 2008, the World Conference on Dialogue was convened in Madrid, to which leaders of all of the world's major faiths were invited. In November of the same year, King Abdullah travelled to New York to address the United Nations and to promote his interfaith initiative, which was well received by world leaders.

The Emergence of National Dialogue

In this context, the national dialogue project in the Kingdom of Saudi Arabia became the sole purpose for the founding of King Abdulaziz Centre for National Dialogue (KACND) in 2003. It stemmed from the vision of the Custodian of the Two Holy Mosques, King Abdullah Bin Abdulaziz Al Saud, to achieve coexistence and to open up interfaith and intercultural dialogue internally and externally. This richly endowed project has, within the space of ten years, become a noticeable force for disseminating the culture of dialogue and its diverse values within the society. Ultimately, it hopes to instill dialogue as an aspect of life, culture, thought, custom and tradition. This is the Centre's core mission and to achieve its mission, the Centre has designed and taken a number of approaches, including youth participation and broad intellectual approaches to discussing issues of national importance with government and private sectors. These are aimed at the stated goal of spreading the culture of dialogue and consolidating the values of modesty and tolerance.

The approach of moderation is primarily referring to the moderation of thinking, in orientation, in the opinion, in subtraction, and in dealing with various issues, such as moderation in all affairs of life, with integrity on the constants. To pursue the value of moderation, it requires a continuation rooted in values including concepts of tolerance, dialogue and acceptance of the other, despite its inconsistency with the essence of religion, which is the essence of the privacy of the Kingdom and one of the determinants of cultural differentiation and civilization.

The Centre believes that dialogue creates cooperation and unity in making a difference in the world through a common human endeavor. Thus the KACND explicitly aims to build a bridge of communication between members of the Saudi society, promote unity amongst all people, and to reinforce values of moderation and tolerance. It has been perceived as one of the most prominent achievements of the period following the September 11 attacks. The Center played a major role in raising awareness of the importance of expressing views and ideas through dialogue and peace.

The Three Paths of Dialogue

King Abdulaziz Center for National Dialogue has been perusing a goal of spreading the culture of dialogue and tolerance in Saudi Arabia. This goal is met through two methods: (1) national conferences for intellectual dialogue and training from which a number of projects and programs have stemmed; (2) youth dialogue programs in order to motivate young people to participate in social change, foster their social responsibility and encourage the spirit of service and volunteerism; (3) cross-culture dialogue through diverse programs aimed at equipping individuals with awareness of the Other, and building bridges between cultures and cultivating qualities in the Saudis so that they can serve as cross-cultural ambassadors.

(1) National Conference

National conferences are held every year in order to address certain matters concerning the Saudi society. Up to now, the Center has held ten national conferences. In 2003, the King called for holding the first national dialogue conference entitled "*International Conventions and Relations and their Impact on National Unity*". It aimed at reaching a common vision on how to deal with other cultures especially amid the aftermath of the September 11 attacks. Religious and political leaders were invited to participate from all over the regions. The conference resulted in a number of recommendations including establishing an independent center for national dialogue to regulate such conferences; which was later on called *The King Abdulaziz Center for National Dialogue*. Among the recommendations also was reinforcing relations between different religious sects and political and intellectual orientations in the Saudi society; bridging cultural and social gaps between Saudi Arabia and other countries; and adopting values of moderation and acceptance in the Saudi society while maintaining religious and national identities.

The 2nd National conference aimed to develop a comprehensive view on extremism and moderation where the participants agreed on general religious frameworks that identify values of moderation and justice. The 3rd conference tackled women issues regarding education, employment, and national ID regulations for women. This conference contributed in creating a new era of women empowerment in all domains of the society. After that, realizing that about 70% of the Saudi society is composed of youth, it was a must to tackle youth issues. Thus, the fourth national conference discussed best practices and suggested solutions for empowering youth and how to engage them in the society. One of the most prominent results of the youth conference was launching *the King Abdullah Scholarship Program,* which opened up opportunities for thousands of young Saudis to study abroad in different majors. The program covers students' tuitions as well as their family expenses and even allocates monthly salaries for these students. The program's main objective is to lead the country towards an era of development and prosperity by providing the best education for its young nation. It not only had a positive economic effect, but it also contributed in developing Saudi youth socially and culturally through allowing them to experience other cultures and get to know new people. Indeed the King Abdullah Scholarship program is a unique program that is not seen elsewhere.

In 2015, and amid reoccurrences of terrorism and extreme acts, the Center decided to hold its 10th conference under the title *"Extremism and its effect on National unity"*. Through opening up dialogue on this topic, the Center seeks to reassess educational systems and look into the different social backgrounds leading to extreme acts. It also aims at bringing up solutions to prevent or deal with intellectual deviation that leads to extremism especially among youth.

Before holding the main conference, the Center holds a series of preparatory meetings in multiple locations around the Kingdom to give everyone a chance to participate, especially giving women the equal opportunities to participate. Participants are invited from all sectors of the society including intellectual orientations, religious sects, age groups, and government and private sectors. Moreover, The Center pays attention to maintain the traditional approach characterized by *"Majlis"* in convening dialogue. *Majlis* is an Arabic word meaning a place of sitting. Traditionally, it is important to have a respectful figure in a *Majlis* whom is responsible for running the dialogue uninterruptedly, systematically but not randomly within a specific timeframe; allowing each and every participant to have a say on a given issue.

The conference usually continues for 2–3 days in order to ensure that there is space for discussing all topics related to the topic chosen to be discussed. By the end of the conference, participants meet the King in person to discuss with him a brief on the conference and submit the final recommendations. Afterwards, the King addresses related sectors to look into executing the recommendations as soon as possible. These local conferences are a historical and cultural extension of the "Majlis" concept that took place in almost every Saudi house since the establishment of Kingdom hundreds of years ago by King Abdulaziz. The founder's sons continued applying this system of directly receiving citizens to discuss pressing issues and get to know their different views. This was also the same case for Sheiks of tribes and princes appointed in other towns whom always welcome open meetings with people. Afterwards, due to the expansion of the country and increasing population this system was structured in a different way such as the Shoura Council and the conferences organized by KACND.

(2) *Youth dialogue programs*

In order to prepare the society for dialogue, the KACND provides many training programs to equip citizens with required dialogue skills such as listening, effective speaking, and dialogue ethics. These programs target the four main different elements of the Saudi society including the religious institutes, families, schools, and the media. Moreover, the Center has initiated youth programs including Tamkeen Youth Dialogue Program, Dialogue Caravan, and Dialogue Café.

Tamkeen "Empowerment" is a program in which youths are given the opportunity to express ideas and participate in finding practical solutions for issues they are usually criticizing and complaining about in their society. After ideas can be turned into proposals to be put through a voting process which aims to identify the strongest proposal. Once selected, the proposal is further developed with the support of relevant experts and then handed to the related sector for execution.

In order to promote the role of youth in spreading the culture of dialogue and to help them develop their communication skills, KACND started the

Dialogue Caravan (DC) in 2010. The DC is a project involving 47 trained volunteers who focused on reaching out to people in rural areas. The first phase of the Dialogue Caravan was implemented in areas around Riyadh. The volunteers camped throughout a whole weekend in rural localities with a view to promote dialogue and tolerance within schools, families and mosques. By the end of the first phase, the Dialogue Caravan had been carried out in 11 towns, 3841 people had been trained, and thousands were reached through school assemblies, the Friday Prayer, weekly sermon, and so forth.

Dialogue Cafés are occasions where youths gather together in a public venue to discuss a certain issues in a friendly informal atmosphere. This project not only aims at spreading the culture of dialogue in the rural areas, but also stimulates volunteerism and encourages young people to activate their sense of social responsibility and develop a sense of belonging.

The main conclusion drawn by the participants to the "eye-opening exploration" was that "dialogue and tolerance are the only way for peace and unity", and that through perseverance and a selfless attitude, volunteers could build more harmony among diverse people.

(3) Cross-cultural dialogue programs

Given the fact that more than 9 million foreigners live in Saudi Arabia today, and in an era of rapid technological breakthroughs, preparing Saudis to become representatives for their country and training them on cross-cultural dialogue became a must. Therefore, the Center launched a number of international programs including Jusoor "Bridges", the Ambassador Program for Cross-Cultural Dialogue, Messengers of Peace in cooperation with the International Scouts Organization, and the King Abdullah Program for Peace in cooperation with UNESCO.

In order to address the Saudis studying and working abroad as well as expats living in the Kingdom, the Center launched Jusoor "bridges" project which is a set of guidebooks communicating to parents and educators on how to create positive cross-cultural dialogue. It also published short stories targeting children and teenagers to raise awareness of diversity and openness to the other. Furthermore, Jusoor publications are applied as training programs during children's summer camps.

The Ambassador Program for Cross-Cultural Dialogue aims to promote communication with non-Saudis living in the kingdom. The program first started as a formal meeting entitled: *"The Two Kingdoms"*, involving a British youth delegation as well as young Saudis. Other British boys and girls already living in the Kingdom also joined the British delegation which visited the three main cities in the Kingdom: Riyadh, Jeddah and Dammam. To their amazement, British residents were as surprised as British visitors when they first met Saudi youths. Although they have been already living in Saudi Arabia for years, this was actually the first time these young Britons had deep conversations with any young Saudis. This initial meeting prompted KACND to come up with a program that gives Saudis and non-Saudis living in Saudi Arabia a chance to get to know each other and explore each other's cultures.

In 2008, the Center started holding small sessions where Saudis were invited along with other nationalities for cross-cultural encounters and for reaching a better understanding of each other in this way. It first began as a meeting with the Japanese community, where Japanese and Saudi students gathered to simply talk, discuss and share experiences and knowledge. During this session, participants were asked: what do you know about each other's' culture? Saudi students eagerly answered; mentioning names of famous Japanese cartoons, devices, actors and even football players. However, to everyone's surprise the Japanese students did not know anything about the Saudi culture. It was obvious then that this was due to the fact that current circumstances surrounding the Japanese community living in Saudi Arabia (as well as other non-Saudis) did not create or open up opportunities for Saudis to mingle with non-Saudis. This was the result of strict security measures following some terrorist incidents at that time.

Saudi participants (and the Center as well) felt that they are responsible for not reaching out to other cultural communities in a country where more than nine million expatriates live. As a result, the idea of establishing a Saudi-Japanese friendship club emerged. Maher Al Otaibi, a language student at King Saud University, proposed the idea as he was studying the Japanese language. Maher cooperated with Miyu Nakamura, the daughter of the Japanese ambassador in Saudi Arabia at that time, to establish a club called "SAKURA[2] of the Kingdom". SAKURA organized all kinds of cultural events and artistic experiences for both Saudis and Japanese youths including language lessons, cooking classes, sports, book clubs, and art sessions. Following the success of SAKURA, another club was established in Japan, which was named "Lavender of Japan", referring to one of the famous flowers that grows in the desert of Saudi Arabia. It did not stop here, in 2011 when Tohoku earthquake and the Tsunami hit east Japan, a group of Saudi youths rushed to Japan to help their friends and support them. Their quick response and determination to stand beside the Japanese people in this hard time reflected a enduring relation and genuine friendship that started with an encounter amongst a small group of young people.

All these dynamic activities and associations between the two countries led mothers who accompanied their sons and daughters to request organizing similar activates with Saudi mothers. This resulted in taking the idea of cultural gatherings to a more organized formal level. Therefore, in 2009 the Center launched "The Ambassador Program for Cross-cultural Dialogue". The program targeted all nationalities living in the Kingdom from different group ages: children, youth, and adults.

The first phase of the program focused on adults and high school students in the form of a three-hour dynamic workshop. It included icebreaking activities, open discussions, and joint art activities. Following each workshop, the program was modified and something new was added. Between 2009 and 2013, the Center had successfully held 31 workshops with different nationalities including Japan, Philippines, India, Italy, Denmark, USA, United Kingdom, South Africa, Norway, Sweden, Turkey, Canada, and Pakistan. In addition, two high-level meetings were held for the ambassadors' wives with Saudi women academics and Shoura Council[3] members.

The workshop usually starts with an Icebreaking activity which involves physical interaction and fun games such as Bingo. After that, the participants rotate into groups to discuss three topics of their choice in an open informal atmosphere. By the end of the workshop, participants get a contact list of their new friends to keep in touch. The goal is not only to open up channels of discussion, but also to keep these channels open even after the event ends. These workshops are designed this way because the Center realizes the need for random and spontaneous conversations in the Saudi society especially with other nationalities.

At the Same time, the Center activated the Ambassador Program among high school students. The experience with youngsters took the program to another level. It proved that most of our children have the same common grounds and interests regardless of faith and nationality. They read the same books, watch the same shows, share the same habits, and experience the same feelings and emotions. They were surprised by "how common" they were rather than "how different", and that is the drive of the Ambassador Program: commonness not difference.

Another amazing thing about students at this age is their eagerness. They would go back home and talk to their parents about their experience with Saudi students and how they made new friends. This effect of bonding and communication thus also touches the parents who are very pleased to see their children excited and happy. The center was hoping that these students will be a true support for the issues facing Saudi Arabia today just like the children of ARAMCO in the 50's who supported Saudis soon after the 9/11 attacks and defended them against stereotyping because they truly knew the Saudis.

However, despite the Center's efforts and proactivity, the process of opening up communication channels between cultures remains to be a two-way one. If participants aren't willing to reach out even after the event, then the goal cannot be achieved. For this reason by the end of every session, a list of participants' contact information is distributed as future plans between the two parties are discussed. Another important aspect is feedback, which is taken by the end of each session anonymously through a simple feedback form.

On an international level, the Center has signed many memorandums of understanding with important organizations to develop programs that aim at promoting dialogue and common human values such as compassion, modernization, respect for cultural diversity, and tolerance. For example, *The King Abdullah bin Abdulaziz International Program for a Culture of Peace and Dialogue* (KAICIID) was launched with UNESCO in order to prepare training programs and hold events to spread the culture of peace and dialogue among people. The program seeks to make dialogue and peace a way of life, challenge misunderstandings that prevail in some societies, and enrich peoples' lives culturally throughout the world. In addition, the Center has in many occasions cooperated with the world Scout Organization to promote training on the culture of dialogue through the "Messengers of Peace Program".

Another milestone in the journey of the Center was holding *the International Youth Conference for Volunteering and Dialogue*, which was organized in cooperation between the Saudi Ministry of Education, King Abdul Aziz Center for National Dialogue and the UNESCO. This event was held within King Abdullah Program for Dialogue and Peace, which is implemented by the UNESCO and funded by the Government of Saudi Arabia. The goal of the conference was to provide a platform for exchanging experiences and perspectives among young participants from different countries around the world. The conference mainly focused on giving youth participants an opportunity to tell stories and encourage discussions in the areas of volunteerism and dialogue. Participants from around the world were nominated and invited to the Conference and each young person had the opportunity to showcase his/her work in a side gallery that was created as an addition to the main conference to ensure maximum benefit and exposure to new ideas. Young people also connected with each other through cultural events, artistic experiences, folkloric dancing and traditional sightseeing trips.

The founding of the King Abdullah bin Abdulaziz International Centre for Interreligious and Intercultural Dialogue 'KAICIID' was yet another extension of King Abdullah's vision. As we shall see in the case study of KAICIID in this book, it is a partnership of the Kingdom of Saudi Arabia, Republic of Austria and Kingdom of Spain. KAICIID aims at strengthening the values of cooperation and coexistence, promoting cultural exchange, and spreading peace, security and stability among the people of the world through conducting studies and workshops related to its goals and objective.

Conclusion

Overall, KACND has been paving the way towards creating a culture of dialogue and peace in a quite challenging country. The Center has gradually but successfully trained more than 1 million citizens in 45 cities on dialogue communication skills through certifying about 3100 trainers in the field.

During the course of ten years, we have been working on spreading the culture of moderation, tolerance and dialogue to create a renewed lifestyle and approach based on dialogue. This has been achieved through implementing various programs and activities locally and internationally, with consideration of the demographic and geographic aspects of the Saudi society. We have went through (and still are going through) several different phases during which we faced numerous challenges, such as rejection from others, fear of losing our national and religious identity, being criticized based on what media reflects especially regarding women, political wars in Arab regions, and more importantly the need to learn how to deal with the ever increasing Islamic phobia. Our beloved King Abdullah passed away in early 2015, however his vision of achieving coexistence is more alive among us than ever. By exploring KACND's journey of dialogue and peace, it is clear that King Abdullah's vision is reflected in programs that had a tangible impact nationally and internationally, a vision that involved different countries and benefited thousands of people locally and internationally. Saudi Arabia has put forth all these efforts to build bridges of communication, love, and understanding among its people and people of the world. We will never give up on our dream to contribute in building a more beautiful world and creating a better future for our children immersed in love, tolerance and peace through dialogue and reviving the true essence and message of Islam which is *"peace"*.

Notes

1. Hadith refers to all the sayings of Prophet Mohammad.
2. Sakura is a special kind of cherry blossom that grows in Japan only.
3. Shoura *(consultative)* Council is the formal advisory body of Saudi Arabia. Council members are permitted to purpose draft laws, interpret laws, examine annual reports, and advise the King on policies and economic plans.

Epilogue

This collection of essays was inspired by the Spirit of Humanity (SoH) 2014 Forum in Reykjavik, Iceland, which met under the title of 'Love and Compassion in Governance'. When this title was chosen, there was some suggestion that the word "Love" should be omitted, as it was thought it would be unlikely to attract participants, particularly those from the world of politics and business. Nevertheless, the word was kept and the Forum turned out to be of enormous energy and impact, reflecting the love and care that all of those who attended were bringing to their work, including those in politics and the business world.

Since that time, the SoH Forum has become more convinced that it was right to speak of Love, for as these essays have shown a shift in consciousness is underway, and its form is such that it can only be understood in the language of connection, relationship and mutuality—the language of Love.

It is thus reassuring to hear from those who have studied the behaviour of humankind that we are, in truth, *Homo sapiens-amans*, in other words, 'loving animals' and that our concern for the well-being of others, including other people, species and the eco-system, arises naturally from our living in the 'biology of love' because 'love is our natural manner of being' and that love can only be cultivated by living it (Romesin, Verden-Zöller, 2008).

As the book has illustrated, these matters of Love are not so easy to wrestle with, especially at a systemic level, across the disciplinary, cultural and national boundaries. To aspire for governance that is based on connection, relationship and reciprocity requires a return to our true humanness, the loving nature that deeply resides in each of us. In very small ways, the contributors of these essays have managed to do just that, to show that it is possible to break away from the desire for control and the need for domination by being Love in action, and by living our values.

However, despite this new story and the testimony of hope that it offers, there remain many questions concerning the central inquiry to which this book was intended to point. These include the following: Are there key aspects of values-based governance that are universally applicable? What are the practical consequences of following the 'flourishing of all' agenda? How might such an agenda be expressed in terms of the rule of law and accountability? How does values-based governance support social and economic objectives and democratic ends? Does compassionate governance require new forms of organisation and if so what might those new forms be? There are also questions concerning how, in detail, these propositions might be captured in the book be put into practice, for instance, in healthcare and education.

These are questions of central importance, not least to the community of the SoH Forum. The essays in this book give some sense of direction, but more work must be done.

What is now clear is that the answers to the questions can only arise, and are arising, from a necessary shift of consciousness. As the first stanza of the Buddha's *Dhammapada* tells us: 'With our thoughts we make the world'. Finding our way requires, as a pre-condition, that we see the world as it truly is, deeply interconnected, and that we proceed as we truly are, deeply interconnected. For this adventure, Love matters.

References

Adam, B. (2012). 'Convergence for Future Generations' talk given at the 2012 Social Ethics conference, University of Newport, UK, April, 2012.
Addiss, D. G. (2013a). 'Epidemiologic models, key logs, and realizing the promise of WHA 54.19'. *PLoS Negl Trop Dis.* 7(2): e2092. doi:10.1371/journal.pntd.0002092.
Addiss, D. G. (2013b). 'Global elimination of lymphatic filariasis: A mass uprising of compassion', *PLoS Negl Trop Dis.* 7(8): e2264. doi:10.1371/journal.pntd.0002264.
Addiss, D. G. (2014). 'A fresh wind for realizing human potential', *Huffington Post*, 17 April 2014.
Allen, T. J., & Henn, G. (2006). *The Organization and Architecture of Innovation: Managing the Flow of Technology*. New York: Routledge.
Andersen, R.M., Truscott, J.E., Brooker, S. J. & Hollingsworth, T.D. (2013) 'How effective is school-based deworming for community-wide control of soil-transmitted helminths? *PloS Negl Trop Dis* 7(2): e2027. doi:10.1371/journal.pntd.0002027.
Annan, Kofi (1998). *Speech to the World Conference of Ministers Responsible for Youth*, 8 August, 1998.
Armstrong, K. (2006). *The Great Transformation: The World in the Time of Buddha, Socrates, Confucius, and Jeremiah*, London: Atlantic.
Armstrong, K. (2011). *Twelve Steps to a Compassionate Life*. New York: Random House.
Aronson, E., Stephan, C., Sikes, J., Blaney, N., & Snapp, M. (1978). *The Jigsaw Classroom*. Beverly Hills, CA: Sage.
Arthus-Bertrand, Y., & Besson, L. (2009). 'Home', https://archive.org/details/HOME_English
Badiner, A.H, (2002). *Mindfulness in the Marketplace: Compassionate Responses to Consumerism*. Berkeley, CA: Parallax Press.

Batson, D. (2008). *Empathy-Induced Altruistic Motivation*, Inaugural Herzliya Symposium, 2008.
Batson, C. D. (2011). *Altruism in Humans*. New York: Oxford University Press.
Battat, R., Seidman, G., Chadi, N., Chanda, M.Y., Nehme, J., Hulme, J., Li, A., Faridi, N., & Brewer, T. F. (2010). 'Global health competencies and approaches in medical education: A literature review', *BMC Medical Education 10*: 94. http://www.biomedcentral.com 1472-6920/10/94.
Beaglehole, R., & Bonita, R. (2010). 'What is global health?' *Global Health Action 3*: 5142. doi: 10.3402/gha.v3i0.5142.
Beaumier, C. M., Gomez-Rubio, A. M., Hotez, P. J., & Weina, P. J. (2013). 'United States military tropical medicine: Extraordinary legacy, uncertain future'. *PLoS Negl Trop Dis* 7(12): e2448. doi:10.1371/journal.pntd.0002448.
Berry, T. (1999). *The Great Work: Our Way into the Future*. New York: Bell Tower.
Berry, W. (1973). *The Country of Marriage*. New York: Harcourt Brace Jovanovich, Inc.
Bersagel Braley, M. (2014). 'The Christian Medical Commission and the World Health Organization', in Idler, E., ed. *Religion as a Social Determinant of Global Health*. Oxford, UK: Oxford University Press, 298–319.
Biermann, F. (2014) *Earth System Governance: World Politics in the Anthropocene*. Boston, MA: MIT Press.
Biermann, F., Betsill, M. M, Gupta, J., Kanie, N., Lebel, L., Liverman, D., Schroeder, H. & Siebenhüner, B. (2009) Earth System Governance: People, places and the planet. Science and implementation plan of the Earth System Governance Project, Earth System Governance Report 1, IHDP Report 20 Bonn, IHDP: The Earth System Governance Project.
Block, P. (2009). *Community: The Structure of Belonging: Easy Read Comfort Edition*. Oakland, CA: Berrett-Koehler.
Bohm, D. (1990). *On Dialogue*. David Bohm Seminars: Ojai, CA.
Bokova, I. (2013) Speech at the Bejing launch, 'The Hangzhou Declaration: Heralding the next era of human development'. http://www.unesco.org/new/en/unesco/resources/the-hangzhou-declaration-heralding-the-next-era-of-human-development/#sthash.RGbZQ4Lx.DnnI3Rs1.dpuf
Braham, R. L. (2014). 'The assault on the historical memory of the Holocaust', Hungarian Spectrum, 22 March, 2014. http://hungarianspectrum.org/2014/03/22/randolph-l-braham-the-assault-on-the-historical-memory-of-the-holocaust/
Brooks, D. (2014). 'The deepest self', *New York Times,* http://www.nytimes.com/2014/03/14/opinion/brooks-the-deepest-self.html?_r=1
Brown, P. J. (2014). 'Religion and global health', in Idler E., ed. *Religion as a Social Determinant of Global Health*. Oxford, UK: Oxford University Press, 273–97.
Brown, T. M., Cueto, M., & Fee, E. (2006). 'The World Health Organization and the transition from international to global public health', *Am J Public Health* 96: 62–72.
Brunettia, A., & Wederb, B. (2003). 'A free press is bad news for corruption', *Journal of Public Economics* 87(7–8), pp. 1801–1824.

Brysk, A., & Wehrenfennig, D. (2010). 'My brother's keeper'? Inter-ethnic solidarity and human rights. *Studies in Ethnicity and Nationalism, 10*(1), 1–18. doi:10.1111/j.1754-9469.2010.01067.x.

Buber, M. (1970). *I and Thou* (W. Kaufmann, Trans.). New York: Scribner.

Čehajić-Clancy, S., Effron, D. A., Halperin, E., Lieberman, V., & Ross, L. D. (2011). Affirmation, acknowledgment of in-group responsibility, group-based guilt, and support for reparative measures. *Journal of Personality and Social Psychology, 101*(2), 256–270. doi:10.1037/ a0023936.

Cadman, D. (2014). *Love Matters*. Aldborough: Zig Publishing.

Campbell, W. C. (2012). 'History of avermectin and ivermectin, with notes on the history of other macrocyclic lactone antiparasitic agents', *Curr Pharm Biotechnol, 13*: 853–865.

Capra, F. (1997). *The Web of Life: A New Synthesis of Mind and Matter*. London: Flamingo.

Chirot, D., & McCauley, C. (2006). *Why Not Kill Them All: The Logic and Prevention of Mass Political Murder*. Princeton, NJ: Princeton University Press.

Climate Change (2014). https://ipcc-wg2.gov/AR5/images/uploads/WG2AR5_SPM_FINAL.pdf

Comte-Sponville, A. (1996). *A Small Treatise on the Great Virtues*, a Holt Paperback. Climate Change (2014). https://ipcc-wg2.gov/AR5/images/uploads/WG2AR5_SPM_FINAL.pdf

Constitution of the Republic of South Africa, 1996, Preamble. http://www.constitutionalcourt.org.za/site/constitution/english-web/preamble.html

Cornell, S., Prentice, I. C, House, J. I., & Downy, C. J. (eds.). (2012). *Understanding the Earth System: Global Change Science for Application*. Cambridge: Cambridge University Press.

Cuomo, C. (1998) *Feminism and Ecological Communities*. London: Routledge.

Dalai Lama (1992) *Worlds in Harmony: Dialogues on Compassionate Action*. Berkeley, CA: Parallax Press.

Dalai Lama (1999). *Ancient Wisdom, Modern World: Ethics for a New Millennium*. New York: Little, Brown.

Dalai Lama (2000). *Ancient Wisdom, Modern World: Ethics for a New Millennium*. (New Ed.). London: Abacus.

Dalai Lama (2001) *Open Heart*, Hodder and Stoughton.

Dalai Lama (2002). 'Dialogues'. In R. J. Davidson and A. Harrington (eds.), *Visions of Compassion: Western Scientists and Tibetan Buddhists Examine Human Nature*, pp. 90–91, 225–227. New York: Oxford University Press.

Daniel, J. C., and Hicks, K. H. (2014). 'Global health engagement: Sharpening a key tool for the Department of Defense'. *Center for Strategic and International Studies*, 1–14. Washington, DC.

Danieli, Y. (1985). 'The treatment and prevention of long-term effects and intergenerational transmission of victimization: A lesson from Holocaust survivors and their children.' In C. R. Figley (Ed.), *Trauma and Its Wake* (pp. 295–313). New York: Brunner/Mazel.

Darwin (1839). *A Naturalists Voyage Round the World: The Voyage oof the Beagle.*

Davidson, R. J., & Begley, S. (2012). *The Emotional Life of Your Brain: How Its Unique Patterns Affect the Way You Think, Feel, and Live—And How You Can Change Them.* New York: Hudson Street Press.

De Schutter, O. (2014). The transformative potential of the right to food, report to the UN Human Rights Council, UN General Assembly: New York.

Deutsch, M. (1973). *The Resolution of Conflict: Constructive and Destructive Processes.* New Haven, CT: Yale University Press.

Dodge, K. A., Bates, J. E., & Pettit, G. S. (1990). Mechanisms in the cycle of violence. *Science,* 250, 1678–1683.

Dossey, L. (1991). *Meaning and Medicine.* New York: Bantam.

Dossey, L. (1993). *Healing Words.* San Francisco: Harper.

Dunbar, R. (2010). *How Many Friends Does One Person Need?: Dunbar's Number and Other Evolutionary Quirks.* New York: Faber & Faber.

———. (2011): Personal mobility erodes communities. http://www.wired.co.uk/magazine/archive/2011/07/ideas-bank/robin-dunbar.

Edelman (2014). *Edelman Trust Barometer 2014 Annual Global Study,* http://www.edelman.com/insights/intellectual-property/2014-edelman-trust-barometer/about-trust/executive-summary/

Edelman, 2014. *Edelman Trust Barometer 2014 Annual Global Study,* http://www.edelman.com/insights/intellectual-property/2014-edelman-trust-barometer/about-trust/executive-summary/

Eisenberg, N., Fabes, R. A., Spinrad, T. L. (2006). Prosocial development. In W. Damon (Ed.), *Handbook of Child Psychology, Volume 3: Social, Emotional, and Personality Development* (5th ed., pp. 646–718). New York: Wiley.

Eisler, R. (2008). *The Real Wealth of Nations: Creating a Caring Economics.* San Francisco: Barrett-Koehler.

Eliade, M. (1959). *The Sacred and the Profane* (Vol. 11). London: Harcourt Brace Jovanovich.

Elworthy, S. (1996). *Power and Sex: A Book About Women.* Shaftesbury: Element.

Elworthy, S. (2014). *Pioneering the Possible: Awakened Leadership for a World That Works.* Berkeley, CA: North Atlantic Books.

Farley, J. (1991). *Bilharzia: A History of Imperial Tropical Medicine.* New York: Cambridge University Press.

Farmer, P. (2013a). 'Health, healing and social justice: Insights from liberation theology'. In M. Griffin & J. Weiss Block (eds.), *In the Company of the Poor: Conversations with Dr Paul Farmer and Fr. Gustavo Gutierrez,* pp. 35–70. Maryknoll, NY: Orbis Books.

Farmer, P. (2013b). 'Conversion in the time of cholera'. In M. Griffin & J. Weiss Block (eds.), *In the Company of the Poor: Conversations with Dr Paul Farmer and Fr. Gustavo Gutierrez,* pp. 99–145. Maryknoll, NY: Orbis Books.

References

Fein, H. (1979). *Accounting for genocide: Victims and survivors of the Holocaust*. New York, NY: Free Press.

Footprint Network (2015). http://www.footprintnetwork.org/en/index.php/GFN/page/w0rld_footprint/

Foege, B. (2012). A personal communication, Task Force for Global Health, Dectaur, Georgia, April 26, 2012.

Frank, R. H. (1988). *Passions within Reason: The Strategic Role of the Emotions*, p. 236. New York: W. W. Norton & Company.

Frenk, J., & Moon, S. (2013). 'Governance challenges in global health'. *N Engl J Med*, 368: 936–42, doi: 10.1056/NEJMra1109339.

Galtung, J. 1981. 'Social cosmology and the concept of peace', *Journal of Peace Research*, 18(2): 183–199.

Gill, S., & Thomson, G. (2012) *Rethinking Secondary Education: A Human Centred Approach*. London and New York: Pearson, Routledge.

Gladwell, M. (2000). Designs for working. The New Yorker, 11, 60–70.

Gladwell, M. (2006). *The Tipping Point: How Little Things Can Make a Big Difference*. New York: Hachette Digital, Inc.

Goetz, J., Keltner, D., & Simon-Thomas, E. (2010). 'Compassion: An evolutionary analysis and empirical review'. *Psychol Bull*, 136, 351–374.

Goffman, E. (1959). *The Presentation of Self in Everyday Life*. New York: Anchor Books.

Goleman, D. (2007). *Social Intelligence*. New York: Random House.

Gopfert, A., Mohamedbhai, H., Mise, J., Driessen, A., Shakil, A., Fitzmaurice, A., & Graham, W. (2014). 'Do medical students want to learn about global health?' *Glob Health Action* 7: http://dx.doi.org/10.3402/gha.v7.23943

Goshen-Gottstein, A. (ed.) (2014). *The Religious Other: Hostility, Hospitality, and the Hope of Human Flourishing*. London: Lexington Books.

Gostin, L.O. (2012). 'A framework convention for global health: Health for all, justice for all'. *J Am Med Assn, 307*: 2087–2092.

Gostin, L.O. (2014) Global polio eradication: Espionage, disinformation, and the politics of vaccination, *Millbank Q*, 92: 413–417. This was published in line on 9th September 2009 at doi: 10.1111/1468-0009.12065.

Gow, J. (2002). 'The HIV/AIDS epidemic in Africa: Implications for U.S. policy'. *Health Affairs, 21*: 57–69.

Green, D. (2012). *From Poverty to Power: How Active Citizens and Effective States Can Change the World*. New York: Oxfam International.

Griffin, M., & Weiss Block, J. (2014). *In the Company of the Poor: Conversations with Dr. Paul Farmer and Fr. Gustavo Gutierrez*. Maryknoll, NY: Orbis Books.

Gunaratana, B.H. (2001). *Eight Mindful Steps to Happiness: Walking the Buddha's Path*, Wisdom Publications.

Gutierrez, G. (2003). *"We Drink From Our Own Wells': The Spiritual Journey of a People*. Maryknoll, NY: Orbis Books.

Gutierrez, G. (2013). 'Conversion: A requirement for solidarity'. In M. Griffin & J. Weiss Block, *In the Company of the Poor: Conversations with Dr. Paul Farmer and Fr. Gustavo Gutierrez*, pp. 71–93. Maryknoll, NY: Orbis Books.

Habermas, J. (1990). Moral Consciousness and Communicative Action, Polity Press: Cambridge.

Hagelin, J. (2009). 'Can group meditation bring world peace?' YouTube video 4:05 posted by *Transcendental Meditation,* October 6, www.youtube.com/watch?v=yVFa6W tuxu8

Hammack, P. L. (2011). *Narrative and the Politics of Identity: The Cultural Psychology of Israeli and Palestinian Youth.* New York: Oxford University Press.

Hardin, R. (2013). 'Government without trust'. *Journal of Trust Research, 3*(1), pp. 32–52.

Harding, D. (2002). *On Having No Head: Zen and the Rediscovery of the Obvious.* Carlsbad, CA: The Shollard Trust.

Harvey, A. (2012) (3). *Radical Passion.* Berkeley, CA: North Atlantic Books.

Henry, R. & Stobbe, M. (2014). 'American Doctor With Ebola Arrives in Us', *The World Post,* August8, 2014. http://www.huffingtonpost.com/2014/08/02/emerican-doctor-ebola_n_5643628.html

Hill, D. R., Ainsworth, R. M., & Partap, U. (2012). 'Teaching global public health in the undergraduate liberal arts: A survey of 50 colleges'. *Am J Trop Med Hyg 87*: 11–15.

Hungarian spectrum, 22 March.

Hunter, D. J., & Fineberg, H. V. (2014). 'Convergence to common purpose in global health'. *N Engl J Med, 370*: 1753–5. doi: 10.1056/NEJMe1404077

Institute for Economics and Peace (2013). 'Pillars of peace: Understanding the key attitudes and institutions that underpin peaceful societies', Sydney, Australia.

International Council for Science (ICSU) (2013) 'What is earth system science?' www.essp.org (now www.icsu.org/future-earth).

International Institute for Democracy and Electoral Assistance (2004). 'Voter turnout in Western Europe since 1945', http://www.idea.int/publications/voter_turnout_weurope/upload/Full_Reprot.pdf

IPCC 2014, *Summary for Policymakers; Climate Change 2014: Impacts, Adaptation, and Vulnerability. Part A: Global & Sectoral Aspects. Contribution of Working Group II to the First Assessment Report of the Intergovernmental Panel on Climate Change* [Field, C. B., V. R. Barros, D. J. Dokken, J. J. Mach, M. D. Mastrandrea, T. E. Bilir, M. Chatterjee, K. L. Ebi, Y. O. Estrada, R. C. Genova, B. Girma, E. S. Kissel, A. N. Levy, S. MacCracken, P. R. Mastrandrea, and L. L. White (ed)]. New York: Cambridge University Press, pp. 1–32.

IUCN (2013). 'Changes in numbers of species in the threatened categories (CR, UR, VU) from 1996 to 2013 (IUCN Red List Version 2013.1) for the major taxonomic groups on the Red List', table 2, *The IUCN Red List of Threatened Species,* last modified June 8, 2013, www.iucnredlist.org/documents/summary/statistics/2013_1_RL_Stats_Table_2.pdf

Jackson, T. (2009) *Prosperity Without Growth.* London: Earthscan.

References

Jolly, R. (ed.) (2001). *Jim Grant—UNICEF Visionary*. New York: UNICEF.

Kelman, H. C. (1990). 'Applying a human needs perspective to the practice of conflict resolution: The Israeli-Palestinian Case'. In J. Burton (Ed.), *Conflict: Human Needs Theory* (pp. 283–297). New York: St. Martin's Press.

Kerry, V. B., Walensky, R. P., Tsai, A. C., et al. (2013). 'US medical specialty global health training and the global burden of disease'. *J Glob Health 3*(2): 020406.

Keynes, J. M. (1936). *The General Theory of Employment, Interest and Money*. London: Palgrave Macmillan.

King, U. (1989) *The Spirit of One Earth: Reflections on Teilhard de Chardin and Global Spirituality*. New York: Paragon House.

Kiser, M., Jones, D. L., & Gunderson, G. R. (2006). 'Faith and health: Leadership aligning assets to transform communities'. *Internat Rev Mission 95* (376–377), 50–58.

Klimecki, O. M., Leiberg, S., Ricard, M., & Singer, T. (2013). Differential pattern of functional brain plasticity after compassion and empathy training. *Social Cognitive and Affective Neuroscience*. Retrieved from http://scan.oxfordjournals.org/content/early/2013/04/10/scan.nst060.short

Koca, D. (2013). 'CONVERGE Synthesis input' in Parker et al., (2013) CONVERGE *Transdisciplinary Synthesis for Knowledge Transfer*, Bristol, UK: Schumacher Institute.

Konnikova, M. (2014). The Limits of Friendship. New Yorker. http://www.newyorker.com/science/maria-konnikova/social-media-affect-math-dunbar-number-friendships.

Koplan, J. P., Bond, T. C., Merson, M. H., Reddy, K. S., Rodriguez, M. H., Sewankambo, N. K., & Wasserheit, J. N. (2009). 'Towards a common definition of global health'. *Lancet, 373*, 1993–1995.

Kornikova, M. (2014). 'The limits of friendship', *New Yorker*. http://www.newyorker.com/science/maria-konnikova/social-media-affect-math-dunbar-number-friendships

Kristinsdottir S. M., Ragnarsdottir K. V., Davidsdottir D. and the CONVERGE Project Team (2013). The CONVERGE Process. Institutes of Earth Sciences and Sustainable Development, University of Iceland.

Krog, A. (2006). *Body Bereft*. Johannesburg: Umuzi.

Krog, A. (2011) Body Bereft, Cape Town : Random House Struik

Laloux, F. (2014). *Reinventing Organizations: A Guide to Creating Organizations Inspired by the Next Stage of Human Consciousness*. Millis, MA: Parker-Nelson.

Lancet (2009). 'What has the Gates Foundation done for global health'? *Lancet, 373*: 1577.

Landrigan, P. J., Ripp, J., Murphy, R. J. C., Claudio, L., Jao, J., Hexom, B., Bloom, H. G., Shirazian, T., Elahi, E., & Koplan, J. P. (2011). 'New academic partnerships in global health: Innovations at Mount Sinai School of Medicine'. *Mt Sinai J Med., 78*(3): 470–482. doi:10.1002/msj.20257.

Larson, J. S. (1996). 'The World Health Organization's definition of health: Social versus spiritual health'. *Social Indicators Research, 38* (2): 181–192.

Latour, B, & Weibel, P. (eds.) (2005). *Making Things Public: Atmospheres of Democracy.* Cambridge, MA: The MIT Press.

Layard, R. (2006). Happiness and public policy: A challenge to the profession. *The Economics Journal, 116* (510), C24–33.

Lederach, J. P. (2005). *The Moral Imagination: The Art and Soul of Building Peace.* New York: Oxford University Press.

Leenerts, M. H., Koehler, J. A., & Neil, R. M. (1996). 'Nursing care model increases care quality while reducing costs'. *Journal of Association of Nurses in AIDS Care, 7* (4), 37–49.

Levinas, E. (1969). *Totality and Infinity.* Pittsburgh, PA: Duquesne University. 14th printing.

Lieberfeld, D. (2009). Lincoln, Mandela, and qualities of reconciliation-oriented leadership. *Peace and Conflict: Journal of Peace Psychology, 15,* 27–47.

Lieberman, M. D. (2013). *Social: Why Our Brains Are Wired to Connect.* New York: Oxford University Press.

Ligon, G. S., Hunter, S. T., & Mumford, M. D. (2008). 'Development of outstanding leadership: A life narrative approach'. *The Leadership Quarterly, 19* (3), 312–334.

Macfarlane, S. B., Jacobs, M., & Kaaya, E. E. (2008). 'In the name of global health: trends in academic institutions'. *J Public Health Policy, 29,* 383–401.

Macy, J. (1988). 'Taking heart: Spiritual exercises for social activists'. In Eppsteiner, F. (ed.), *The Path of Compassion,* p. 203. Berkeley, CA: Parallax Press.

Macy, J. (1991). '*World as Lover, World as Self*'. Berkeley, CA: Parallax Press.

Magona. S. (2012). *From Robben Island to Bishopscourt: The Biography of Archbishop Njongonkulu Ndungane.* Cape Town, SA: New Africa Books.

Maguen, S., Metzler, A. J., Litz, B. T., Seal, K. H., Knight, S. J., & Marmar, C. R. (2009). The impact of killing in war on mental health symptoms and related functioning. *Journal of Traumatic Stress, 22* (5), 435–443. doi:10.1002/jts.20451.

Makgoba, T. (2011). Address delivered at the Red-Card Corruption Pledge Convention, August 31, 2011. The Council for the Advancement of the South African Constitution. http://www.casac.org.za/?news

Makgoba, T. (2014). To the Laos—The church reclaims her prophetic vocation—April 2014. http://archbishop.anglicanchurchsa.org/2014_04_01_archive.html

Makgoba, T. (2014a). Address to a 'Procession of Witness' to Parliament, April 19, 2015: http://archbishop.anglicanchurchsa.org/2014/04/archbishop-thabo-makgobas-address-to.html

Makgoba, T. (2014b). South Africa's New Struggle - Beyers Naude Memorial Lecture, 27 October 2014: http://archbishop.anglicanchurchsa.org/2014/10/south-africas-new-struggle-beyers-naude.html

Makgoba, T. (2014, December 28). 'Make change happen for good of all'. *Sunday Independent,* Johannesburg, December 28, 2014, p. 14.

Makgoba, T. (2015). 'It is time for the new struggle'. *Sunday Independent,* Johannesburg, January 11, 2015. http://www.iol.co.za/sundayindependent/it-is-time-for-the-new-struggle-1.1804316

Mandela, Nelson (2000). Address on receiving the Freedom Award of the National Civil Rights Museum, 22 November 2000.

Manji, F., & O'Coill, C. (2002). 'The missionary position: NGOs and development in Africa'. *International Affairs, 7*, 567–583.

Margulis, L., & Sagan, D. (2002) *Acquiring Genomes: A Theory of the Origin of Species.* New York: Basic Books.

Marmot, M., & Wilkinson, R. G. (2006). *Social Determinants of Health*, 2nd ed. New York: Oxford University Press.

Maslow, A. H. (1971). *The Farther Reaches of Human Nature.* New York: Viking.

McCoy, D., Chand, S., & Sridhar, D. (2009). 'Global health funding: how much, where it comes from and where it goes', *Health Policy and Planning, 24*, 407–417, doi:10.1093/heapol/czp026.

McLurcan. D. & Hinton, J. (2015). *How on Earth: What If Not-for-profit Enterprise Were at the Heart of the Global Economy by 2050?* White River Junction, VT: Chelsea Green.

McNair, R. M. (2002). *Perpetration-induced Traumatic Stress.* London: Praeger.

McNeill, D. P., Morrison, D. A., & Nouwen, H. J. M. (1982). *Compassion: A Reflection on the Christian Life.* Garden City, NY: Doubleday & Company.

McTaggart, L. (2001). *The Field.* Shaftesbury: Element, p. 125.

Mectizan Donation Program (2014). 'Onchocerciasis treatments approved'. Available from: http://www.mectizan.org/achievements/onchocerciasis-treatments-approved

Merson, M. H (2014). 'University engagement in global health'. *N Engl J Med 370*: 1676–1678.

Meyer, A. (2000). *Contraction and Convergence: The Global Solution to Climate Change,* Cambridge: Schumacher Briefing, Green Books.

Millis, D. M. (2013). *Conversation, the Sacred Art: Practicing Presence in an Age of Distraction.* Woodstock, VT: SkyLight Paths Publishing.

Mischel, W. (2014). *The Marshmallow Test: Mastering Self-Control.* New York: Little, Brown and Company.

Mitchell, E. Institute of Noetic Sciences. http://www.noetic.org/about/history

Mohammed, M., & Thomas, K. (2014). 'Enabling community and trust: Shared leadership for collective creativity.' *The Foundation Review, 6* (4), Article 10.

Monaghan, A. (2014). 'Shadow banking system a growing risk to financial stability–IMF', *The Guardian*, 1 October.

Mwenda, S. (2011). 'The Africa Christian Health Associations platform: Showcasing the contributions of CHAs'. *Contact, 190*, 2.

Nagase, M. (2012). 'Does a multi-dimensional concept of health include spirituality? Analysis of Japan Health Science Council's discussions on WHO's 'definition of health' (1998)'. *International Journal of Applied Sociology, 2* (6): 71–77, doi:10.5923/j.ijas.20120206.03.

Nagel, T. (1970). *The Possibility of Altruism*, Princeton University Press, 77.

National Development Plan 2030. 2012. *Republic of South Africa, 2012.* http://www.gov.za/issues/national-development-plan-2030

New Economics Foundation (2004). A wellbeing manifesto for a flourishing society www.neweconomics.org/gen/z-sys_publicationdetail.aspx?pid=193

Newman, M. A., Sime, A. M., & Corcoran-Perry, S. A. (1991). 'The focus of the discipline of nursing'. *Advances in Nursing Science, 14*, 1–6.

Nicole, W. (2014). 'Seeing the forest for the trees: How "one health" connects humans, animals, and ecosystems'. *Environ Health Perspect, 122* (5): A122–A129.

Noor, M., Brown, R., Gonzalez, R., Manzin, J., & Lewis, C. A. (2008). 'On positive psychological outcomes: What helps groups with a history of conflict to forgive and reconcile with each other'? *Personality and Social Psychology Bulletin, 14* (6), 819–833. doi:10.1177/ 0146167208315555.

NPR (2011) *Don't Believe Facebook; You Only Have 150 Friends*. http://www.npr.org/2011/06/04/136723316/dont-believe-facebook-you-only-have-150-friends.

Nowak, M., & Highfield, R. (2011). *SuperCooperators* (Reprint.), pp. 271–272 and 280. New York: Free Press.

Page 127, para 2, NPR (2011) Don't Believe Facebook; You Only Have 150 Friends. http://www.npr.org/2011/06/04/136723316/dont-believe-facebook-you-only-have-150-friends.

O'Connell, M. H. (2009). *Compassion: Loving Our Neighbor in an Age of Globalization*. Maryknoll, NY: Orbis Books.

Omar, R. (2013). *Interfaith Reflections on the Fight Against Corruption*. Cape Town: Religious Leaders Forum.

Oxfam International (October 2014). New York: Oxfam GB International.

Paine, T. (1856). *The Political Writings of Thomas Paine*. Boston: J. P. Mendum.

Palmer, M. & Wagner, K. (2013). ValuesQuest: The search for values that will make a world of difference, Club of Rome: Zurich.

Palmer, P. J. (1987). 'Community, conflict, and ways of knowing: Ways to deepen our educational agenda'. *Change: The Magazine of Higher Learning, 19* (5), 20–25.

Palmer, P. J. (1990). *The Active Life: A Spirituality of Work, Creativity, and Caring*. San Francisco, CA: Harper & Row.

Palmer, P. J. (2004). *A Hidden Wholeness: The Journey Toward an Undivided Life*. John Wiley & Sons.

Palmer, P. J. (2009). *A Hidden Wholeness: The Journey Toward an Undivided Life*. New York: John Wiley & Sons.

Paluck, E. L. (2009). 'Reducing intergroup prejudice and conflict using the media: A field experiment in Rwanda'. *Journal of Personality and Social Psychology, 96*, 574–587. doi:10.1037/a0011989.

Parker, J. (2010). 'Care in the global system' in *Interdisciplinarity and Climate Change: Transforming Knowledge and Practice for Our Global Future*, R. Bhaskar, C. Frank, K-G. Hoyer & P. Naess (eds.). London: Routledge.

Parker, J. (2014) *Critiquing Sustainability, Changing Philosophy*, London: Routledge.

References

Pascale, R. T., Sternin, J., & Sternin, M. (2010). *The Power of Positive Deviance: How Unlikely Innovators Solve the World's Toughest Problems* (Vol. 1). Cambridge, MA: Harvard Business Press.

Patterson, G. (1998). 'The CMC story: 1968–1998', *Contact* (161–162): 3.

Pearlman, L.A. (2013). 'Restoring self in community: Collective approaches to psychological trauma after genocide'. *Journal of Social Issues*, 69, 111–124.

Peck, M. S. (1987). *The Different Drum: The Creation of True Community—The First Step to World Peace*. Liverpool: Arrow.

Piketty, T. & Goldhammer, A. (2014). *Capital in the Twenty-First Century*, Harvard University Press.

Pinker, S. (2012). *The Better Angels of Our Nature: Why Violence Has Declined*. New York: Penguin.

Pinker, S. (2014). *The Village Effect: How Face-to-face Contact Can Make Us Healthier, Happier, and Smarter*. New York: Random House LLC.

Plumwood, V. (1993) *Feminism and the Mastery of Nature*. London: Routledge.

Poole, R. (1991) *Morality and Modernity*. London: Routledge.

Post, S. G. (2003). *Unlimited Love: Altruism, Compassion, and Service*, p. vi. West Conshohocken, PA: Templeton Foundation Press.

Puchalski, C., Ferrell, B., Virani, R., Otis-Green, S., Baird, P., Bull, J., Chochinov, H., Handzo, G., Nelson-Becker, H., Prince-Paul, M., Pugliese, K., & Sulmasy, D. (2009). 'Improving the quality of spiritual care as a dimension of palliative care: The report of the Consensus Conference'. *J Palliat Med*, *12* (10), 885–904. doi: 10.1089/jpm.2009.0142.

Putnam, R. D. (2000). *Bowling Alone: The Collapse and Revival of American Community*. New York: Simon and Schuster.

Ray, G. (2013). 'The ocean is broken', *Newcastle Herald* (Australia), www.theherald.com.au/story/1848433/the-ocean-is-broken

Reeler, B. (2013). 'Tarisiro' email to author.

Reifenberg, S. (2013). Afterword in M. Griffin & J. Weiss Block (eds.). *In the Company of the Poor: Conversations with Dr Paul Farmer and Fr. Gustavo Gutierrez*, pp. 180–197. Maryknoll, NY: Orbis Books.

Rhodes, R. (1999). *Why They Kill*. New York: Knopf.

Ricard, M. (2006). *Happiness: A Guide to Developing Life's Most Important Skill*. New York: Little, Brown and Company.

Ricard, M. (2015). *Altruism: The Power of Compassion to Change Yourself and the World*. New York: Little, Brown and Company.

Ricard, M., Lutz, A., & Davidson, R. J. (2014). Mind of the meditator. *Scientific American*, *311* (5), 38–45. doi:10.1038/scientificamerican1114-38.

Ricard, M. (2015). *Altruism: The Power of Compassion to Change the World*, Atlantic Books.

Richerson, P. J., & Boyd, R. (2004) *Not by Genes Alone: How Culture Transformed Human Evolution*. Chicago: University of Chicago Press.

Rignot, E., Velicogna, I., Broeke, M. R., Monaghan, A., & Lenaerts, J. T. (2011). 'Acceleration of the contribution of the Greenland and Antarctic ice sheets to sea level rise'. *Geographical Research Letters 38*, no. 5, 2011: doi:10.1029/2011GL046583.
Rockström, J., & Klum, M. (2012). *The Human Quest: Prospering Within Planetary Boundaries*. Stockholm: Bokförlaget Langenskiöld.
Rogers, M. E. (1970). *An Introduction to the Theoretical Basis of Nursing*. Philadelphia, PA: FA Davis.
Rogers, M. E. (1992). 'Nursing science and the space age'. *Nursing Science Quarterly, 5*, 27–34.
Rogers, M. E. (1994). 'The science of unitary human beings: Current perspectives'. *Nursing Science Quarterly. 2*, 33–35.
Romesin, H. M., & Verden-Zöller, G. (2008). *The Origin of Humanness in the Biology of Love*, ed. P. Bunnel. Charlottesville, VA: Imprint Academic.
Romesin, H. M., & Verden-Zöller, G. (2012). *The Origin of Humanness in the Biology of Love*. N.p.: Andrews UK Limited.
Roosevelt, F. D. (1937). *Second Inaugural Address, January 20, 1937*. The Franklin D. Roosevelt Presidential Library and Museum.
Rose-Ackerman, S. (2013). *Corruption: A Study in Political Economy*. Waltham, MA: Academic Press.
Royal Society (2009). 'Geo-engineering the climate: science, governance and uncertainty', RS Policy document 10/09, Royal Society.
Sachs, J. D. (2008). *Common Wealth: Economics for a Crowded Planet*. New York: Penguin Press.
Sagi, A. (2002). *Albert Camus and the Philosophy of the Absurd*, Editions Rodopi BV, 170.
Sandow, D., & Allen, A. M. (2005). 'The nature of social collaboration: How work really gets done'. *Reflections: The SoL Journal, 6* (2–3), 2–3.
Schippa, C. (2012). 'Iceland's resilience offers guidance to Europe', *Financial Times*, 2 September 2012 http://www.ft.com/cms/s/0/a9671762-f385-11e1-b3a2-00144feabdc0.html#axzz3TwB2FdH0
Siegel, D. J. (2010). *Mindsight: The New Science of Personal Transformation*. New York: Bantam.
Sitzman, K., & Watson, J. (2014). *Caring Science, Mindful Practice. Implementing Watson's Human Caring Theory*. New York: Springer.
Snower, D. J. (2014). http://www.global-economic-symposium.org/symposium-2014/news/opening-address-ges-2014-dennis-j.-snower
Staub, E. (1989). *The Roots of Evil: The Origins of Genocide and Other Group Violence*. New York: Cambridge University Press.
Staub, E. (1998). 'Breaking the cycle of genocidal violence: Healing and reconciliation'. In J. Harvey (Ed.). *Perspectives on Loss* (pp. 231–238). Washington, DC: Taylor & Francis.

References

Staub, E. (2003). *The Psychology of Good and Evil: Why Children, Adults and Groups Help and Harm Others*. New York: Cambridge University Press. doi:10.1017/CBO9780511615795.

Staub, E. & Bar–Tal, D. (2003). *Genocide, mass killing and intractable conflict: roots, evolution, prevention and reconciliation*. In D. Sears, L. Huddy, and R. Jervis (Eds.), Handbook of political psychology. New York: Oxford University Press.

Staub, E. (2005). 'The roots of goodness: The fulfillment of basic human needs and the development of caring, helping and nonaggression, inclusive caring, moral courage, active bystandership, and altruism born of suffering". In G. Carlo & C. Edwards (Eds.), *Nebraska Symposium on Motivation: Vol. 51. Moral Motivation Through the Life Span: Theory, Research, Applications* (pp. 33–72). Lincoln: University of Nebraska Press.

Staub, E. (2006). 'Reconciliation after genocide, mass killing or intractable conflict: Understanding the roots of violence, psychological recovery and steps toward a general theory'. *Political Psychology, 27* (6), 867– 894. doi:10.1111/j.1467-9221.2006.00541.x.

Staub, E. (2011). *Overcoming Evil: Genocide, Violent Conflict and Terrorism*. New York: Oxford University Press.

Staub, E. (2013). 'Building a peaceful society: Origins, prevention, and reconciliation after genocide and other group violence'. *American Psychologist, 68* (7), 576–589.

Staub, E. (2014a). 'Reconciliation between groups: Preventing (new) violence and improving lives". In Deutsch, M., & Coleman, P. *The Handbook of Conflict Resolution: Theory and Practice*. 3rd Edition. San Francisco: Jossey-Bass Publishers.

Staub, E. (2014b). 'The challenging road to reconciliation in Rwanda: Societal processes, interventions and their evaluation'. *Journal of Social and Political Psychology, 2* (1), 505–517, doi:10.5964/jspp.v2i1.294.

Staub, E. (2015). *The Roots of Goodness and Resistance to Evil: Inclusive Caring, Moral Courage, Altruism Born of Suffering, Active Bystandership and Heroism*. New York: Oxford University Press.

Staub, E., & Pearlman, L.A. (2006). Advancing healing and reconciliation. In Barbanel, L., & Sternberg, R. (Eds). *Psychological Interventions in Times of Crisis*. New York: Springer Verlag.

Staub, E., & Pearlman, L. A. (2009). 'Reducing intergroup prejudice and conflict: A commentary'. *Journal of Personality and Social Psychology, 96,* 588–593. doi:10.1037/a0014045.

Staub, E., & Vollhardt, J. (2008). 'Altruism born of suffering: The roots of caring and helping after experiences of personal and political victimization'. *American Journal of Orthopsychiatry, 78,* 267–280. doi: 10.1037/a0014223.

Staub, E., Pearlman, L. A., Gubin, A., & Hagengimana, A. (2005). 'Healing, reconciliation, forgiving and the prevention of violence after genocide or mass killing: An intervention and its experimental evaluation in Rwanda'. *Journal of Social and Clinical Psychology, 24* (3), 297–334. doi:10.1521/jscp.24.3.297.65617.

Strang, H., Sherman, L., Angel, C. M., Woods, D. J., Bennett, S., Newbury-Birch, D., & Inkpen, N. (2006). 'Victim evaluations of face-to-face restorative justice conferences: A quasi-experimental analysis'. *Journal of Social Issues*, 62, 281–306. doi:10.1111/j.1540-4560.2006.00451.x.

Tarnas, R. (1991). *The Passion of the Western Mind: Understanding the Ideas That Have Shaped Our World View*, New York: Ballantine.

Task Force for Global Health (2011). Compassion in global health. Richard Stanley Productions, http://www.taskforce.org/press-room/videos/compassion-global-health-video

TEEB (2010). The Economics of Ecosystems and Biodiversity, http://www.teebweb.org/Portals/25/TEEB%20Synthesis/TEEB_SynthReport_09_2010_online.pdf accessed 1.8.2012.

Tom Crompton et al., (2010). *Common Cause: The case for working with our cultural values*, September 2010. http://assets.wwf.org.uk/downloads/commom_cause_report_pdf

Thomson, G. (1987). *Needs*. New York: Routledge.

Thomson, G. (2002). *On the Meaning of Life*. Boston: Wadsworth.

Tolle, E. (2005). *A New Earth: Awakening to Your Life's Purpose*, New York: Penguin.

Uhl, C. (2003). *Developing Ecological Consciousness: Paths to a Sustainable Future*. Lanham, MD: Rowman & Littlefield Publishers.

UNESCO (2007). *Philosophy: A School of Freedom*, UNESCO: Paris. http://unesdoc.unesco.org/images/0015/001541/154173E.pdf

UNGA (2013). 'A life of dignity for all: accelerating progress towards the Millennium Development Goals and advancing the United Nations development agenda beyond 2015'. *Report of the Secretary-General*, UNGA Report, 26 July.

Uniting to Combat Neglected Tropical Diseases (2014). *Delivering on Promises and Driving Progress*. 46pp. http://unitingtocombatntds.org/sites/default/files/document/NTD_report_04102014_v4_singles.pdf

Valent, P. (1998). 'Child survivors: A review'. In J. Kestenberg & C. Kahn (Eds.), *Children Surviving Persecution: An International Study of Trauma and Healing*. Westport, CT: Praeger.

Values and Frames (2015). 'Common cause', *The Case for Working with Values and Frames*', retrieved from http://valuesandframes.org/

Vanier, J. (1989). *Community and Growth*. Mahwah, NJ: Paulist Press.

Varshney, A. (2002). *Ethnic Conflict and Civic Life: Hindus and Muslims in India*. New Haven, CT: Yale University Press.

Vitello, P. (2012). 'Steve Ben Israel, 74, a living theater performance artist', *The New York Times*, 17 June, p. A22.

Volkan, V. D. (2001). 'Transgenerational transmissions and chosen traumas: An aspect of large group identity'. *Group Analysis*, 34, 79–97. doi:10.1177/05333160122077730.

Vollhardt, J. R., & Staub, E. (2011). 'Inclusive altruism born of suffering: The relationship between adversity and prosocial attitudes and behavior toward disadvantaged outgroups'. *American Journal of Orthopsychiatry, 81* (3), 307–315. doi:10.1111/j.1939-0025.2011 .01099.x.

Walsh, R. N. (1999). *Essential Spirituality: The 7 Central Practices to Awaken Heart and Mind.* Hoboken, NJ: John Wiley.

Warneken, F., & Tomasello, M. (2006). 'Altruistic helping in human infants and young chimpanzees'. *Science, 311* (5765), 1301.

Watson, J. (1979). *Nursing. The Philosophy and Science of Caring.* Boulder, CO: University Press of Colorado.

Watson, J. (2005). *Caring Science as Sacred Science.* Philadelphia: FA Davis.

Watson, J. (2008). *Nursing. The Philosophy and Science of Caring. New Revised edition.* Boulder, CO: University Press of Colorado.

Watson, J. (2010). *Postmodern Nursing and Beyond.* Boulder, CO: Watson Caring Science Institute.

Watson, J. (2014a). 'Social/moral justice from a caring science cosmology'. In P. N. Kagan, M. C. Smith, & P. L. Chinn, (eds.), *Philosophies and Practices of Emancipatory Nursing: Social Justice in Praxis.* New York: Routledge.

Watson, J. (2014b). 'Integrative nursing: Caring science, human caring, and peace'. In M. J. Kreitzer & M. Koithan (eds.), *Integrative Nursing*, pp. 101–108. New York: Oxford University Press.

Weiss, E. (1989). *In Fairness to Future Generations: International Law, Common Patrimony, and Intergenerational Equity.* Washington, DC: Transnational Publication and the United Nations University.

WHO (1978). 'Declaration of Alma-Ata. International Conference on Primary Health Care'. *WHO Chron, 32* (11): 428–30.

WHO (2006). *World Health Report 2006,* Geneva, Switzerland: WHO, pp 1–17.

WHO (2010). *First WHO Report on Neglected Tropical Diseases: Working to Overcome the Global Impact of Neglected Tropical Diseases,* Geneva, Switzerland: WHO.

WHO. Preamble to the Constitution of the World Health Organization as adopted by the International Health Conference, New York, 19-22 June, 1946; signed on 22 July 1946 by the representatives of 61 States (Official Records of the World Health Organization, no. 2, p. 100) and entered into force on 7 April 1948.

Wijkman, A., & Rockstrom, J. (2012). *Bankrupting Nature: Denying Our Planetary Boundaries.* London: Routledge.

Wilkinson, R. and Pickett, K. (2010). *The Spirit Level: Why More Equal Societies Always do Better,* Penguin.

Wolpe, H., & McDonald, S. (2008). 'Democracy and peace building: Rethinking the conventional wisdom'. *The Round Table, 97* (394), 137–145. doi:10.1080/00358530 701844742.

Worthington, E. L. Jr., & Drinkard, D. T. (2000). 'Promoting reconciliation through psychoeducational and therapeutic interventions'. *Journal of Marital and Family Therapy, 26,* 93–101.

WWF Global–Living Planet Index (n.d.) http://wwf.panda.org/about_our_earth/all_publications/living_planet_index2/, www.who.int/about/definition/en/print.html

Yardley, W. (November 6, 2013). 'Clifford Nass, who warned of a data deluge, dies at 55', *New York Times*, http://www.nytimes.com/2013/11/07/business/clifford-nass-researcher-on-multitasking-dies-at-55.html?_r=0

Zander, R. S., & Zander, B. (2000). *The Art of Possibility: Transforming Professional and Personal Life*. New York: Penguin.

Ziegler, M. (2010). A soap opera for peace in Rwanda. *Peace Magazine*. Retrieved from http://peacemagazine.org/archive/v26n4p16a.htm, October–December.

Contributors

David G. Addiss is studied public health at The Johns Hopkins University. He co-founded and co-directed the World Health Organization's Collaborating Center for Control and Elimination of Lymphatic Filariasis in the Americas. In 2006, David joined the Fetzer Institute in Kalamazoo, Michigan, where he directed a research program in science and spirituality. He taught global health and epidemiology at Kalamazoo College, where he was a Fellow at the Arcus Center for Social Justice Leadership. David is currently Director of Children Without Worms (CWW), based at the Task Force for Global Health in Decatur, Georgia, USA. In 2014, David completed a Buddhist chaplaincy training program at Upaya Zen Center, Santa Fe, New Mexico, USA, and was ordained a lay minister. He co-founded the Center for Compassion and Global Health.

Fatima Al-Bishri is an interpreter and Programme Supervisor at King Abdulaziz Center for National Dialogue (KACND). She is interested in women empowerment and cultural dialogue. In 2008, Fatima was co-founder of the Ambassador Program for Cross Cultural Dialogue. Since then (7 years) she has been responsible for organizing and running cross-cultural workshops in an aim to open up channels of communication between Saudis and non-Saudis; among women in particular. In 2011, she was nominated among the top twenty youth leaderships in the Kingdom. In 2013, Fatima worked with the UNESCO in organizing the Youth Conference for Volunteering and Dialogue. She has also participated lately in organizing national meetings for women held by KACND in many regions around Saudi Arabia tackling topics concerning the Saudi society including extremism and national unity.

Amal y. al-Moallimi is the Head of female branch at King Abdul Aziz Center for National Dialogue (KACND), and a member of the International Dialogue team. She is a Fellow at the Oxford Centre for Islamic Studies, United Kingdom and has 21 years of experience working in the field of education, training and social development. As a certified Consultant for the Family Dialogue Program and Master Trainer in communication skills, a certified trainer for "Developing Thinking Skills" from Saudi Ministry of Education and Consultant in T.V. production for dialogue programs in Saudi Channel One television, Amal has trained nearly 5,000 people on communication skills and cultural dialogue and conducted several studies in social, educational and cultural dialogue fields. Amal is a member of several of charities and local committees.

Scilla Elworthy is a peace builder and the founder of the Oxford Research Group, a non-governmental organisation she set up in 1982 to develop effective dialogue between nuclear weapons policy-makers worldwide and their critics, for which she was nominated three times for the Nobel Peace Prize. She served as its executive director from 1982 until 2003, when she left that role to set up Peace Direct, a charity supporting local peace-builders in conflict areas. In 2003 she was awarded the Niwano Peace Prize. From 2005 she was adviser to Peter Gabriel, Desmond Tutu and Richard Branson in setting up The Elders. She is a member of the World Future Council and in 2012 co-founded Rising Women Rising World, a growing, vibrant community of women on all continents who take responsibility for building a world that works for all.

Kul Chandra Gautam is a distinguished international civil servant, development professional, public policy expert, and human rights activist. He was Deputy Executive Director of UNICEF and Assistant Secretary-General of the United Nations. Currently, Kul informally advises Nepal's senior political and civil society leadership on the peace process, consolidation of democracy and socio-economic development. He also serves on the boards of a number of international and national foundations, charitable organizations and public private partnerships. Kul also served as Special Advisor to the Prime Minister of Nepal on International Affairs and the Peace Process. Internationally, he is Chair of the Council of the World Day of Prayer and Action for Children (Japan/USA); Chair of the Audrey Hepburn Children's Fund (USA); an International Trustee of Religions for Peace (USA); South Asia Food and Nutrition Security Initiative (World Bank), amongst other chairmanships.

Heiða Kristín Helgadóttir is an Icelandic politician. She was the Campaign Manager for the Best Party which won in the Mayor's election and served as General Manager of the Best Party in 2010–2014. She was the

National Committee Chairman of the Bright Future party 2012–14 and the Vice-Chairman for the Welfare Committee of Reykjavik. Heiða is a Freelance Columnist and Public Speaker and is currently TV Presenter of the 365 Broadcasting Corporation. She also writes and edits articles on socio-political issues for local newspapers and online media in Iceland and give talks and presentations on feminist-based approaches and leadership within the contingent nature of contemporary politics. She is on the board of various Icelandic companies and organizations.

Dadi Janki is the Spiritual Head of the Brahma Kumaris World Spiritual University (BKWSU). She joined the BKWSU as a founding member in 1937 at the age of 21. In the 1950s she established numerous BK centres throughout India. In 1974 she established the first BK centre outside of India, in London, UK. Under her guidance and inspiration, centres now exist in 110 countries. Dadi Janki's uniqueness lies in her unswerving optimism and a heart that is rich with compassion. She has redefined the concept of freedom in the West by placing it within the context of the ancient wisdom of the East. Internationally acknowledged as a great teacher and mentor, she continues to offer inspiration to many people who are searching for peace and harmony in their heart and in their homeland.

Polly Higgins is a barrister, author and international environmental lawyer advocating a different approach to preventing the destruction of our planet. Voted by the Ecologist as one of the 'World's Top 10 Visionary Thinkers' for her earlier work advancing the Universal Declaration of Planetary Rights, Polly has submitted a second proposal to the United Nations: the Crime of Ecocide. She argues that ecocide is a 5th Crime Against Peace, yet to be recognised alongside Genocide, Crimes Against Humanity, War Crimes and Crimes of Aggression. Polly was nominated 'The Planet's Lawyer' by the 2010 Performance Awards, has been named one of the top 'unreasonable people' in the world by the cult US online magazine Planet Green for refusing to accept the norm. She has been hailed by the *Guardian* as one of their Green Heroes working for the right kind of environmental change. Polly is author of *Eradicating Ecocide* (Shepheard-Walwyn, 2010).

Steve Killelea is an accomplished entrepreneur who dedicates most of his time and fortune to sustainable development and peace. Steve founded Integrated Research Ltd, one of Australia's leading software companies. In 2000, he established The Charitable Foundation, one of the largest private overseas aid organizations in Australia. In 2007 Steve founded the Institute for Economics and Peace, an international think tank dedicated to building a greater understanding of the interconnection between business, peace and economics with particular emphasis on the economic benefits of peace. Steve currently serves on a number of influential Company Boards, Advisory Boards and President Councils. In 2010 he was honoured as Member of the Order of Australia for his service to the global peace movement and the provision of humanitarian aid to the developing world. In 2013 Steve was nominated one of the "Top 100 Most Influential People in Armed Violence Reduction" by the UK group Action on Armed Violence.

The Most Revd. Dr Thabo Makgoba has served as the Anglican Archbishop of Cape Town, and Metropolitan (that is, head) of the Anglican Church of Southern Africa, since January 2008. He is the youngest person elected to this office. In 2008 he was decorated by the Archbishop of Canterbury, Dr. Rowan Williams, with the Cross of St Augustine for his role within the Anglican Communion. He is currently the chair of the Anglican Communion Environmental Network. In 2009 Dr Makgoba received the degree of Doctor of Divinity, honoris causa, from the General Theological Seminary (of the Episcopal Church) in New York City and in 2013 Huron University College, London, Ontario Doctor of Divinity, jure dignitatis. Later in 2009 he earned a PhD from the University of Cape Town, for a thesis on *Spirituality in the South African Mining Workplace* (published in 2012). He received the Ernest Oppenheimer Memorial Trust Scholarship to support this research. In February 2012 he was inaugurated as the Chancellor of the University of the Western Cape.

Derek Masselink is an ecologist, designer, educator and community animator. He is founder and lead curator of ŦELÁNET Centre for Innovation and Peace, a positive place-based, change-focused organization located in the Salish Sea on the northwest coast of North America. He is an Associate Faculty Member in the School of Environment and Sustainability at Royal Roads University, teaching and working in the areas of transformative leadership and governance for sustainability. In 2014, Derek was re-elected as a local trustee with the Islands Trust on North Pender Island under the banner of the Bright Future Party—an electoral organization that he founded and now leads. Derek grew up on the west coast and interior of British Columbia, Canada. He currently lives, works and farms with his family on North Pender Island, British Columbia.

Mohammed H. Mohammed is a program officer at the Fetzer Institute, Michigan, USA. He has worked in the area of philanthropic programmatic management as well as corporate research developing new technologies and business models before transitioning to his current role. His trainings straddle human-computer interaction, anthropology, design, and the humanities. He also has experience in international development and social innovation.

Jenneth Parker is the Research Director at the Schumacher Institute. She received Msc from London School of Economics in Philosophy and an interdisciplinary DPhil from the University of Sussex drawing on ethics, philosophy of science and social movement theory to discuss eco-feminist ethics for sustainability. She has recently worked with the University of Bristol QUEST Earth System Science climate change team on interdisciplinary synthesis and as a researcher on the EU-funded CONVERGE project. She is a former Co-Director of the international Education for Sustainability distance learning Masters programme set up by NGOs after the first Earth Summit in 1992 at London South Bank University, and has worked on the African Commonwealth Scholars programme.

Matthieu Ricard was born in France and studied classical music, ornithology and photography. He received a PhD. in cellular genetics at the Institut Pasteur under Nobel Laureate François Jacob. After that, Matthieu decided to forsake his scientific career and concentrate on Tibetan Buddhist studies. He has lived in the Himalayas since 1972 and has been a Buddhist monk for 37 years at the Shechen Monastery in Nepal. Since 1989 he has accompanied HH Dalai Lama to France, acting as his personal interpreter. He has been awarded the French National Order of Merit for his involvement and his efforts to preserve the Himalayan cultures. Matthieu is a bestselling author, has translated and edited numerous books on Tibetan Buddhism and is highly praised for his vast knowledge of Tibetan religion and culture.

Ervin Staub is a Professor of Psychology Emeritus at the University of Massachusetts, Amherst, and Founding Director of its PhD program in the Psychology of Peace and Violence. He received his PhD at Stanford, taught at Harvard and was a visiting professor at Stanford, the University of Hawaii, and the London School of Economic and Political Science. He has worked in many real-world settings, including Rwanda, Burundi and the Congo on reconciliation, with the L.A. police to reduce the use of unnecessary force, in schools to raise caring and non-violent children. He was also President of the International Society for Political Psychology and of the Society for the Study of Peace, Conflict and Violence. Ervin is the author of many books.

Kurian Thomas is a program officer at the Fetzer Institute, Michigan, USA. His work combines philosophical understanding and practical applicability for human development. Over the past 15 years, Kurian has worked in many countries with practitioners, researchers, and policy makers. Previously, Kurian was associated with Oxfam based in Hong Kong as the focal person for program quality and accountability. Kurian has also served as the Adviser for Learning and Impact at Save the Children UK, and as Knowledge Manager with the Centre for Good Governance, India. He earned his Post Graduate Programme in Management from Xavier Institute of Management India, and a Master's Degree in Public Administration from the Maxwell School of Citizenship and Public Affairs at Syracuse University, USA.

Garrett Thomson is the CEO of the Guerrand-Hermès Foundation for Peace. He also teaches philosophy at the College of Wooster where he holds the Compton Chair. He has a PhD from Oxford University, England. He is the author of 18 books including *On the Meaning of Life* (Wadsworth, 2002), *Needs* (Routledge, 1987), and *Bacon to Kant* (Waveland, 2013). He co-edited the six volumes of the *Longman Standard History of Philosophy* with Prof. D. Kolak (Longman, 2006). He has also taught at universities in Colombia and the U.K.

Stewart Wallis is the Executive Director of New Economics Foundation. He graduated in Natural Sciences from Cambridge University, followed by a Masters Degree in Business and Economics at London Business School. He spent seven years with the World Bank in Washington DC working on industrial and financial development in East Asia. He then worked for Robinson Packaging in Derbyshire for nine years, the last five as Managing Director, leading a successful business turnaround. He joined Oxfam in 1992 as International Director with responsibility, latterly, for 2500 staff in 70 countries and for all Oxfam's policy, research, development and emergency work worldwide. He was awarded the OBE for services to Oxfam in 2002. His interests include: global governance, functioning of markets, links between development and environmental agendas, the future of capitalism and the moral economy.

Jean Watson is Distinguished Professor and Dean Emerita, University of Colorado Denver, College of Nursing Anschutz Medical Center, where she held the nation's first endowed Chair in Caring Science for 16 years. She is founder of the original Center for Human Caring in Colorado and is a Fellow of the American Academy of Nursing; past President of the National League for Nursing; founding member of International Association in Human Caring and International Caritas Consortium. Her latest activities include Founder and Director of non-profit foundation Watson Caring Science Institute. In October 2013 Jean was inducted as a Living Legend by the American Academy of Nursing, its highest honor.

Index

Page number with an *f* indicate a figure.

A

Abdulaziz Al Saud, King, 222, 232
acceptance, defined, 179
accountability, 154–155
acknowledgment of harm done, 187–188
active bystanders, 183, 190
activities, relationships of with
    goals, 82, 90
Addiss, David, 75, 107, 119n1
adversarial contact, 184
affordable health care, 168, 173
African National Congress, 171
African Program for Onchocerciasis
    Control, 118
AIDS/HIV patients, 200
Al-Bishri, Fatima M., 166, 221
All Candidates meeting, 217
Allen's Curve, 127
Alma-Ata Declaration, 109, 113
Al-Moallimi, Amal y., 166, 221
altruism
    born of suffering, 186–187
    compassion and, 11
    defined, 42
    end to suffering, 46–47
    nature of, 11, 42–46
    obstacles to overcome, 47–49
    overview, 39–42
Ambassador Program for Cross-Cultural
    Dialogue, 228, 230
ambassadors' wives, 230
Amish settlements, 127
Amplified Field, 20
Ancient Wisdom, Modern World: Ethics for a New Millennium (Dalai Lama), 49
Anglican Church, 168
Annan, Kofi, 172
Anthropocene age/era
    altruism and, 41
    compassion and, 103
    economic globalisation, 101
    environment and, 52, 96
    hope and, 102
    human population and, 97
    human unity and, 98
    United Nations and, 99
apartheid, 173–174
Arab Peninsula (KSA), 222
Arab Spring, 66
Arabian American Oil Company (Saudi
    ARAMCO), 222–223, 230–231
Armenian genocide, Turkey, 188
Armstrong, Karen, 27, 127
Arthus-Bertrand, Yann, 26
Article 73, United Nations, 153, 154
Ashoka, Indian Emperor, 64
Aung San Suu Kyi, vii
Austria, KAICIID and, 232
authentic leadership, 164
awareness, processes to increase, 18
Aziz, Mohammed, 108

B

Bank N.V., 123
banking system, 53, 60
Barnes, Hazel, 199
Batson, Daniel, 11, 39, 42
Beijing Conference on Women (1996), 65
La Benevolencija Humanitarian Tools Foundation, 182–183
Berry, Wendell, 216
Best Party (Besti Flokkurinn), 206–207, 209–210
The Better Angels of Our Nature (Pinker), 39
Better Reykjavik (Betri Reykjavik), 210
Bhutan, Kingdom of, 195
biblical precepts, 168–169
Bill & Melinda Gates Foundation, 110, 117
bio-capacity, 95, 96, 97, 99, 100
blazing intelligence, 21–22
Block, Peter, 123
Bohm, David, 124
bonds, compared to equity, 85
Boston University, 197–198
Bowling Alone (Putnam), 122
Boyd, R., 40
brain development, 39–40
Brandt, Willy, 188
Brazil, breastfeeding campaign, 67–68
Bright Future Iceland (Björt framtíð), 219n2, 219n3
Bright Future Party (Canada)
  future of, 218–219
  membership form, 219n4
  as officially registered party, 216
  purple as official color, 217
Bright Future Party (Iceland), 209–210
British children in Saudi Arabia, 228–229
Brooks, David, 123–124
Brown, Peter, 112
Buddha, Siddartha Gautam, 64, 236
Buddhism, 44–45
bureaucrats, relationship to politicians, 208
business environment, as Pillar of Peace, 139, 140
businesses, duty to care, 150–151

C

Cadman, David, 98
Cairo International Conference on Population and Development (1994), 65
Camus, Albert, 46
Capital in the 21st Century (Piketty), 53
capitalism, 51
Carative Processes, 202
Carbon Markets, 96
care, as a legal duty, 150–151
Caring Economics, 194–195
caring ideology, 182
Caring Science
  described, 193–194
  infinite field of universal Love as foundation, 195
  at University of Colorado, 197
case law, 158
Catholic Church. *See* Roman Catholic Church
causality, 146, 146f
causes of suffering, as Noble Truth, 47
Center for Strategic and International Studies, 114–115
Centre for Compassion and Global Health, 119n1
Centre for Nursing Research, 199
cessation of suffering, as Noble Truth, 47
challenges, mirror or magnifying glass process, 18
children
  British and Saudi youth program, 227–228
  bullying and active bystanders, 190–191
  natural socialization, 189–190
  UNICEF, 189–190
Christian Medical Commission, 113
Christianity, 104n2
citizens, politicians' duty to, 208
civil law, 155
climate change
  drama of, 96
  Framework Convention on Climate Change, 27

Index

global warming, 25–26, 52
runaway climate change, 95
Strategic and International
  Studies, 101
as symptom of Earth system
  collapse, 101
climate science, as part of ESS, 95
climate stabilisation, 97
Clinical Associate Dean of Nursing in
  University School of Nursing, 200
clinical nursing doctorate
  (ND degree), 197
Clinical Research faculty, 200
Clinical Teaching Associates, 200
Clinical Teaching Hospital
  partnerships, 200
Clinical-Educational Practitioners, 200
COE pay, 53
coexistence, 180–181
cold peace, 180
Cold War era, 65–69
Colorado Centre for Human Caring,
  197–200
commemorations, 186
Common Cause (Crompton), 56
common good, 56
communal value, 121
Communism, 28
Communist Party, 170
'Community, Conflict, and Ways of
  Knowing' (Palmer), 125
community and communities
  defining who we are, 74
  experience of, 128–129
  face-to-face communities, 128, 129
  of faith, 113
  of freedom, 122, 123–126, 127,
    129, 130
  online community, 102, 128
  roles of, 102, 124
  as sacred bond, 126–131
  stages in building of, 131
  transformative, 122
companies
  conceptions of rational aims of, 80
  defined, 87, 89
  duty to care, 150–151

instrumental conception of, 90
minimal rational aims of, 83, 85
purposes of, 83
See also corporations
compassion
  challenges to in global health, 114–117
  as form of altruistic love, 44–46
  global health as manifestation of,
    111–114
  globalisation of, 107–119
  and the inner landscape, 103
  love and, 94, 98, 101–102
  term usage, 4
  as value connected to peace, 135, 136
compassionate governance
  aspects of, 12
  in corporations, 79–91
  for global health, 117–119
compassionate ideology. *See* caring
  ideology
competence, as value connected
  to peace, 135–136
competition, 59
Comte-Sponville, André, 46
conference participants, 226–227
conflict, Unified Field and, 19
consciousness
  caterpillar transformation
    compared to, 24–25
  elements of, 10, 15
  intelligence, 21–22
  interconnectedness, 17–21
  masculine-famine balance, 22–24
  perspective, 16–17
Constitution of the Republic of South
  Africa, 170–171
constructive visions, 189
consumerist modernity, 95, 101, 103
contact information for future friendships,
  230–231
contemplative neuroscience, nature of, 40
Contraction and Convergence (Meyer), 99
control of one's life, need for, 185
Convention on Biological Diversity, 27
Convention to Combat
  Desertification, 27
CONVERGE project, 93, 97, 99, 105n9

convergence
  contribution of, 93–105
  cultural challenges for in global system, 101–103
  defined, 99
  difference and diversity in, 102–103
  key principles of, 100
  purpose of, 99–100
Convergent Globalisation, 100
Convergent Vision, 100
cooperation, 49
Copenhagen Summit on Social Development (1995), 65
core values, 56
corporate culture, radical rewrite of, 90
corporations
  aims of, 83, 85
  concept of, 79
  defined, 83–87, 89, 92n3
  duty to care, 150–151
  as instrument, 83–85
  as persons, 85–87
  redefinition of, 90
  values of, 80, 87–91
  See also companies
corruption
  low levels of, as Pillar of Peace, 139, 141, 142*f*
  in South Africa, 174–175
Council for a Parliament of the World's Religions, 123
Cowee, John, 198
creation, blazing intelligence of, 21–22
creativity, 59
Crime Against Peace, 155, 156
Crime of Genocide, 156
Crimes Against Humanity, 156
Crimes of Aggression, 156
criminal law
  accountability and, 154–155
  civil law *vs.*, 155
Crompton, Tom, 56
cross-cultural dialogue programs, 228–232
Cueranderos, 196
cultural ecocide, 155
cultural evolution, 40

cultures, prioritising values, 5
Custodian of the Two Holy Mosques (King Abdullah), 224

D

Dalai Lama, vii, 40–41, 44, 45, 47, 49, 112
Dammam, Saudi Arabia, 228–229
Darwin, Charles, 46, 134, 135
'Days of Tranquility for Children, El Salvador,' 68
decision-making
  long-term, 59
  value-based, 5–6, 169, 172
  wisdom and, 33–35
deep listening, 125, 130, 132n3
defensive aggression, 185–186
democracy, a caring God and, 168
democratic deficit, 144
democratic economic governance, 59, 60
Democratic Peoples Republic of Korea, 66
Denver Nursing Project in Human Caring, 197, 200–201
destructive ideology, 189
devaluation, 183–184
development
  crisis between science and, 96
  current model of, 101
Dhammapada (Buddha), 236
dialogue
  as mission of KACND, 224–225
  three paths of, 225–232
Dialogue Café, 227–228
Dialogue Caravan (DC), 227–228
dialogue skills training, 227, 232
distribution of resources, 60–61
diversified ownership, 59
dividends, as cost of capital, 85
Doctor of Nursing Practice Degree (DNP), 197
donations to Caring Centre, 201
Drinkard, Dewitt, 180
Duarte, Jose Napoleon, 68
Duke University, 197–198
Dunbar, Robin, 122, 127

Index

E

Earth community, 151, 160n3
Earth Summit (1992), 65
Earth System crisis, 94
Earth System governance, 97–98
Earth System Science (ESS), 95–96
Ebola outbreak, 107, 115
ecocide, defined, 160n2
  See also Law of Ecocide
Ecocide Act (proposed), 156–157
Eco-geo-engineering, 97
Economic Evaluation of Biodiversity project, 95–96
economic policies and happiness, 195
economic system
  alternative solutions, 54–56
  banking system, 53, 60
  capitalism, 51
  Keynesianism, 57
  myths and half-truths, 55
  neo-liberalism, 57–58
  new system vision, 58–61
  power, influence of, 54–55
  as scientific system, 55
  status of, 51–54
  values, 56
Eco-Spirituality, 123
Ecosystem services, 95
Ecovillages, 123, 131, 132n2
education for all, 168, 173
Einstein, Albert, 10
Eisler, R., 194–195
El Salvador, 'Days of Tranquility for Children,' 68
electronic communication, 128
Eliade, Mircea, 126
Elworthy, Scilla, 10, 15
empathy, 40, 45
employment, 52–53
en+theos, 123
Enabling Acts, 152–153
Encyclopedia Britannica, 126
End Ecocide on Earth, 157
ends, means and, 81, 82

environment
  consciousness transformation and, 24–25
  evolution of, 41
  global warming, 25–26, 52
  sustainability, 52
  will to care for, 27–28
  See also Law of Ecocide
equity
  concept of, 84
  role of in sustainability, 100
equity holders, 84
Era I (body physical thinking), 194
Era III thinking terms, 196
Era of the Truth, 64
ethic of belonging, as science principle, 196
European Community, 190
Even It Up: Time to End Extreme Inequality (Oxfam International), 52–53
expatriates. *See* non-Saudis
experiential understanding, 181
extended altruism, 46
external identities, 31
extremism
  National conference on, 226
  national unity and, 226
  western views of Saudis, 223
extrinsic values, 56
Ezekiel (prophet), 172

F

Facebook
  Pender Island Forum group, 215–216
  virtual social connections, 121
facilitation format, in communities of freedom, 129–130
faith
  interfaith initiative, 224
  interpretation of, 223–224
  value traditions and, 98, 102, 104n3
  See also specific religions by name e.g. Islam, Hinduism
Faith Alliance for the Future, 94, 96
faith communities, 113

famine-masculine balance, 22–24
Farmer, Paul, 109, 117
FAVI (metal manufacturing company), 126
fear-based decision-making, 33
fearlessness in politics, 208, 210
Federation of Southern Gulf Islands Trust, 212
feedbacks, 95
feeling effective, need for, 185
Female Community Health Volunteers (FCHV), 68–69
Fetzer Institute, 124, 126
fiduciary duty, 153
financial systems, 60
Fineberg, H. V., 110, 111
"first do no harm" principle, 150
Fischer, Antony, 57
flourishing, 9, 74
Foege, Bill, 108, 116
followers, leader ideology and, 182
food security, 97–98
Ford, Loretta, 197
Four Noble Truths (Buddha), 46–47
4th National conference, on youth empowerment, 226
Framework Convention on Climate Change, 27
Frank, Robert, 48
freedom
    communities of, 122, 123–126, 127, 129, 130
    human narratives of, 96
Freud, Sigmund, 39
Frieden, Thomas, 115
Friedman, Milton, 57

G

Galtung, Johan, 133, 137, 138
Gandhi, Indira, 149
Gardening the Planet, 97
Gautam, Kul Chandra, 12, 63
genocide workshops, 181
Geo-engineering, 97
Geothermal Power Plant (Orkuveitan), 208, 209

global challenges, meaningful and ethical response to, 94
Global Financial Crisis, 135, 142
global governance
    accountability, 154–155
    claiming the space, 157–158
    framing the narrative, 158–159
    greatness, aspiring to, 152–153
    Law of Ecocide, 155–156
    legal duty to care, 150–151
    naming the offences, 158
    sacred trust of civilisation, 153–154
    trusteeship, 156–157
global health
    as academic discipline, 110
    challenges to compassion in, 114–117
    compassionate governance for, 117–119
    described, 107–108
    as example of globalisation of compassion, 107–119
    future of, 116
    key principles of, 118
    as manifestation of compassion, 111–114
    as notion, 108–109
    as objective, 109–110
    as radical proposition, 116
    as system, 110–111
    understanding of, 108–114
Global National Happiness Index (GNHI), 195
Global Peace Index (GPI), 138, 142, 142*f*
global principles, 102
global public sphere, 102
global sustainability, 101
global values, 135, 136
global warming, 25–26, 52
    See also climate change
globalisation, re-thinking of, 99
Gnarr, Jón
    Best Party founder, 165
    as comedian and political aspirant, 206
    mayoral functions, 210
    met Masselink, 213
    as new mayor of Reykjavik, 207–208

goals
  relationships of with activities, 82, 90
  requirements of, 82
  of work, 82–83, 88
godly peace, 172
Golden Rule, 168–169
goodness, 30–31
Gorbachev, Mikhail, 65
Gore-Tex, 127
governance
  defined, 4, 63–64, 167
  effective governance, 145*f*
  human values, 70
  Millennium Development
    Goals, 65–69
  per Mandela, 168
  politics and, 163
  purpose of, 163
  requirements of good governance, 79
  spirit of humanity, 64–65
  traditional concepts of, 63
  transformation of, 121–132
  as value-based decision-making,
    5–6, 169
  See also global governance
government, as Pillar of Peace, 139–140
Grameen Bank, 123
Grant, James P., 66, 67
Grant, Jim, 116, 118
greatness, aspiring to, 152–153
gross domestic product (GDP)
  vs. GNHI, 195
Gross National Happiness Index of
  Bhutan, 122
group ideology, 182
group traumas, 185
growth at any cost model, 101
Gunaratana, Bhante Henepola, 44–45
Gutierrez, Gustavo, 107, 117

H

Habermas, J., 104n4
Hadith, 223, 233n1
Hagelin, John, 18–21
Happy Planet Index, 132n1
harm
  acknowledgment of, 187–188
  defined, 86, 157–159
  principle of, 150
harmony, sustainable, 48–49
Harrison, Jim, 9
Harvey, Andrew, 28
Hayek, Friedrich, 57
health
  definition of, 113, 137
  global. *See* global health
  social determinants of, 109
  See also World Health
    Organization (WHO)
health care, 168, 173, 195
health equity, 109
Heiligenfeld (medical service company),
  126
Hejaz region (west Saudi Arabia), 222
Helgadóttir, Heiða Kristín, 165, 205,
  206, 219n1
Higgins, Polly, 76, 149
Himalayan spiritual journey, 16–17
Hinduism, 64
Hobbes, Thomas, 39
Holocaust, 188
Home (film), 26
hope and connection, 102
housing, 173
Hübl, Thomas, 19–20
human capital
  high levels of, as Pillar of Peace,
    139, 142*f*
  wide definition of, 141
human dignity, 56
human growth
  activities that contribute to, 136
  measurement of, 122
human progress, dominant narratives of, 95
human rights, 96
human sustainable development
  project, 94
humanitarian cease-fires, 68
humility, 35
Humphrey, Hubert, 112
Hunter, D. J., 110, 111
Hutus, experiential
  understanding with, 181

I

Iceland
  Bright Future Iceland, 219n2, 219n3
  Bright Future Party, 209–210
  downsizing and restructuring, 209
  financial crisis, 206, 209
  political landscape, desire to change, 206–207
  Reykjavik, 2, 65, 206–207
  Social Democrat Party, 208
  town hall meetings, 210
ideology of unity, 182
ignorance, 45, 47
individualism, 39, 98, 101, 124
individuals, relationship to society, 146–147, 146*f*
information, as Pillar of Peace, 139, 141, 142*f*
inner strength, 11, 29–31
Institute for Economics and Peace (IPE), 136, 138, 141, 143
instrumental rationality, 81, 82, 83, 85
instrumental value, 80, 81, 82, 87, 88, 89, 90, 92n2
intent, 149, 150, 152
interconnectedness, 17–21, 134, 135
intergenerational equity, 48
International Conventions and Relations and their Impact on National Unity, 225–226
International Criminal Court (ILC), 150, 155
International Human Dimensions (IHDP), 97
International Panel on Climate Change (IPCC), 95
International Scouts Organization, 228, 231
International Union for the Conservation of Nature, 25
International Youth Conference for Volunteering and Dialogue, 231
intestinal worm infections, 118–119
intrinsic value
  of activities, 83, 90
  defined, 56
  instrumental value and, 80–81
  as non-instrumental value, 73, 92n1
  work as, 82–83, 87, 88
Islam
  correct interpretation of faith, 223–224
  mission of KACND and, 223–224
Islamophobia, 66, 166, 223, 232
Islands Trust Council, Southern Gulf Islands, 212
isolation, 222, 228–229
Israel, Ben, 112
Israel-Palestine relations, 184, 189
ivermectin (onchocerciasis treatment), 108

J

Janki, Dadi, 10–11, 29
Japanese in Saudi Arabia, 229
Jeddah, Saudi Arabia, 228–229
Jeremiah (prophet), 172
joint projects, value of, 183–184
joint-stock company, 84
Journal of Conflict Resolution, 18–19
Jusoor "Bridges" project, 228
justice, 172, 187–189

K

KACND. *See* King Abdulaziz Center for National Dialogue
Kasser, Tim, 56
Keynes, Maynard, 55
Keynesianism, 57
Khmer Rouge, 183–184
Killelea, Steve, 76, 133
King, Ursula, 93
King Abdulaziz Center for National Dialogue (KACND)
  established by, 226
  mission of, 223
  trainer certification, 232
King Abdullah bin Abdulaziz initiative for interfaith and intercultural dialogue, 224

Index 267

King Abdullah bin Abdulaziz International Program for a Culture of Peace and Dialogue (KAICIID), 230–232
King Abdullah Program for Peace with UNESCO, 228
King Abdullah Scholarship Program, 226
King Soopers' grocery store food donations, 201
Kingdom of Saudi Arabia, 222
Koplan, J. P., 107, 110
Kristinsdottir, S. M., 100
Kristoff, Nicolas, 67
Krog, Antjie, 172
KSA. *See* Arab Peninsula

L

land projects, 151
"Lavender of Japan" club, 229
Law of Ecocide
  Crime Against Peace proposal, 155
  duty to care, 77
  Ecocide Act, 156–157
  justification for, 155
  origins of, 149–150
Law of Moses, 169–170
Layard, Richard, 195
leader ideology, 182
leaders and leadership
  authentic leadership, 164
  components of effective leadership, 145
  decision-making, 33–35
  defined, 4
  form of in communities of freedom, 130–131
  inner strength, 29–31
  love, power of, 31–33
  model of, 144–145
  need for set of values to guide choice of, 135
  nourishing self, 36–37
  servant leadership, 163, 167, 176
  serving society, 35–36
Lee, Robert E., 182
Levinas, E., 196
liberal individualism, 98

liberation, 47
liberation theology, 109, 112, 114
life
  control of one's, 185
  sacredness of, 156, 158
  satisfaction with, 41, 53–54
  spiritual, 10
  values and, 79
"Like Death in my Arms" (Krog), 172
limited liability, 83–84
Lincoln, Abraham, 118, 182
listening, 34, 125, 130, 132n3
loans, as negotiable instrument, 85
local conferences before national one, 226–227
Local Trust Areas, Southern Gulf Islands, 212
long-term thinking for the seventh generation, 59
love
  altruistic, 44–46
  compassion and, 94, 98, 101–102
  power of, 31–33
  source of, 11
  term usage, 3–4
'Love and Compassion in Governance' (SoH forum), 93, 94
loving-kindness, 45

M

MacFadyen, Ivan, 25
Macy, Joanna, 117
Madina, Saudi Arabia
  as prophet Mohammad mosque location, 222
  as sacred city, 221
magical thinking, 28
Magnet hospitals, 196
Maher Al Otaibi, 229
Majlis (place of sitting), 227
Makgoba, Thabo, 164, 167
Making Things Public: Atmospheres of Democracy (Latour and Weibel), 167
Makkah, Saudi Arabia

King Abdullah bin Abdulaziz
  initiative for interfaith and
  intercultural dialogue, 224
  as prayer direction, 222
  as sacred city, 221
Mandela, Nelson, vii, 1, 23, 168,
  175, 182
"Manifesto" (Berry), 216
masculine-famine balance, 22–24
Masselink, Derek
  career background, 165
  as North Pender Island Trustee,
    212–213
  as officially registered candidate, 216
  re-imaging of politics, 205
  at Royal Roads University, 213
material value, 121
Matthew, Gospel of, 168–169
McTaggart, Lynne, 20
means, and ends, 81, 82
media
  coverage of moral issues by, 144
  coverage of political processes by, 143
meditation, 19–21, 44
Merck & Co., Inc., 108, 118
Messengers of Peace program, 228, 231
Millennium Development Goals, 65,
  66, 69
Millennium Ecosystems Report, 52
mirror or magnifying glass process, 18
Mistri, Shaheen, 18
Mitchell, Edgar, 15, 28
Miyu Nakamura, "SAKURA of the
  Kingdom" club, 229
moderation, aspects of, 225
Mohammed, Mohammed H., 75, 121
monk allegory as campaign turning
  point, 217
moral judgments, 46
Morphogenetic Field, 20
Mother Teresa, 23, 112
motivation, values and, 144–145
Mugabe, Robert, 19
Musekeweya (New Dawn;
  radio drama), 183

N

Nagel, Thomas, 42
Nass, Clifford, 129
National Development Plan, 168
national dialogue conferences, 225–227
nationalities included in cross-cultural
  workshops, 230
natural altruism, 45–46
natural socialization, 189–190
natural systems, 59
needs *vs.* wants, 87, 92n7
negative assumptions, 33
negative peace, 137, 138
neighbours, as Pillar of Peace, 139, 140,
  142*f*
neo-liberalism, 57–58
Nepal, women's empowerment, 68–69
neuroplasticity, 40
New Age dreaming, 28
New Economics Foundation (NEF),
  58–59
Newton, Isaac, 15
9/11 attacks, 223, 225
Noble Eightfold Path, 47
non-instrumental value, 80, 81, 87, 89
non-market economy, 59
non-Saudis
  Ambassador Program for Cross-
    Cultural Dialogue for, 228
  isolation for security reasons, 228–229
Non-Self Governing Territories
  (NSGTs), 153
North Pender, British Columbia
  Best and Bright Future parties, 205
  Bright Future Party on, 213–214
  election victory, 217–218
  location, 211
  overdevelopment danger, 211–212
nourishing the self, 36–37
Nowak, Martin, 49
numbers, practical numbers for
  community of freedom, 127–128
Nurse Practitioner programmes, 197
nursing education, decline in, 197–198

Index

O

occupation, exposure to other cultures from, 222
Old Testament, 170
onchocerciasis (river blindness), 108–109, 118
online community
  benefits of, 128
  role of in global public sphere, 102
openness in politics, 208
Ornament of Sutras (Buddha), 47
Ostrom, Elinor, 104n7
Overcoming Evil (Staub), 183
ownership, 59, 84, 92n4, 151, 158
Oxfam International, 52–53

P

Paine, Thomas, 176
Palme, Olof, 149
Palmer, Parker, 121, 125, 128
Parker, Jenneth, 75, 93
passive bystanders, 182
Patagonia, 126
path (Noble Eightfold Path), 47
peace
  definition of, 137
  departments of, 137
  as in everyone's self-interest, 134
  as guiding principle, 147, 147*f*
  importance of, 134–137
  measurement of, 137–145
  negative peace, 137, 138
  pillars of. *See* Pillars of Peace
  Positive Peace/positive peace, 133, 138
  role of in encouraging prosperity, 143
  values connected to, 135
Peace & Conflict Centers, 136
peaceful society, factors in creation of, 136
Pearlman, Laurie Anne, 181
Peck, M. Scott, 124, 131
Pele, breastfeeding campaign in Brazil, 67–68
Pender Island Forum Facebook group, 215–216
perpetrator-victim meetings, 188
persons, defined, 86
perspective, 16–17
phosphorus, in food production, 97, 98*f*
Pickett, Kate, 53
Piketty, Thomas, 53
Pillars of Peace, 133, 138–148, 139*f*, 142*f*
Pinker, Steven, 39
Pinker, Susan, 128
Planetary health, 194
Plautus, 39
Plumwood, Val, 104n6
political ineffectiveness, 135
political landscape
  conflicting promises, 207
  desire to change, 206–207
politicians, relationship to bureaucrats and citizens, 208
politics
  defined, 167
  duty to care, 150
  fearlessness in, 210
  focus on main objectives and convictions, 210–211
  joy and laughter in, 214–215
  non-partisan politics, 213–214
  value-based decision-making, 172
positive contact, 183–185
positive identity, need for, 185
positive ideology, 33, 189
Positive Peace/positive peace, 133, 138
Post, Stephen, 42
Post-2015 Development Agenda, 143
poverty, as demeaning, 168
power
  economic, 54–55
  masculine-famine balance, 22
practices and symbols, in communities of freedom, 130, 132n4, 195–196
Prakasmani, Dadi, 29
profits, importance of retained, 89
Psalm 85:10, 114
psychological needs, 185
public leaders, as servants, 163, 167, 176
Public Protector, 170
public sphere, characterization of, 102
Putnam, Robert, 122

R

radical/rooted trust in politics, 214–215
radio programs on reconciliation, 182–183, 186, 190
Ramsey, George, 132n2
rationality
  concept of, 80, 82
  instrumental rationality, 81, 82, 83, 85
Reagan, Ronald, 57, 65
reconciliation
  defined, 179–180
  shared futures with, 181–182
  violence prevention and, 180
reflective leadership, 195
reflective practices, 130
religious extremism, 66
resources
  distribution of, 60–61
  equitable distribution of, as Pillar of Peace, 130, 139, 142f
  feeding frenzy for, 97
  internal, 36
  natures, 27–28
Resources for Human Development (RHD), 126
respect
  difference and diversity in convergence, 102–103
  use of term, 94
  value of, 34
restorative justice, 188
Reykjavik, Iceland
  mayoral and council election, 206–207
  Summit of 1986 (US-USSR relations), 65
  as world capital of peace, 2
Ricard, Matthieu, 11, 39
Richerson, P. J., 40
right to life, 156
rights of others, as Pillar of Peace, 139, 140, 142f
Riyadh, Saudi Arabia
  British and Saudi children meeting in, 228–229
  Dialogue Caravan in, 228
Rogers, Martha, 196

Roman Catholic Church
  intermediary in El Salvador, 68
  liberation theology, 109, 112, 114
Romans, St. Paul's letter to, 171
Rome Statute, ILC, 150, 155
Roosevelt, Franklin D., 168
Royal Roads University, 213
rule of three, 127
runaway climate change, 95
rural development, 168
Rwanda
  constructive visions, 189
  genocide workshops, 181
  informational healing, 185
  non-discrimination laws, 189
  origins of violence information, 188
  radio programs on reconciliation, 186
  sources of change, 185

S

sacred trust of civilisation, 153–154
sacredness of life, 158
Sakura, 233n2
"SAKURA of the Kingdom" club, 229
Salish people, 211
Salish Sea, 211
Sartre, Jean-Paul, 199
satisfaction with life, 41, 53–54
Saudi Arabia
  aid for Japanese earthquake and tsunami, 229
  British children in, 228–229
  Dammam, 228–229
  Hejaz region, 222
  Japanese in, 229
  Jeddah, 228–229
  Kingdom of, 222
  Makkah, 221, 222, 224
  for non-Saudis, 228
  non-Saudis, 228–229
  people of, 222, 230
  Riyadh, 228–229
  terrorism, rejection of, 223–224
  as victim of terrorism, 224
Saudi Ministry of Education, 231
Saudi-Japanese friendship club, 229

scapegoating, 183–184
School of Nursing National Advisory Visiting Board, 199
Schumacher Institute, 93, 94
science, crisis between science and development, 96
2nd National conference, on extremism, 226
secular state, 104n3
security, need for, 185
self-awareness, 30–31, 33–34
self-centeredness, 124
self-discovery, 123
self-governance, 152
selfishness, 41–42
self-nourishment, 36–37
servant leadership, 163, 167, 176
shamanic practices, 196
shared resources, 27–28
shareholders, 84, 85, 92n5, 150
Sheldrake, Rupert, 20
Shoura Council, 227, 230, 233n3
Siegel, Daniel, 21
silence, 30, 34, 36
Silver, Henry, 197
slip-n-slide cancer benefit, 217
Smith, Adam, 55
Snower, Dennis, 47–48
social capital, 121, 122, 123, 128
social connections, 121
social equity, 126, 136
social justice, 100, 109, 114, 115, 188–189
social media
  Facebook, 121, 215–216
  in political campaigns, 216
Social Progress Index, 132n1
society and societies
  prioritising values, 5
  relationship of individuals to, 146–147
  serving, 35–36
sociocracy model, 130, 131
solace ministries, 186
soul, nature of, 30
South Africa
  Constitution, 170–171
  National Development Plan, 168

recent decay of public morality, 170
seen as religious country, 170, 177
Southern Gulf Islands Trust, 211–212
Spain, KAICIID and, 232
The Spirit Level (Wilkinson and Pickett), 53
spirit of humanity, historical perspective, 64–65
Spirit of Humanity (SoH) Forum (2012), 2
Spirit of Humanity (SoH) Forum (2014), 2, 93, 94, 123, 213, 235–236
spiritual journey, 16–17
spiritual life, integrating with public service, 10
spiritual revolution, 49
Staub, Ervin, 164, 179, 181
Steelcase, 127
stewardship, 56
stories and storytellers, 1
strength, inner, 11, 29–31
suffering
  born of, 186–187
  end to, 46–47
Super Radiance, 20
survival of the fittest, 134
Sustainable Development Goals (2015), 66, 99
sustainable harmony, 48–49
symbols and practices, in communities of freedom, 130, 132n4, 195–196
systems, lack of belief in, 134

T

Tamkeen "Empowerment" program, 227
Tamkeen Youth Dialogue Program, 227
Tang Ke, 149
Task Force for Global Health, 114, 118
technology
  benefits of, 129
  role of, 128
Ten Carative factors from Watson Theory, 201, 202
Ten Commandments, 175
10th National conference, on extremism and national unity, 226

terrorism, Saudi Arabia's rejection of, 223–224
terrorism attacks (2001), 223, 225
Thatcher, Margaret, 57
Theory of Human Caring, 197, 200
The Theory of Moral Sentiments (Smith), 55
3rd National conference, on women's issues, 226
Thomas, Kurian, 75, 121
Thomson, Garrett, 74, 79
tipping points, 95
Tohoku earthquake and Tsunami, Japan, 229
Tolle, Eckhart, 28
trainer certification for dialogue communication skills, 232
transcendence, human narratives of, 96
Transcendental Meditation, 20–21
transformative communities, 122
Tree of Life in Zimbabwe, 19–20, 28n1
tropical medicine, 114
trustees and trusteeship
　Article 73, UN, 153, 154
　duty to care, 150–151
　Ecocide Act and, 156–157
Trusteeship Council, United Nations, 156
truth of suffering, as Noble Truth, 47
Turkey, Armenian genocide and, 188
Tutsis, experiential understanding with, 181
Tutu, Desmond, vii
Twelve Steps to a Compassionate Life (Armstrong), 127
twelve-step program, 127
"The Two Kingdoms" meeting, 228

U

Ubuntu, vii–viii, 2–3
UNESCO, 228, 231
UNICEF, 65, 66–69, 116
Unified Field, 19, 24, 28
United Nations
　anthropocene and, 99
　Article 73 (trusteeship), 153, 154
　Cold War era, 65–69
　Convention to Combat Desertification, 27
　Framework Convention on Climate Change, 27
　International Law Commission, 155
　King Abdullah's interfaith initiative, 224
　Millennium Development Goals, 65, 66, 69
　Millennium Ecosystems Report, 52
　Sustainable Development Goals, 66
　Trusteeship Council, 156
　UNESCO, 228, 231
　UNICEF, 65, 66–69
United States Agency for International Development (USAID), 69
United States, Central Intelligence Agency (CIA), 115
Uniting to Combat Neglected Tropical Diseases, 111
unity consciousness, 18
universal symbols, 130, 132n4, 195–196
University of Colorado School of Nursing, 197–198

V

value
　instrumental, 73, 80, 81, 82, 87, 88, 89, 90, 92n2
　non-instrumental, 73, 80, 81, 87, 89
value-based decision-making, 169, 172
value-error, 80
values
　conceptions of, 79–83
　core values, 56
　of corporations, 80, 87–91
　extrinsic, 56
　global values, 135, 136
　in governance, 3, 10
　intrinsic. *See* intrinsic value
　living of life as, 79
　and motivation, 144–145
　shared values, 126–127
victims of violence, 185

Index

Vienna World Conference on Human Rights (1993), 65
The Village Effect (Pinker), 128
violence
  influences to create or prevent, 181–182
  meditation as prevention technique, 19–21
  victims of. *See* victims of violence
violence begets violence, 185
Vishnu, 196
visions, constructive *vs.* destructive, 189
Volkan, Vamik, 185

W

Wallis, Stewart, 3, 11–12, 51
Walsh, Roger, 126
wants *vs.* needs, 87, 92n7
War Crimes, 156
warm peace, 181
Watson, Jean, 165, 193, 198
Watson Theory of Human Caring, 201–203
The Wealth of Nations (Smith), 55
Weber, Arnold, 198
Weiss, Edith Brown, 48
well-being, 73–74, 92n2
well-functioning government, as Pillar of Peace, 139–140
Western paradigm, corruption as, 174–175
Westernized hospital model of care, 193–194
Wilkinson, Richard, 53
Wired (magazine), 122
wise mind, 24

women's issues, 226
work
  goals of, 82–83, 88
  as having intrinsic value, 82–83, 87, 88
  as having non-instrumental value, 87
  micro-economic conception of, 83
  ultimate instrumental benefit of, 89
work ethic, 136
workplace settings, disruption of, 122
World Bank, 63–64, 110, 111
World Conference on Dialogue, 224
World Council of Churches, 113
World Economic Forum (2009), 58–59
World Health Assembly, 113
World Health Organization (WHO)
  definition of, 113, 137
  as global tapestry of influence, 110
  health for all vision, 109
  institutions invested in, 112
  intestinal worm infections control program, 118
  ivermectin, for onchocerciasis, 108
World Meteorological Organization (WMO), 25
World Summit on Children (1990), 65
Worthington, Everett, 180

Y

youth dialogue programs, 227–228
youth empowerment, 226
Yunus, Muhammad, 123

Z

Zuma, Jacob, 174–175